T0330083

THE SOUTH SEA BUBBLE
AND IRELAND

THE SOUTH SEA BUBBLE
AND IRELAND

Money, Banking and Investment, 1690–1721

Patrick Walsh

THE BOYDELL PRESS

First published 2014
The Boydell Press, Woodbridge

ISBN 978-1-84383-930-9

The Boydell Press is an imprint of Boydell & Brewer Ltd
PO Box 9, Woodbridge, Suffolk IP12 3DF, UK
and of Boydell & Brewer Inc.
668 Mt Hope Avenue, Rochester, NY 14620-2731, USA
website: www.boydellandbrewer.com

A CIP catalogue record for this book is available
from the British Library

The publisher has no responsibility for the continued existence or
accuracy of URLs for external or third-party internet websites referred
to in this book, and does not guarantee that any content on such
websites is, or will remain, accurate or appropriate

This publication is printed on acid-free paper

Typeset by BBR, Sheffield

This book is dedicated to Niamh with much love

Contents

Preface

This book is about the impact of one international financial crisis on people and places removed from its centre. It was written during another one. Readers seeking lessons from the experiences of Irish investors in the South Sea Company to help escape the post-2008 global financial crisis may not, however, find them in this book. Nevertheless this project, which was conceived in late 2007, and which was started in earnest a year later as the Eurozone crisis hit Ireland, was researched and written with the storms of the current crisis raging in the background. The impact of these contemporary events on its content is, however, if anything, of the unconscious variety. Despite occasional temptations, direct parallels have been avoided, although readers may wish to draw their own inferences. If the global economic circumstances within which this book was written were rather precipitous this has, however, been a good time to be involved in financial and economic history with these sub-disciplines enjoying new levels of popular and scholarly attention. This renewed interest in what were previously arcane subjects has helped to make writing this book a much easier task. Financially this research was initially funded by a two-year postdoctoral fellowship awarded by the Irish Research Council for Humanities and Social Sciences, which allowed me to develop my ideas in the congenial and supportive environment of the School of History and Archives at University College Dublin. This book could not have been completed without the excellent work of the archivists and librarians in the many archives and libraries in which I have worked, and it is a pleasure to acknowledge in particular their vital contribution at a time when so many repositories are suffering from ill-judged and short-termist budgetary constraints.

My colleagues at UCD, and subsequently in Trinity College Dublin and University College London, have made researching and writing this book a mostly pleasant task. The lively exchange of ideas, puns and the reciprocal reading of each other's work made working with my fellow postdocs Ian Campbell, Niamh Cullen, Ciara Meehan and Kevin O'Sullivan in the Belfield fishbowl a particular joy. Ivar McGrath meanwhile, frequently and always with infectious good humour, went beyond the bounds of what might be expected from a postdoctoral mentor offering encouragement, friendship and constructive criticism. Without him this book would have been very different, and may never have been finished. Among his many contributions was an introduction to the 'Money, Power and Print' international interdisciplinary research group. Their biannual colloquia, organized by Dr McGrath in tandem with Chris Fauske and Rick Kleer, have proved invaluable in widening my knowledge of the British financial revolutions, and it is with pleasure that I acknowledge the advice and support of my fellow participants over the last seven years. Special thanks are also due to Michael Brown, John McAleer, David O'Shaughnessy, Lisa Griffith and the Economic History Society, who have invited me to speak on this subject at events in Aberdeen, the Institute of Historical Research, Warwick, Trinity and Durham.

Several colleagues have commented on previous drafts of parts of this book, offered suggestions on specific points, pointed me in the direction of sources or assisted in various other ways. Here I am especially grateful to Ann Carlos and Anne Laurence for their robust critiques of earlier drafts. Particular thanks are also due to Juliana Adelman, Robert Armstrong, John Bergin, Maurice Bric, Stephen Conway, Vivien Costelloe, Mary Daly, Christine Desan, David Dickson, Eoin Drea, Rowena Dudley, Aaron Graham, Marnie Hay, Edward James, James Kelly, Caitriona MacDonald, Eoin Magennis, James Maguire, Anthony Malcomson, Anne Murphy, Elaine Murphy, Ruth Musielak, Lean NíChleirigh, Helen Paul, Martyn Powell and Koji Yamamoto for advice on particular points, references and various forms of practical support and interest. At Boydell, I would particularly like to thank Michael Middeke and Megan Milan for their patience, as well as for their encouragement and advice along the way.

My family have, once again, made writing a book much easier. My parents Jim and Jeanne, brothers Cormac and Fergal, and sister Fionnuala have treated my interests in bubbles with appropriate levels of scepticism, while still providing much help and support. Special thanks are due to Jeanne and Fionnuala who have read the book in manuscript, offering much appreciated advice on the placement of wayward commas and other infelicities, though all errors naturally remain my full responsibility. My wife Niamh has read everything, listened to me ramble on about the 'pernicious' South Sea, as well as providing writing refuges in Milan and Sansepolcro. All this, and much more, has been done with her typical good humour and sharply honed historical insights. This book is dedicated to her with much love.

Patrick Walsh
Dublin, 2013

Plates, Figures and Tables

Plates

Figures

Tables

Editorial Note

Unless otherwise stated, dates are given in Old Style, although the year is taken to begin on 1 January rather than 25 March, which in this period was still the formal convention. In quotations from contemporary sources, spelling has been modernized, and punctuation and capitalization standardized, except in cases where the meaning of the original is ambiguous or unclear. All references to money are expressed in £ sterling unless otherwise stated.

Abbreviations

Add MS	Additional Manuscript
BL	British Library
BoE	Bank of England Archives
CJI	*The Journals of the House of Commons of the Kingdom of Ireland*, 3rd edn, 20 vols (Dublin, 1796–1800)
DIB	James McGuire and James Quinn (eds), *Dictionary of Irish Biography*, 9 vols (Cambridge, 2009)
HIP	E. M. Johnston-Liik, *History of the Irish Parliament, 1692–1800: Commons, Constituencies and Statutes*, 6 vols (Belfast, 2002)
HMC	Historical Manuscripts Commission
IAA	Irish Architectural Archive
NLI	National Library of Ireland
NRS	National Records of Scotland
ODNB	H. G. C. Matthew and Brian Harrison (eds), *Oxford Dictionary of National Biography* (Oxford, 2004)
PRONI	Public Record Office of Northern Ireland
SHC	Surrey History Centre
TCD	Trinity College Dublin
TNA	The National Archives (United Kingdom)

Introduction

In late September 1720, the South Sea bubble burst. The South Sea Company's share price which had been rising all summer collapsed more quickly than it had risen, causing the first great British stock-market crash. Its repercussions were felt far beyond the City of London. Its impact was felt right across western Europe from Aberdeen to Amsterdam, from Belfast to Berne and from Limerick to Lisbon. The dramatic rise and fall of the South Sea Company's stock in the summer of 1720 was a source of wonder, excitement and despair for contemporary observers. Some of them had been drawn to invest in the buoyant London financial markets following reports and rumours of the great riches gained by the fortunate. Many of these investors came from outside the English capital and the consequences of their activities, both positive and negative, reverberated beyond the boundaries of the British world. Money flowed into London from Amsterdam, Berlin, Berne, Cork, Dublin and Edinburgh, expanding the market for South Sea Company shares. The gains and losses made by these investors and speculators during the hectic summer of 1720 fed back into their local economies. Profits made in London's Exchange Alley temporarily drove property prices upwards in Scotland, while investment and banking schemes were floated in Dublin and Edinburgh as local projectors responded to the innovations in the metropolitan capital. More negatively, losses incurred as a result of the London crash impacted on provincial banking systems causing short-lived bank runs in Dublin and Edinburgh. These investments from the periphery, their consequences and what they tell us about financial developments in early eighteenth-century Britain and Ireland are the focus of this book.

These are contentious subjects. Much of the extensive scholarly and also popular literature on the rise and fall of the South Sea Company has taken as one of its starting assumptions that the bubble was almost exclusively a London-based episode.[1] Indeed some scholars have seen it as primarily a

---

[1] For the history of the South Sea Company see Adam Anderson, *An Historical and Chronological Deduction of the Origins of Commerce from the Earliest Accounts to the Present Time*, 2 vols (London, 1764); John Carswell, *The South Sea Bubble* (London, 1960); P. G. M. Dickson, *The Financial Revolution in England: A Study of the Development of Public Credit, 1688–1756* (London, 1967), pp. 90–156; H. J. Paul, *The South Sea Bubble: An Economic History of its Origins and Consequences* (London, 2010); and Carl Wennerlind, *Casualties of Credit: The English Financial Revolution 1620–1720* (Cambridge, MA, 2011), pp. 197–234.

crisis of the City, and one influential account has gone so far as to argue that the idea that the bubble impacted on the English provinces, let alone Ireland or Scotland, is one of the great myths surrounding the bubble.[2] The argument presented here suggests that this myth has been too hastily debunked. Instead this book reveals that Irish investors were the third largest group of 'foreign' investors active in London in 1720, behind only the Dutch and the Swiss. It argues that these Irish investments and their consequences, together with those made by Scottish investors, tell us much not just about the bubble itself, but also about the wider experience of the financial revolution in Britain and Ireland during the three decades after the Glorious Revolution of 1688–89. This financial revolution, of which the South Sea bubble was the great crisis, was not just an English phenomenon, and it is a central contention of this study that both it and the bubble can only be fully understood when examined within this wider context.[3] What follows is therefore intended to make a contribution not just to the economic and financial history of Ireland, but crucially also to the wider historiography of the South Sea bubble, and the British and Irish financial revolutions. Before doing this it is necessary first to briefly outline the history of the South Sea Company, emphasizing its transnational and multidimensional aspects in order to establish the context of what follows.

I

The history of the South Sea Company itself demonstrates the importance of seeing the stock-market crash of 1720 within a wider geographical context. From its incorporation in 1711 as a trading company with a monopoly on British trade with South America, the South Sea Company, or to give it its full title *The Company of the Merchants of Great Britain Trading to the South Seas and other Parts of America and for Encouraging the Fishery*, had a global outlook. Established in an era of highly partisan politics and international war, it served a number of the political and financial objectives of Robert Harley's Tory government in Britain.[4] Politically it was intended to be a Tory counterpart to the Whig-dominated East India Company and Bank of England, thereby strengthening the Tory financial position at a time when contemporaries were concerned about the growing power of the Whig

---

[2]   Julian Hoppit, 'The Myths of the South Sea Bubble', *Transactions of the Royal Historical Society*, 6th ser., 12 (2002), 141–65 (p. 158).
[3]   On the financial revolution see Dickson, *Financial Revolution*; Henry Roseveare, *The Financial Revolution, 1660–1760* (London, 1991); and Anne Murphy, *The Origins of English Financial Markets: Investment and Speculation before the South Sea Bubble* (Cambridge, 2009).
[4]   Geoffrey Holmes, *British Politics in the Age of Anne*, rev. edn (London, 1987), pp. 155–8.

moneyed interest. Scholars continue to be divided over the extent of the connections between partisan politics and shareholding in the great corporations of this period, but it is clear that the South Sea Company, in its original incarnation, was closely aligned to Harley's ministry. Economically and diplomatically, the company was conceived as the conduit for the expansion of British trading interests into Spanish South America. This was to be made possible by the company's acquisition in 1713 of the *Asiento* – the sole right to supply African slaves to the Spanish colonies – as part of the Treaty of Utrecht, a concession that was already confidently anticipated in 1711.[5]

The treaty brought an end to the eleven-year War of the Spanish Succession, an extraordinarily expensive conflict, which was fought mostly in Continental Europe and North America. Prosecuting this war had led to an escalation in the size of the English (later British after 1707) national debt, which had risen from £16 million in 1702 at the war's outset, to just over £40 million in 1713.[6] Servicing this unprecedented level of debt posed new and complex challenges for successive ministries in Whitehall. The foundation of the South Sea Company was one of the solutions advanced to solve this conundrum. In return for the grant of the potentially enormously lucrative *Asiento* contract, the South Sea Company undertook to manage a substantial portion of the national debt. In exchange for its incorporating charter, the company absorbed £9,471,320 of the national debt in return for a 6% annual interest payment from the Treasury (this would be reduced to 5% in 1717).[7] The transaction benefited both parties. The company gained its trading charter guaranteeing its monopoly rights and stood to receive guaranteed annual interest payments from the government. The Treasury, meanwhile, transferred to the company a significant portion of its liabilities, some of which had very high yield interest rates, while promising to pay a lower rate of interest on the consolidated debt it now owed the company.[8] The public creditors who had previously lent to the government through a variety of means, including the purchase of bonds, annuities and lottery tickets, now saw their investments in the state transformed into stock in the South Sea Company. This 'debt for equity' swap meant that their fortunes were liable to rise with the assured success of the company, and much effort was expended by the company in advertising the endless possibilities promised by its access to the wealth of the South American continent.[9]

5   Carswell, pp. 60–77; and Paul, pp. 37–9.
6   John Brewer, *The Sinews of Power: War, Money and the English State, 1688–1783* (London, 1989), pp. 114–22.
7   Dickson, *Financial Revolution*, p. 68.
8   For the reasons for these high rates see Hoppit, 'Myths of the South Sea Bubble', p. 142.
9   Wennerlind, pp. 203–8.

The South Sea Company's trading ventures failed to fully realize their imagined potential, at least in the short term. While recent research has made it clear that it was more active in the transatlantic slave trade than many financial historians had given it credit for, the company faced significant geopolitical challenges, notably continued conflict with Spain, which adversely affected its prospects in South America.[10] These trading difficulties were offset by the company's continued expansion into the sphere of public finance. The success of their initial debt for equity swap in 1711 encouraged it to take on more of the government's liabilities, a development the Treasury was keen to support. Over the succeeding nine years the company gradually acquired further elements of the national debt, subsuming for instance the debt owed on lottery tickets first sold in 1710 into its capital in spring and summer 1719. By midsummer 1719 the South Sea Company held £11.7 million or 23% of the British national debt.[11] Its increased concentration on managing the public debt reflected the expertise of the company's leading personalities, many of whose backgrounds lay in the then embryonic financial and banking spheres rather than in mercantile and trading concerns. For instance, John Blunt, George Caswall and Jacob Sawbridge, three of the company's key figures, were formerly leading players in the Hollow Sword Blade Company, none of whose many incarnations from rapier making to Irish property development to banking could be regarded as especially mercantile.[12] Instead their previous careers indicated an aptitude for financial management and calculated risk-taking. It is therefore not surprising that the company increasingly focused its energies on the managing of the national debt and the famous South Sea scheme of 1720 would be the outcome of this prioritization of the trade in stock rather than in slaves and South American produce.

The South Sea Company's intentions would, by summer 1720, stretch to privatizing the entire British national debt. The intellectual origins and practical inspiration of this ambitious scheme lay not in London but in contemporary Paris, where a controversial Scotsman was presiding over a remarkable turnaround in France's national fortunes. In 1714, upon the death of Louis XIV, the French state was virtually bankrupt thanks to the late king's military endeavours and his extravagant expenditure at Versailles and elsewhere. In a desperate bid to rescue their perilous national finances, the regency government of the Duc d'Orléans turned to the controversial

[10] Paul, pp. 54–65; Wennerlind, pp. 218–30; and Shinsuke Satsuma, 'The South Sea Company and Its Plan for a Naval Expedition in 1712', *Historical Research*, 85 (2012), 410–29.
[11] Dickson, *Financial Revolution*, p. 89.
[12] Stuart Bell, '"A Masterpiece of Knavery"? The Activities of the Sword Blade Company in London's Early Financial Markets', *Business History*, 54 (2012), 623–38. See below pp. 29–31.

but brilliant Scottish economist John Law. Having first made his name in London, Law was forced to leave England under a cloud following a fatal duel in 1694. Despite this setback, he then made a reputation for himself as a financial innovator and skilled gambler, first in Edinburgh and then in the royal courts of Europe.[13] His Parisian activities would, however, be on a far bigger scale and would first make, and then ruin, his reputation. Law's first French venture involved the creation of the Banque Générale in 1716, whose notes quickly passed into general circulation, and which by 1717 were the officially sanctioned means to remit tax revenue to the French Treasury. The success of his bank gave Law even greater influence at the French court, and his next proposal, which imitated the South Sea Company's innovative debt for equity conversion, was readily accepted in Paris. It involved establishing an overseas trading corporation along the lines of the English model, which would combine its trading activities with the management of part of the national debt. In 1718, the Company of the West, better known as the Mississippi Company, was established under the direction of Law himself and granted a monopoly on trade with the French colonies in North America. In exchange for these valuable trading privileges, seventy-five million livres worth of government bonds, which were then trading at a 70% discount, were converted into shares in Law's new company, accounting for three-quarters of the corporation's founding capital. Over the next year, Law gathered virtually all of the French state's commercial and colonial activities across the globe under his company umbrella, potentially greatly increasing his personal and corporate revenues. The Mississippi Company's ambitions already dwarfed those of the South Sea Company in London, Law's original inspiration. This became even clearer in August 1719 when, in the company's 'most extravagant transaction', they took over the total French government debt of 1.5 billion livres.[14] Law, by now the most powerful figure in France, had effectively privatized the entire national debt.

The success of Law's 'system' depended, however, on continued investment in his company, and the maintenance of a high share price. Thanks to Law's impressive promotional campaign promising great riches for his shareholders, investors flocked to Paris to invest in the company, further driving up the price of stock, and what became known as the Mississippi bubble began. These investors came not just from France but from right across Europe, with the Dutch and Swiss prominent.[15] Particularly notable were investors from Britain and Ireland, and especially from Scotland, reflecting Law's continuing connections with his homeland, as well as the

---

[13] For further details on Law see Antoin E. Murphy, *John Law: Economic Theorist and Policy Maker* (Oxford, 1997).

[14] Wennerlind, p. 232.

[15] For some quantitative evidence see Larry Neal, *The Rise of Financial Capitalism: International Capital Markets in the Age of Reason* (Cambridge, 1990), pp. 62–79.

influence of the British ambassador to Paris, John Dalrymple, 2nd Earl of Stair.[16] Among these Scottish investors were leading Whig politicians like Archibald Campbell, Earl of Islay, as well as members of the Jacobite diaspora. Some of the Irish Jacobite exiles in Paris were also conspicuous investors, with Law's sometime business partner, the County Kerry-born, French-domiciled banker and economist Richard Cantillon, the most prominent.[17]

The apparent success of Law's scheme in late 1719 attracted the interest of both the ministry in London and the directors of the South Sea Company. Both were anxious to stem the flow of English and Scottish funds to Paris, while both were also intrigued by Law's conversion of the entire French debt into company stock. The South Sea Company began drawing up ambitious plans to replicate Law's scheme. Where once he had copied them, they were now going to return the favour. However their timing was hardly propitious as Law's scheme collapsed in early 1720 when its creator began to meddle too much in the market in an attempt to keep the Mississippi Company's share value rising. Thus as the Mississippi bubble began to crash, what we now call the South Sea bubble began. In January 1720 the South Sea Company proposed to take over the remainder of the British national debt. They offered to reduce the interest rate they charged the government from 1727 onward, while also offering an initial lump sum payment of £3 million to the Treasury. This proposal, which would have turned the company into the world's biggest financial corporation, perhaps unsurprisingly caused concern at the Bank of England, and the Bank felt compelled to propose a counter-offer so as to maintain their dominant position in the British financial system. Over the next two months a duel would be fought both inside and outside parliament to determine which corporation or institution would take over the nation's debt.[18] After a complex and sometimes dirty bidding war, the South Sea Company emerged victorious and what became known as the South Sea Act received royal assent on 7 April 1720.[19] Under its terms, the South Sea Company took control of the majority of the national debt, amounting to £31.5 million, most of which was in the form of long-term irredeemable annuities. Annuitants were encouraged to convert their holdings of government debt into South Sea

---

[16] James Craggs to John Dalrymple, 2nd Earl of Stair, 24 Sep. 1719, in J. M. Graham, *Annals and Correspondence of the Viscount and First and Second Earls of Stair*, 2 vols (Edinburgh, 1875), vol. 2, p. 405; and Patrick Walsh, 'The Bubble on the Periphery: Scotland and the South Sea Bubble', *Scottish Historical Review*, 91 (2012), 106–24 (p. 114).

[17] Antoin E. Murphy, *Richard Cantillon: Entrepreneur and Economist* (Oxford, 1986), pp. 157–90.

[18] Carswell, pp. 98–118.

[19] 6 Geo. I, c. 4, *An Act for Enabling the South Sea Company to Increase Their Present Capital Stock and Fund.*

stock, with future returns coming in the form of company dividends rather than interest payments from the Treasury. This offered great advantages to the government who stood to substantially reduce their annual expenditure on servicing this debt.

The majority of annuitants, convinced by the promises made by the company's directors and its propaganda machine about its trading prospects, by the favourable terms offered to them, and by the contemporaneous reports of great fortunes gained in the ostensibly similar Paris scheme, took up this opportunity. This vote of confidence in the South Sea Company helped to push up its share price, increasing the company's nominal value. As the value of its stock rose, its debt liabilities fell. For instance, if the price of a share doubled from £100 to £200 then that share could now cancel £200 of debt or, if we look at the big picture, £15.5 million (half of £31 million) would clear the whole national debt.[20] This is a rather conservative example as instead of doubling their worth, South Sea shares tripled in value within a week of the passage of the South Sea Act in April 1720. Anticipating additional gains, the company moved to create further stock, selling £2.25 million worth of stock at 300% in mid-April, £1.5 million at 400% just two weeks later, and £5 million at 1,000% in June. Ten weeks later on 24 August 1720 they sold a fourth stock subscription of 1.25 million at 1,000% (equivalent to £12.5 million). Most of this stock was paid for in instalments with individual purchasers paying only 10% of their purchase price as a down payment to the company. The popular demand to enter these subscriptions was reflected in the company's rising share price as figure 0.1 shows.

In tandem with the company's sale of its stock, an active secondary market in South Sea stock developed in London's financial district, which according to some contemporary observers sparked scenes of frenzied crowd activity, although some later scholars have cast doubts upon these reports.[21] The details of such activity remain unclear, but it is certain that South Sea stock quickly became very popular, and its price continued to rise through the summer months, aided and abetted by the willingness of the company's directors to bend the rules of contemporary corporate governance, through corrupt payments to ministers and false dividend issues, to keep the price high. Their ever-rising share price in turn pushed up the prices of other leading stocks such as shares in the Bank of England, East India Company and the Royal African Company, while up to 190 other 'bubble' companies emerged in an attempt to cash in on the investing and speculative boom engulfing the London financial markets.[22] Investors in these companies, and

---

[20] Roseveare, p. 55.

[21] For descriptions of these crowds see Carswell, pp. 140–2 and 155–6, but see Paul, p. 99 for some scepticism on this point.

[22] Hoppit, 'Myths of the South Sea Bubble', pp. 143–4.

Figure 0.1. South Sea Company share price, January to December 1720.

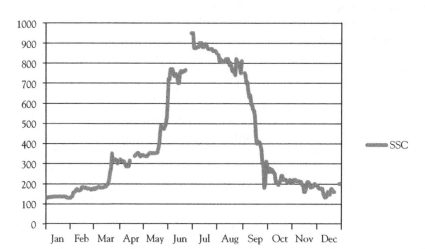

This graph has been created using data from John Castaing's *Course of the Exchange* (London, 1720) collected by Larry Neal, and found in File CEP1700S in the European State Finance Database (http://esfdb.websites.bta.com/table.aspx?resourceid=11346) last accessed on 25 February 2013. The company books were closed in late June/early July so no stock price data is therefore available for this period.

particularly in the South Sea Company as this book makes clear, came from across Britain, Ireland and western Europe making Exchange Alley as the physical locus of the stock market an even more cosmopolitan place than usual.

While the directors of the South Sea Company were delighted with their rising share price, they were also by midsummer beginning to get worried about its sustainability and the threat of competition from some of the newly founded corporations trading on the London markets. Some of the directors decided to realize their own individual paper profits, selling out with considerable fortunes. They also successfully pressurized the government – confirming the directors' close links with the ministry – to introduce a piece of legislation known as the Bubble Act to curtail the multiplicity of corporations then seeking subscribers.[23] Some of these joint-stock enterprises, like one proposing a perpetual motion machine, were rather whimsical while others, like the York Buildings Company and various fishery schemes, were much more viable. This bill was introduced in late June but it was only in August when the Treasury, firmly backed by the South Sea Company, took action against some of these rival enterprises, that the bubble burst. The

23 Roseveare, p. 57.

share price fell from a high of £950 in late July to £750 by the beginning of September. Two weeks later it stood at £500, while by the end of the month it had fallen to £200.[24] The bubble had burst, and with it many paper fortunes disappeared. The fortunate, like the London philanthropist Thomas Guy, had sold out at the top of the market but many more investors had incurred losses, some more dramatic than others. The crash marked the beginning of a new period of recrimination and rebuilding. The company's directors were investigated by parliament, and found guilty of fraudulent manipulation of the market, while their political allies in the English ministry fell from grace, leading to the rise of Sir Robert Walpole.[25] Meanwhile the South Sea Company itself was heavily restructured, with half of its holdings of government debt eventually transferred into new South Sea annuities in 1723. Despite its spectacular losses and the uncovering of gross corporate mismanagement among its directors, the company continued to operate until the middle of the nineteenth century, diversifying its concerns into the whaling trade among others.[26]

Much of this history is well known, and there are few major points of contention. Most debates surrounding the bubble focus on two important topics: first, were the investors in the company behaving rationally or were they participating in a speculative mania? Secondly, what were the consequences of the bubble, both in the short and the long term?[27] This book addresses both issues, drawing particularly on the experiences of individual Irish (and to some extent Scottish) investors, but it also raises another important question: how far geographically did the investment community in 1720 extend, and how much does the answer to that affect how we understand the bubble's consequences?

In doing so, this book starts with a broad interpretation of the meaning and parameters of the concept of the 'financial revolution' and demonstrates why it is appropriate to include Irish and Scottish financial developments within its rubric. It then moves on to explore the bubble through the experiences of the investors from these territories, analysing for the first time both their individual and collective narratives. These are considered in terms of their significance – a notoriously slippery concept – taking into consideration both their relative and absolute contribution to the London capital markets, and the impact of their investments, as much as it can be measured and understood, on their domestic economies. Finally, the influence of both the promise and the reality of the South Sea scheme on Irish 'projects' in

---

24 Dickson, *Financial Revolution*, p. 149.
25 Carswell, pp. 207–25.
26 Paul, pp. 107–10.
27 The rationality of the South Sea scheme is particularly emphasized in Peter Garber, *Famous First Bubbles: The Fundamentals of Early Manias* (Cambridge, MA, 2000), esp. pp. 121–2. See also Paul, pp. 102–3.

1720–22 is explored, and in particular the competing proposals for a national bank. This in-depth analysis demonstrates both how these bank schemes comprised an alternative locus for investment, and how their prospects were affected by the inflation and bursting of the bubble, while offering some insight into the manner in which contemporaries understood events in London. Cumulatively, the arguments and evidence presented here challenge existing interpretations of the bubble and its impact beyond the limits, both physical and mental, of the London stock market.

II

The first section of this book (chapters 1 and 2) interrogates whether it is both desirable and possible to include Ireland and Scotland within our understanding of the 'financial revolution'. The term was first coined by P. G. M. Dickson in his seminal 1967 study *The Financial Revolution in England: A Study in the Development of Public Credit, 1688–1756*, which focused on English financial developments and innovations in the decades after the constitutional and political 'Glorious Revolution' of 1688. These included the foundation of the Bank of England in 1694, the establishment of a funded national debt, the growth of a market for securities, and the emergence of an efficient system of war financing, all of which were crucial to the military and diplomatic successes of the eighteenth-century British imperial state. Since the publication of Dickson's hugely influential study, subsequent scholars have sought to extend the geographical, chronological and thematic boundaries of his enquiry.[28]

Dickson made explicit his sole concentration on English developments, arguing that 'English historians' perennial ignorance of Irish and Scottish developments, and of the reaction of these developments on English ones, cannot, respectfully, be redeemed by substituting "British" for "English" and then continuing to ignore Ireland and Scotland'.[29] Importantly, he did not rule out the possibility that his analysis could be extended northward and westward. Succeeding generations of historians have since taken up this challenge, and a small but important body of scholarship examining Irish and Scottish financial developments now exists.[30] These studies show that

---

[28] For useful collections of international comparative studies see Christopher Storrs (ed.), *The Fiscal-Military State in Eighteenth-Century Europe: Essays in Honour of P. G. M. Dickson* (Farnham, 2009); and Bartolomé Yn-Casalilla and Patrick K. O'Brien with Francisco Comín Comín (eds), *The Rise of Fiscal States: A Global History, 1500–1914* (Cambridge, 2012).

[29] Dickson, *Financial Revolution*, p. xvii.

[30] Daniel Carey and Christopher Finlay (eds), *The Empire of Credit: The Financial Revolution in Britain, Ireland and America, 1688–1815* (Dublin, 2011); C. I. McGrath and Chris Fauske (eds), *Money, Power and Print: Interdisciplinary Studies on the Financial*

both Ireland and Scotland (before the union in 1707) experienced their own distinct varieties of the financial revolution, which while influenced by English developments did not simply repeat or imitate them.[31] Thus Scotland unlike Ireland had a national bank, while Ireland unlike pre-Union Scotland had its own national debt, funded in this case by Irish taxes. This debt, first instituted in 1716, was used to pay for some of Ireland's contribution to the British fiscal-military state, emphasizing that the purpose of Irish fiscal developments followed the same pattern identified by Dickson, and later John Brewer, for England.[32]

Ivar McGrath in his assessment of the Irish experience of the financial revolution has stressed the evolutionary nature of Irish developments, noting continuities with earlier periods as well as the comparatively late appearance of the national debt.[33] In highlighting this evolutionary aspect, his work consciously echoed that of Henry Roseveare who made a significant revision to Dickson's original thesis by drawing attention to the continuities between the financial and fiscal innovations of the Commonwealth and Restoration regimes, and later post-1688 developments.[34] The different chronologies of developments in Ireland, and indeed Scotland and the North American colonies, alert us to the need to interpret the meaning(s) of the financial revolution as broadly as possible.[35] Here it is crucial to disentangle the connections between the political and constitutional revolution of 1688–89 with the more chronologically fluid financial one. This is especially true when considering Ireland and Scotland, where the experiences of 1688–89 were neither necessarily 'glorious' nor 'revolutionary' in the same way that they were in England. The different experiences of the Williamite revolution and their consequences for financial developments in Ireland and Scotland are the subject of chapter 1.

Revolution in the British Isles (Newark, 2008); Sean D. Moore, *Swift, The Book, and the Irish Financial Revolution: Satire and Sovereignty in Colonial Ireland* (Baltimore, 2010); and Patrick Walsh, 'The Irish Fiscal State, 1690–1769', *Historical Journal*, 56 (2013), 629–56.

[31] Walsh, 'Bubble on the Periphery', pp. 111–13.

[32] Brewer, *Sinews of Power, passim*; and C. I. McGrath, '"The Public Wealth is the Sinew, the Life, of Every Public Measure": The Creation and Maintenance of a National Debt in Ireland, 1716–45', in Carey and Finlay (eds), *The Empire of Credit*, pp. 171–208.

[33] C. I. McGrath, 'The Irish Experience of "Financial Revolution" 1660–1760', in McGrath and Fauske (eds), *Money, Power and Print*, pp. 157–88 (pp. 166–8).

[34] Roseveare, pp. 2–3; Carl Wennerlind in *Casualties of Credit* extends the chronology of the financial revolution back to 1620, although this may be stretching the boundaries too far.

[35] On North America see Julian Gwynn, 'Financial Revolution in Massachusetts: Public Credit and Taxation, 1692–1774', *Histoire Sociale – Social History*, 27 (1984), 59–77; and Daniel Vickers, 'The Northern Colonies: Economy and Society, 1600–1775', in *The Cambridge Economic History of the United States I*, ed. Stanley L. Engerman and Robert E. Gallman (Cambridge, 1996), pp. 209–48.

The thematic parameters of Dickson's work have also been significantly extended since he first described the concept of the 'financial revolution'. Particularly pertinent to the present study is the ever-increasing scholarship on early financial markets. Ann Carlos, Anne Murphy and Larry Neal among others have considerably deepened our understanding of how the primary and secondary markets for government debt, and also investments in late seventeenth and early eighteenth-century joint-stock corporations, functioned.[36] Their contribution has allowed a greater understanding of investment in this period to emerge, and has permitted more nuanced work to be carried out on individual schemes and institutions. Significant here in terms of the geographic extension of the 'financial revolution' has been Douglas Watt and W. Douglas Jones' work on the subscriptions to the ill-fated Company of Scotland in the mid-1690s, an approach that has influenced the analysis of the subscriptions to the putative banks of Ireland in chapter 7.[37] The increasing availability of domestic Irish and Scottish investment opportunities indicates the spread and adoption of innovations developed in London, even if their original purposes were altered in the act of translation. Chapter 2 analyses the development of investment opportunities in Ireland and Scotland in the three decades before 1720, examining their different trajectories. Attention is paid here to the emergence of separate and distinct banking and financial sectors in Dublin and Edinburgh, exploring how they both converged and diverged from developments in England. The presence of Irish and Scots men and women as public creditors in Britain and as participants in the London stock market in these years is also investigated showing how, despite the growth of indigenous banking and investment opportunities, London continued to attract capital from Ireland and Scotland.

The multilayered investment and financial activities of the Irish and the Scots, with their participation in both local and metropolitan markets, and the cross-fertilization of ideas and innovations between London, Dublin and Edinburgh, demonstrate the complexities of uncovering an Irish or Scottish financial revolution. While both kingdoms (Scotland before 1707) exhibited some of the characteristics associated with the English financial revolution as described by Dickson and his successors – including innovations in banking, joint-stock companies and a funded national debt in Ireland – developments in each place remained subordinate to those evolving in England.

---

[36] Among other works see Ann M. Carlos and Larry Neal, 'The Micro-Foundations of the Early London Capital Market: Bank of England Shareholders During and After the South Sea Bubble, 1720–25', *Economic History Review*, 59 (2006), 498–538; and Murphy, *Origins of English Financial Markets*, passim.

[37] W. Douglas Jones, '"The Bold Adventurers": A Quantitative Analysis of the Darien Subscription List (1696)', *Scottish Economic & Social History*, 21 (2001), 22–42; and Douglas Watt, *The Price of Scotland: Darien, Union and the Wealth of Nations* (Edinburgh, 2007).

Nevertheless it is possible to see these Irish and Scottish financial processes as revolutionary within their own constitutional, military and political contexts as described in the next two chapters.

III

The limits of the Scottish financial revolution were evident in the failure of the Darien scheme in 1696, which was unsuccessful in its objective of laying the foundations for a Scottish commercial empire in Central America. Ireland experienced no such drama, but the confines of Irish financial development were brought home by the failure of the various schemes for a national bank in 1720–21. They are the focus of the final three chapters of this book, but it is arguable that the willing participation of hundreds of Irish men and women in the South Sea bubble demonstrated the lack of domestic innovation in providing an alternative venue for their capital. Their desire to partake in the opportunities available in London and the impact of their investments on the Dublin financial sector, whether in the form of a run on the local banks or on the fate of domestic schemes, emphasizes the interconnectivity between the Irish and English financial revolutions, and its disruptive, even destructive, potential. The second section of this book (chapters 3–5) investigates for the first time Irish investment in the South Sea Company and its consequences.

Chapter 3 stresses the transnational dimension of the bubble, placing Irish investors firmly within the context of those from other 'foreign' or non-English territories. Although constitutionally and politically complicated, including Irish investors within the 'foreign' category is justified by the presence of alternative potential investment opportunities in Dublin and by the contemporary perception of these investors as a novel and identifiable grouping in London during the bubble. Drawing on the records of the Bank of England in the absence of the South Sea Company's own transfer book and share registers, this chapter offers a quantitative analysis of Irish investment patterns in 1720, outlining where possible the religious, gender and occupational profile of these investors, demonstrating how they fit into broader trends identified by other modern scholars of the bubble.

The following chapter takes a more qualitative approach, examining the investing experience of individuals and family groups. Using a wide range of archival materials, this focus allows us to understand in greater detail the personal motivations and strategies that lay behind the faceless majority of shareholders during the financial revolution. These case studies are therefore valuable beyond their immediate local and familial contexts and, like other similar investigations, inform wider debates about investor behaviour in the early stock market. Such an approach is not unproblematic and important caveats about this research, including in particular how representative the chosen cases are, as well as questions about the difficulty of translating the experience of the individual to that of larger groups, are addressed. Nevertheless, it is shown that the insights gained into the investing activities of the Irish and the Anglo-Irish (where this term is used to describe those whose lives straddled the Irish Sea) tell us much about investment during the bubble and the Anglo-Irish financial nexus more generally.[38] If chapter 4 focuses on individuals, chapter 5 returns to the aggregate dimension, exploring the contested issue of the extent of the influence of the bubble on the Irish economy. Incorporating a variety of statistical and anecdotal evidence, this chapter argues that there was a real impact on the Irish economy in 1720–21 which must, in part at least, be attributed to the effect of the bubble on local credit and monetary institutions, and structures. These include the visible repercussions on the exchange rate between Britain and Ireland, as well as upon interest rates. Here it must be remembered that until the passage of the Act of Union in 1801, Ireland had its own independent currency.[39] Comparative material from Scotland is also employed to emphasize further the wider economic impact of the crash.

The third and final section of this book (chapters 6–8) shifts its attention to look at the influence of the rise and fall of the South Sea Company on the various plans for an Irish national bank. These proposals first appeared in early May 1720 just as the South Sea share price began to attract significant outside investment, and they were finally defeated in late 1721, thanks in part to changes in both investor and political confidence in the aftermath of the London crash. Chapter 6 outlines the origins of the three schemes for a national bank, setting them within the context of the multiplicity of financial and other corporate projects which emerged in Dublin, London and Edinburgh in the period between April and June 1720. The following chapter subjects the surviving bank subscription lists to a close analysis, employing techniques used in studies of the Company of Scotland in the 1690s. It indicates how the subscribers to the various bank schemes can be understood as an alternative Irish investment community during the period of the bubble, showing how hundreds of Irish men and women, Protestants and Catholics, and members of the gentry, merchant and even professional classes, emerged as willing financial backers for a scheme of public credit in 1720.

This scheme collapsed in autumn 1721 in the aftermath of the London crash. Chapter 8 shows how the debates about the bank both within and

---

[38] On the Anglo-Irish see Patrick Walsh, 'Irish Money on the London Market: Ireland, the Anglo-Irish and the South Sea Bubble of 1720', *Eighteenth-Century Life*, 38 (forthcoming 2014).

[39] Thirteen Irish pence were equal to one English shilling. See Joseph Johnston, 'Irish Currency in the Eighteenth Century', in *Bishop Berkeley's Querist in Historical Perspective*, ed. Joseph Johnston (Dundalk, 1970), pp. 52–71.

without the Irish parliament were informed by readings and misreadings of the South Sea bubble. Expanding upon and critiquing the arguments of Sean Moore and Michael Ryder, it reveals how important an effect the bursting of the bubble had on the content and arguments of the flurry of pamphlets produced during this debate, and therefore on the fate of the bank itself.[40] Finally this chapter briefly explores the longer-term resonances that contemporary understandings of the bubble had on Irish economic debate in the eighteenth century. These Irish debates, it is argued, help shed light on the transnational spread of the vocabularies and imagery associated with the South Sea bubble.

IV

Of course, Irishmen also helped to shape this imagery. Jonathan Swift's poems on the bubble, written in Dublin in late 1720, have been seen as crucial in the creation of the modern image of the bubble as a financial folly motivated by greed and corruption. Similarly, the economic thinking of George Berkeley, philosopher and bishop of the Irish diocese of Cloyne, was much influenced by his observations in London during the bubble, leading to the publication of not just the pamphlet *An Essay Towards Preventing the Ruin of Great Britain* in 1721, but also to sections of his famous three-volume work, *The Querist* (1735–37).[41] As well as writing them, Irishmen could also be the subjects of popular commentaries on the bubble. The famous sets of playing cards produced in the aftermath of the crash featured several personalities and stock characters associated with the bubble. These included not only the generic images of stockjobbers and corrupt company directors but also images of investors, some of whom are depicted using various national and ethnic stereotypes. These include readily identifiable images of Jews, Dutchmen, Frenchmen and Scotsmen.[42] This transnational panoply of characters includes the Ten of Clubs featuring an Irishman exclaiming, 'By St Patrick I have sold all my potatoes to buy stock' (see plate 1). The potatoes might be just a reference to a well-worn stereotype, but might also refer to the contemporary perception that the gentlemen of Ireland 'went late into the stocks [and] bought dear', in this instance after the summer's potato harvest.[43] A second man, meanwhile, labeled with the

---

40 Michael Ryder, 'The Bank of Ireland, 1721: Land, Credit and Dependency', *Historical Journal*, 25 (1982), 557–82; and Sean D. Moore, 'Satiric Norms, Swift's Financial Satires and the Bank of Ireland Controversy of 1720–1', *Eighteenth-Century Ireland*, 17 (2002), 26–56.
41 P. H. Kelly, '"Industry and Virtue Versus Luxury and Corruption": Berkeley, Walpole and the South Sea Bubble Crisis', *Eighteenth-Century Ireland*, 7 (1992), 57–74.
42 Paul, pp. 93–4.
43 *London Mercury*, 29 Apr. 1721.

Plate 1. Anon., 'Ten of Clubs', *South Sea Bubble Playing Cards* (London: Printed for Carington Bowles, 1721). Bancroft Collection, Kress Collection of Business and Economics, Baker Library Historical Collections, Harvard Business School.

derogatory term 'Teague', has sold not just his potatoes but also his land to purchase stock but without success. Teague therefore asks his countryman for a position as a footman to make up for his lost income. This commentary, while clearly exaggerated, nevertheless gives an insight into popular images of Irish investment during the South Sea bubble. The remainder of this book seeks to explore these subjects in greater depth, going beyond contemporary caricatures to illuminate the real experiences of Irish men and women in the early financial markets.

1

Varieties of Innovation: Ireland, Scotland and the Financial Revolution 1688–1720

The period between the Glorious Revolution and the South Sea bubble has long been recognized as a particularly significant period in British and Irish financial history. This was the age of the 'financial revolution'.[1] This revolution has traditionally been understood to encompass the series of English financial innovations in the period immediately after the constitutional and political revolution of 1688–89. These included the creation of a national debt, the foundation of the Bank of England in 1694 and the development of a sophisticated system of war financing, all of which enabled William III to continue his continental military conflict with Louis XIV's France following William's ascent to the English, Scottish and Irish thrones. The same period also saw the rise of joint-stock trading companies and the emergence of the London stock exchange as an important financial centre. Rapid developments were also visible in private banking, with a concomitant spread of paper money and bills of exchange as a circulating medium. Cumulatively, these innovations comprised a revolution and have been seen as laying the foundations of modern capitalism.[2]

The fusion of these financial innovations with an increasing centralized and efficient state bureaucracy has led historians, notably John Brewer, to describe the emergence of an English, and after 1707 a British, fiscal-military state. The English/British state's growing ability to mobilize its financial resources, and to develop more efficient and reliable forms of war financing, were crucial to its emergence as a great power in the first half of the eighteenth century. This has been compared favourably with the experience of absolutist France in the same period, encouraging scholars to link Britain's imperial and financial success with the democratic constitutional arrangements ushered in after the revolution of 1688.[3]

---

[1] P. G. M. Dickson, *The Financial Revolution in England: A Study in the Development of Public Credit, 1688–1756* (London, 1967).
[2] Fernand Braudel, *The Wheels of Commerce* (London, 1982), pp. 97–110.
[3] John Brewer, *The Sinews of Power: War, Money and the English State, 1688–1783* (London, 1989); and David Stasavage, *Public Credit and the Birth of the Democratic State: France and Great Britain, 1688–1789* (Cambridge, 2003).

The causal relationship between the political/constitutional and financial revolutions has, however, been subjected to increasing historical scrutiny. Where once scholars spoke of an 'Anglo-Dutch moment', conjuring up images of the importation of 'Dutch finance' into England in King William's baggage train, modern historians have become more sceptical about ascribing a direct causal link between the arrival of the Dutch stadtholder on the English throne and the subsequent revolution in public credit.[4] Instead several scholars have highlighted the continuities that linked developments made during the Restoration and Commonwealth periods, especially in the fiscal realm, with those of the 1690s.[5] In a similar vein, Anne Murphy has shown how sophisticated financial markets were already evident in London in the 1680s, while Steve Pincus has highlighted the modernizing tendencies of James II's English administration in the second half of the same decade.[6] These revisions to previous narratives have complicated received understandings of the period, but they have not fundamentally altered the picture. The revolution of 1688–89 remains a key moment. In England at least, it ushered in an era of greater financial and political stability emphasized by the success of the Williamite regime in raising funds to fight Louis XIV and his allies, first in Ireland and then on the Continent in the 1690s.[7] The much larger sums advanced to the government after the revolution, it has been argued, indicated a greater trust in its ability to repay its creditors. This trust was based on the growing role of parliament as a check on the executive power of the monarch and the government, the key element that differentiated England from France.[8] The establishment of the English national debt and the creation of the Bank of England have been cited as evidence for this 'credible commitment' thesis.[9] It is, however, important to remember that the successes of these innovations were nevertheless not preordained, but instead developed organically in parallel with developments in the political

---

[4]   Anne Murphy, *The Origins of English Financial Markets: Investment and Speculation before the South Sea Bubble* (Cambridge, 2009), p. 4.

[5]   Henry Roseveare, *The Financial Revolution, 1660–1760* (London, 1991); M. J. Braddick, *The Nerves of State: Taxation and the Financing of the English State, 1558–1714* (Manchester, 1996); and D'Maris Coffmann, *Excise Taxation and the Origins of Public Debt* (Basingstoke, 2013).

[6]   Steve Pincus, *1688: The First Modern Revolution* (London, 2009), esp. pp. 143–78.

[7]   D. W. Jones, *War and Economy in the Age of William III and Marlborough* (Oxford, 1988), *passim.*

[8]   On this see Gary W. Cox, 'Was the Glorious Revolution a Constitutional Watershed', *Journal of Economic History*, 72 (2012), 567–600.

[9]   Douglas North and Barry Weingast, 'Constitutions and Commitment: The Evolution of Institutions Governing Public Choice in Seventeenth-Century England', *Journal of Economic History*, 49 (1989), 802–32. See also D'Maris Coffmann, Adrian Leonard and Larry Neal (eds), *Questioning Credible Commitment: Perspectives on the Rise of Financial Capitalism* (Cambridge, 2013).

and parliamentary spheres. Within this context it is therefore important to explore the relationship between financial developments and the different experiences of the 'Glorious Revolution' in Ireland and Scotland.

Here we return to the complex and occasionally problematic question about the application of the concept of the 'financial revolution' to Ireland and Scotland. Increasingly, scholars have answered this question in the affirmative, although always with the caveat that each country's experience of 'revolution' was different, both from each other's and from the English experience.[10] It is clear from the investigations of Carey, McGrath and others that the English model cannot simply be superimposed onto Ireland or Scotland. This is plainly evident in McGrath's nuanced argument regarding the evolutionary rather than revolutionary aspects of Irish developments. Instead these cases need to be examined within their own evolving constitutional, political and economic contexts. This chapter does just that: examining Irish and Scottish financial developments within these contexts and analysing the reasons for their different trajectories, while also asking what they can tell us about the broader situation in the period between the Williamite revolution and war of 1688–91 and the South Sea bubble of 1720. It is first necessary to outline the very different experiences of the Glorious Revolution as witnessed in Ireland and Scotland.

I

The Glorious Revolution of the winter of 1688–89 and the post-revolution constitutional settlement helped define the contexts and contours of the English financial revolution. If its Irish version did something similar in terms of financial developments, the Irish experience of the revolution of 1688–89 was however very different. Neither 'bloodless' nor 'glorious', Ireland instead became a theatre of war for three years from late 1688 to late 1691. The War of the Two Kings had a profound effect on Irish society, establishing as it did the political, religious and social structures that would define eighteenth-century Ireland.[11] These in turn would influence the distinctive character and experience of the financial revolution in Ireland. Among the

10 Daniel Carey and Christopher Finlay (eds), *The Empire of Credit: The Financial Revolution in Britain, Ireland and America, 1688–1815* (Dublin, 2011); C. I. McGrath and Chris Fauske (eds), *Money, Power and Print: Interdisciplinary Studies on the Financial Revolution in the British Isles* (Newark, 2008); and Patrick Walsh, 'The Bubble on the Periphery: Scotland and the South Sea Bubble', *Scottish Historical Review*, 91 (2012), 106–24.

11 On the revolution in Ireland see Tim Harris, *Revolution: The Great Crisis of the British Monarchy, 1685–1720* (London, 2006), pp. 422–76; D. W. Hayton, *Ruling Ireland, 1685–1742: Politics, Politicians and Parties* (Woodbridge, 2004), pp. 8–35; P. H. Kelly, 'Ireland and the Glorious Revolution, from Kingdom to Colony', in *The Revolutions of*

most significant consequences of the Williamite victory in Ireland was the consolidation of political and financial power within the hands of a powerful minority, the Anglican landed elite. Their defence of this dominant position would inform Irish political and financial developments in the succeeding decades, but how did they achieve this hegemony?

Such an outcome was far from certain in November 1688 when William III landed on the southern coast of England, instigating the chain of events that would lead to the removal of his father-in-law James II from the British and Irish thrones. Under James II, Ireland had undergone radical political changes in the three years that followed his accession. Members of the Catholic majority, excluded from positions of political and civil power since the early decades of the seventeenth century, were appointed to most of the major offices of state, whether in the army, judiciary or the revenue.[12] Overseeing this Catholicization of the Irish civil and military administrations was Richard Talbot, Earl of Tyrconnell, a leading Catholic aristocrat whom James had appointed as his Irish lord deputy.[13] Tyrconnell not only cashiered Protestant army officers, he also remodelled Irish local government ensuring that there would be a Catholic majority in any future Dublin parliament. This 'revolution' in Irish government would have significant consequences when James was deposed from his English throne.

First, it made Ireland an ostensibly attractive launching pad from which James could begin his campaign to regain his English and Scottish kingdoms. Secondly, it ensured that when James did indeed arrive in Ireland in March 1689 he would be met by both a friendly Catholic administration in Dublin and a disgruntled, disaffected Protestant population largely concentrated in the northern province of Ulster, where Tyrconnell's policies had had little effect on the ground.[14] The stage was now set for a civil war between supporters of both James and William, who had upon his acceptance of the English crown in early 1689 become *de facto* King of Ireland. The situation became even more complex when James, on arriving in Dublin, decided to call a parliament, the first to be summoned since that called by Charles II in 1661.

Unlike that previous assembly, which was exclusively Protestant in its membership, almost all the members of James' parliament were Catholic, although representatives from the northern parts of Ulster were conspicuous

---

1688, ed. Robert Beddard (Oxford, 1991), pp. 162–90; and J. G. Simms, *Jacobite Ireland, 1685–91* (London, 1969).

12 Simms, *Jacobite Ireland*, pp. 19–43.

13 Tyrconnell's appointment as lord deputy rather than lord lieutenant, the usual higher-ranking title granted to the chief governor, indicates that he was not fully trusted by James' ministers at Whitehall. For biographical details see James McGuire, 'Talbot, Richard (1630–91)', in *DIB*.

14 Not all Irish Protestants actively resisted James' measures. See R. G. Gillespie, 'Irish Protestants and James II', *Irish Historical Studies*, 28 (1992), 124–33.

by their absence. Intended as a mechanism for raising funds through taxation for the anticipated military conflict with William's forces, it instead entered the history books as an agency for Catholic revolution. If made effective, its legislative programme would, in Tim Harris's words, have amounted to a 'genuine revolution, transferring political, religious and economic power to a new ruling class'.[15] Central to this was the proposed overturning of the 1662 Act of Settlement, which would have undone the Restoration land settlement, and put the majority of Irish landed property back in the hands of the Catholic elite who made up the great majority of the parliament's membership. Also potentially of huge significance in the 1689 parliament was the declaration that the English parliament did not have the right to legislate for Ireland, combined with the assertion that the English House of Lords was not the final court of appeal in Irish legal cases, and in addition the passage of an act setting aside the Navigation Acts, which curtailed Irish trade with the American Colonies.[16] Attempts to repeal Poynings' Law, which gave the English and Irish privy councils a crucial, even controlling, role in the passage of Irish legislation, were however frustrated by James II.[17] Nevertheless these were potentially radical political and constitutional departures. Their effectiveness depended, however, upon Jacobite military success on the battlefields of Ireland.

Initially James' forces achieved some military success in north-west Ulster before being thwarted by the fortitude of the defenders of the northern city of Londonderry.[18] The conflict quickly escalated as multinational armies entered the field on both sides. The presence of French and Walloon forces fighting alongside James' Irish army in opposition to the combined English, Dutch, Danish, French Huguenot and Irish Protestant troops who made up the army loyal to William, emphasized that this was not just a local quarrel but one with potentially profound consequences for British and European affairs. The decisive engagement of this bloody three-year conflict, during which over 25,000 men died, came on 1 July 1690 when William, himself recently arrived in Ireland, met James in battle along the banks of the river Boyne. A comprehensive victory saw the Williamite forces secure Dublin, and James flee his kingdoms for a second time, never to return. William too departed from Ireland soon after, leaving his Anglo-Dutch troops to prosecute the war under the command of General Ginkel, later 1st Earl of Athlone. Following an extremely bloody defeat at Aughrim, County Galway,

---

15 Harris, p. 444.
16 On the Navigation Acts see L. M. Cullen, *An Economic History of Ireland since 1660* (London, 1972), pp. 37–8; and Thomas Truxes, *Irish-American Trade, 1660–1783* (Cambridge, 1988), pp. 29–33.
17 C. I. McGrath, *Ireland and Empire, 1692–1770* (London, 2012), pp. 43–4 and 54.
18 The best account of the war in Ireland remains Simms, *Jacobite Ireland, passim*, but see also Richard Doherty, *The Williamite War in Ireland, 1688–91* (Dublin, 1998).

almost exactly a year after the Boyne, and a protracted siege at Limerick, the Jacobite forces surrendered in late 1691.[19]

The ensuing Treaty of Limerick marked the final defeat of Catholic Ireland. Over twelve thousand of James' soldiers, including many representatives of the surviving Catholic aristocracy and gentry, departed for France as part of the terms of surrender, where many enlisted leading to the formation of the celebrated Irish brigades of the eighteenth-century French military.[20] Many of those who remained in Ireland saw their estates confiscated, and the final vestiges of their political power diminished. This process would be confirmed when the second wholly Protestant, postwar Irish parliament assembled in Dublin in 1695. Among its first actions was to destroy the records of James' 'patriot parliament', confirming the earlier declaration made by the English parliament in 1690 that the 1689 legislation was deemed to be null and void.[21] Both the 1695 Irish assembly and succeeding parliaments would further bolster the position of the Protestant victors through the passage of the legislation collectively known as the Penal Laws. This legislation served to reduce the capacity of the surviving Catholic elite to offer a violent or military threat to Protestant Ireland, and crucially also to lessen their economic and social influence, by targeting their religion, property and their access to the professions.

This penal legislation passed by the Irish parliament was directed primarily at Catholics but also used against Protestant Dissenters (i.e. those Protestants who were not adherents of the Anglican Church of Ireland faith). It has been much studied and is a subject that lies largely outside the scope of this book.[22] Nevertheless it is important to briefly consider its economic and financial impact. Much of the legislation, notably the 1704 Act to Prevent the Further Growth of Popery, targeted Catholic economic interests, especially their property. Under this act Catholics were forbidden to purchase land, and could only take up leaseholds up to a maximum of thirty-one years. Such restrictions emphasized one of the identifiable reasons behind these legislative measures, namely a desire to reduce the economic and political power of the propertied Catholic elite. That this was successful is evident from the oft-cited statistic that the Catholic share of total landownership fell from around 14% in 1704 to 5% by 1778.[23] This figure of 5%, long dominant in

---

19 Harris, pp. 445–50.
20 Nathalie Genet-Rouffiac 'The Irish Jacobite exiles in France, 1692–1715', in *The Dukes of Ormonde, 1610–1745*, ed. Toby Barnard and Jane Fenlon (Woodbridge, 2000), pp. 195–210.
21 McGrath, *Ireland and Empire*, p. 44.
22 For a valuable overview of the literature see James Kelly, 'The Historiography of the Penal Laws', in *New Perspectives on the Penal Laws*, ed. John Bergin, Eoin Magennis, Lesa Ni Mhunghaile and Patrick Walsh (Dublin, 2011), pp. 27–54.
23 J. G. Simms, *The Williamite Confiscation in Ireland, 1690–1703* (London, 1956), p. 195.

the historiography of this subject has, however, been vigorously challenged by historians who now see it as a rather exaggerated and misleading statistic. Nevertheless it is clear that the 1704 act and subsequent legislation in 1709 – the so-called 'Discover's Act' – had a detrimental impact on the Catholic landowning class.[24] Catholic economic activity was restricted in other ways too, with barriers placed in the way of full membership of trade guilds and in the recruitment of apprentices, regulations which when enforced reduced economic capacity. The exclusion of Catholics from participation in local politics, and from military and civil employments through the introduction of a sacramental test clause in 1704, reduced further their economic potential. The 'test' also impacted on Protestant Dissenters, excluding the Presbyterian mercantile class hitherto dominant in the northern cities of Belfast and Derry from full involvement in civic life in these cities. Their exclusion from borough corporations also made it much more difficult for Protestant Dissenters to be returned to parliament.[25]

Historians have expended considerable energy debating the economic impact of the Penal Laws. Maureen Wall's argument, first developed in the 1950s, that the eighteenth century saw a rising Catholic mercantile and moneyed interest, is now largely recognized as an unduly optimistic assessment.[26] Instead David Dickson has shown how members of the Church of Ireland continued to dominate the urban economy, especially in the two principal cities, Cork and Dublin, for the majority of the period.[27] Nevertheless it is clear that Catholics were not entirely absent from the burgeoning world of Irish finance, both at home and abroad. Some Catholic merchants, as we shall see, invested in the schemes for a national bank in 1720, while others were active in the slave trade and in the East India and Ostend companies.[28] The Catholic Irish diaspora, whether in London, Paris or elsewhere, were also active investors in foreign stock markets. Among such investors were members of the large Jacobite diaspora who had migrated to France in the 1690s, including not just deposed aristocrats, military officers and clerical figures, but also bankers, such as the Paris-based Daniel Arthur and Richard Cantillon, as well as merchants, many of whom retained

[24] S. J. Connolly, *Religion, Law and Power: The Making of Protestant Ireland, 1660–1760* (Oxford, 1992), pp. 147–8 and 309–10; and McGrath, *Ireland and Empire*, pp. 33–4.

[25] Hayton, *Ruling Ireland*, pp. 186–208.

[26] Maureen Wall, 'Catholics in Economic Life', in *The Formation of the Irish Economy*, ed. L. M. Cullen (Cork, 1968), pp. 37–51.

[27] David Dickson, 'Catholics and Trade in Eighteenth-Century Ireland: An Old Debate Reconsidered', in *Endurance and Emergence: Catholics in Ireland in the Eighteenth Century*, ed. T. P. Power and Kevin Whelan (Dublin, 1990), pp. 85–100.

[28] Nini Rodgers, *Ireland, Slavery and Anti-Slavery: 1612–1865* (Basingstoke, 2009), pp. 124–44.

contacts and connections with relations in Ireland.[29] Their potential financial muscle is evidenced by the probably exaggerated estimates of contemporaries of the extent of the capital outflow that accompanied the migration to France after the Treaty of Limerick. One supposedly well-informed French authority claimed that they extracted £150,000 or half a million livres out of Ireland, which he claimed amounted to half the circulating cash in the Irish economy. Even if treated with caution, these figures point to a significant outflow of funds, most of which would never return to Ireland.[30]

Similar unease about the outflow of cash from Ireland, reflecting wider contemporary anxieties about the scarcity of specie in the kingdom, accompanied the first major Presbyterian out-migration from Ulster in the years 1718–20. These years saw the first major wave of Irish migration to the North American colonies with around four thousand emigrants, mostly from Ulster, crossing the Atlantic.[31] Official concerns, such as there were, at this mass population movement were predominantly about the exodus of hard cash and the failure of some of the emigrants to settle their debts. This reflected the economic motivations that lay behind much of this migration. Many of those departing had benefited from cheap leases in the postwar land market of the 1690s, leases that were now being called in and reset at higher rents. Rather than pay these increased prices, many of these tenants, who were often first-generation settlers of Scottish origin with few ties to Ireland, chose to seek new opportunities in North America. Others preferred to leave because of the continuing legal disabilities directed at Presbyterians under the 1704 test clause, but it is probable that the economic imperative, increased by bad harvests in 1718, was more significant in determining the timing of their exodus. Nevertheless the departure of these relatively prosperous emigrants (many were tenant farmers) hints at the impact of the Penal Laws on the early eighteenth-century Ulster Presbyterian economy.[32]

The effect of these laws on both the Irish Catholic and Protestant Dissenting communities was significant in determining the character of the Irish financial revolution. Only Irish Anglicans enjoyed unfettered access to the political and civic institutions of the state in the decades after the Williamite revolution. Although numerically in the minority, comprising approximately 20% of the population, they enjoyed almost complete control of land ownership and political power. In a largely agrarian economy this meant that they monopolized much of the available capital. In effect they

---

[29] Antoin E. Murphy, *Richard Cantillon: Entrepreneur and Economist* (Oxford, 1986). See also Genet-Rouffiac, pp. 204–9.

[30] Genet-Rouffiac, p. 204.

[31] Patrick Griffin, *The People With No Name: Ireland's Ulster Scots, America's Scots Irish and the Creation of the British Atlantic World* (Princeton, 2001), pp. 67–9.

[32] Patrick Walsh, 'Free Movement of People? Responses to Emigration from Ireland, 1718–30', *Journal of Irish and Scottish Studies*, 3 (2010), 221–36.

dominated the pool from which potential public creditors were likely to be drawn. Members of the various Protestant Dissenting communities, whether Presbyterians, Quakers or Huguenots, would in time become significant financial players at least relative to their ratio of the total population, but in the early years of the eighteenth century they still largely remained politically alienated, albeit with significant exceptions as will be discussed in the next chapter. Catholics, on the other hand, remained even more financially isolated, both as a consequence of penal legislation and also because of their own church's scruples about usury. The official teachings of the Catholic Church disbarred its adherents from lending at interest, therefore reducing further their financial capacity. Within an Irish context, a Catholic bishop, James Gallagher of Raphoe, argued in the 1730s that these restrictions should be lifted considering the already punitive effects of the Penal Laws. His appeals to the Vatican went unheard, and it was not until the 1780s that legislation was introduced in Ireland allowing Catholics to lend without damaging their conscience.[33] Echoing the debates in continental European Catholicism on this subject in the first half of the eighteenth century, Gallagher's appeal is significant for the light it sheds on contemporary Catholic concerns.[34] Adherence to Catholic teachings on usury was not however all-encompassing and some Catholics, notably the Dillons, a Galway banking family, and others with émigré links, continued to be active moneylenders.[35] By the mid-eighteenth century, Catholics also comprised a significant element among Irish public creditors, suggesting eventual active participation in the Irish financial revolution, if this phenomenon is viewed within a long-term context.

II

The Irish Protestant elite had emerged victorious in 1691, but victory brought its own challenges. Three years of conflict had caused significant disruption to the Irish economy, while the war had been expensive to prosecute.[36] Furthermore William III expected that this expenditure would be recouped from Irish sources. His emphasis on raising the necessary revenues locally

---

[33] 23 & 24 Geo. III, c. 55 [Irish], An Act to Remove Doubts and Scruples. Dickson, 'An Old Debate Revisited', p. 92.

[34] Cathaldus Giblin, 'Catalogue of Material of Irish Interest in the Collection Nunziatura di Fiandra, Vatican Archives: Part 5, vols 123–132', Collectanea Hibernica, 9 (1966), 7–70 (pp. 69–70). I am grateful to Prof. Christine Desan of Harvard Law School for helpful discussions on the European theological and legal contexts.

[35] Cullen, Economic History, p. 74.

[36] For the economic impact of the war see Alan J. Smyth, 'The Social and Economic Impact of the Williamite War on Ireland, 1688–91' (Ph.D., Trinity College Dublin, 2013).

was made clear when, upon his initial arrival at Carrickfergus in June 1690, among his first acts as King of Ireland was the nomination of new revenue officers for the areas nominally within his control.[37] Immediate control of the Irish financial bureaucracy needed to be established, which was quickly achieved in the northern counties of Ulster where Tyrconnell's Jacobite revolution of the late 1680s had failed to take hold. The rapid return of Irish tax revenues to their pre-war levels by the mid-1690s demonstrates how successful the Williamite authorities in Dublin were at regaining local control throughout the kingdom.[38]

However, the existing fiscal structures were never on their own going to pay for the massive military expenditure laid out in Ireland in 1689–91. Soldiers had to be paid, the bill for supplies had to be settled, and fortifications, cities and towns had to be rebuilt. Figuring out how to meet these challenges became one of the major issues that would occupy members of the Irish Anglican political elite over the next decade. They would address them in two ways: first, through the time-honoured mechanism for settling early modern Irish military debts, namely by the confiscation and redistribution of the landed estates of the vanquished, and secondly, through the imposition of parliamentarily sanctioned additional taxation. Analysing each of these methods highlights different aspects of the Irish experience of the financial revolution.

The confiscation of much of the landed property of the defeated Irish Jacobites conformed to a pattern established in the aftermath of previous sixteenth and seventeenth-century conflicts. By late 1691 over 750,000 acres had been forfeited to the crown and were vested in the hands of the Irish revenue commissioners.[39] Disposing of these estates would prove time-consuming and complicated as different interests competed over the best way to distribute this bounty.[40] William III was eager to reward his generals and 'favourites' with Irish property, and duly granted enormous estates to influential individuals such as General Ginkel, newly ennobled following his Irish victories as Earl of Athlone, and Joost Van Keppel, the Earl of Albemarle, among others. These actions were opposed by the English parliament who saw them as an abuse of royal prerogative and preferred instead to sell the forfeited estates to fund the vast sums expended fighting the war in Ireland. They hoped to realize £1 million from such sales.[41] To

---

[37] C. I. McGrath, 'The Irish Revenue System: Government and Administration 1689–1702' (Ph.D., University of London, 1997), p. 11.

[38] Patrick Walsh, 'The Irish Fiscal State, 1690–1769', *Historical Journal*, 56 (2013), 637.

[39] Simms, *Williamite Confiscation*, p. 194.

[40] Simms, *Williamite Confiscation*, pp. 82–120.

[41] Anon., *Proposals for Raising A Million of Money out of the Forfeited Estates in Ireland Together, With the Answer of the Irish to the Same, and a Reply Thereto* (London, 1694); and John Trenchard, *A Letter From A Soldier to The Commons of England Occasioned by an Address Now Carrying On By The Protestants in Ireland, In Order to Take Away the Fund Appropriated For the Payment of the Arrears of the Army* (London, 1702).

this end, the Westminster parliament in 1700 successfully resumed the royal grants made by the King to his favourites, and dispatched parliament-appointed trustees to Ireland to sell the confiscated estates at the maximum price they could achieve.

Upon arrival in Dublin the Trustees of Forfeited Estates found their task was more difficult than anticipated. Irish Protestants who in good faith had purchased substantial estates from the King's royal grantees before the Act of Resumption, were seeking compensation for their losses, while complex disputes over title took up much of the Trustees' time.[42] The so-called 'Protestant purchasers' were eventually compensated, but their experience shows that Irish 'property rights' were less inalienable than those guaranteed by Westminster across the Irish Sea. The possibility of confiscation or resumption of legitimate investments by the London or Dublin legislatures suggests that the application of the concept of 'credible commitment' to Ireland is not entirely unproblematic.[43] Nevertheless, the Trustees were able to complete their task, even if they failed to realize the anticipated profits from the Irish forfeitures.

The lower than expected yield from the confiscated Jacobite estates can be attributed to a number of factors. Uncertainties about title, created both by the restoration of some formerly attainted Jacobites to their estates and the problems faced by the 'Protestant purchasers', led to reduced demand and therefore lower prices at the Trustees' auctions in 1702–03. Such uncertainties made investment in these estates risky, but it also could lead to greater rewards, with some Irish purchasers, like the rising Whig political star, William Conolly, acquiring huge estates at bargain prices.[44] The lower purchase prices at the Trustees' auctions could also be attributed to a more general slump in the Irish economy at the turn of the century, and also to shortages of surplus capital in the Irish economy.[45] If Irish Protestants were unable to take full advantage of the opportunities created by these adverse market conditions, there were external investors willing to speculate in Irish land.

The most significant of these was the Hollow Sword Blade Company, later of course to achieve notoriety as the South Sea Company's banker. Its investments in Irish property demonstrate the complexities of situating Ireland within the parameters of the financial revolution. Ireland could be, as we

[42] Simms, *Williamite Confiscation*, pp. 124–6; and Patrick Walsh, *The Making of the Irish Protestant Ascendancy: The Life of William Conolly, 1662–1729* (Woodbridge, 2010), pp. 50–60.
[43] I am very grateful to Anne Laurence for discussions on this topic, and for sharing with me an unpublished paper on the complexities of applying North and Weingast's 'credible commitment' thesis to Ireland.
[44] Walsh, *Making of the Irish Protestant Ascendancy*, p. 60.
[45] Cullen, *Economic History*, pp. 30–1; and Stuart Bell, '"A Masterpiece of Knavery"? The Activities of the Sword Blade Company in London's Early Financial Markets', *Business History*, 54 (2012), 623–38 (p. 632).

29

shall see, both a source of capital for investments in England's public credit and private corporations, and a venue for English corporations to invest their capital. The Hollow Sword Blade Company's Irish activities fall into the latter category and mark a significant point in its evolution from rapier manufacturers to financiers. Established in the early 1690s, it quickly diversified from its original business as a military cutler. Its decision to convert swords into ploughshares by purchasing an Irish property portfolio was the latest manifestation of an evolving business model, and was made possible by a clause in its original incorporating charter, which allowed it to hold landed property.[46] By autumn 1702 it had spent £200,000 on estates scattered across Ireland with a combined annual rent roll of £20,000, equating to a very competitive price of ten years' purchase. In order to pay for these acquisitions the directors issued new stock in the company, another privilege allowed under the terms of its original charter. The Hollow Sword Blade Company encouraged holders of outstanding army pay debentures to exchange them for stock in the company, which would be backed by Irish landed security. These debentures, a form of unsecured government debt, were then trading on the open market at a discount of 85% so both parties gained from these transactions. This innovative scheme meant that the English government received payment for its own land in Ireland in the form of its own pay obligations, which it could then cancel.[47]

This outcome was attractive both to the government and to the Hollow Sword Blade Company, whose directors anticipated profitable returns on their Irish investments. They hoped to increase these profits still further by offering mortgages to other purchasers of forfeited Jacobite estates, a measure which brought the company into conflict with the Bank of England, who saw it as an encroachment on their still recently established banking privileges. The Bank initiated legal proceedings against the company, which responded by continuing to publicly challenge the Bank, defending its right to carry out banking functions. This animosity between the two corporations foreshadowed the Bank's conflict with the South Sea Company in 1720. The Hollow Sword Blade Company's 'Irish adventure' was not, however, a success. Its Irish rents never reached the levels anticipated in 1702 and by 1710 the company directors had mostly extricated themselves from their Irish interests.[48]

Daniel Defoe, in a famous description of the Hollow Sword Blade Company's directors in his 1719 pamphlet *An Anatomy of Exchange*

---

[46] For the Hollow Sword Blade Company see W. R. Scott, *The Constitution and Finance of English, Scottish, and Irish Joint Stock Companies to 1720*, 3 vols (Cambridge, 1912), vol. 3, pp. 435–42; John Carswell, *The South Sea Bubble* (London, 1960), pp. 30–9; and Bell, 'A Masterpiece of Knavery'.

[47] Carswell, p. 35.

[48] Anon., *The Case of the Governor and Company for making Hollow Sword Blades* (London, 1709). *Dublin Intelligence*, 8 Oct. 1709, 22 Apr. 1710; and Bell, pp. 633–4.

Alley, recounts how they escaped from their 'Irish adventure' with 'great mortification'.[49] This outcome he attributed to their 'knavery' and greed as well as to their failure to comprehend the complications of the business in which they were engaged. Modern historians have repeated the latter charge describing how the Hollow Sword Blade Company was unable to negotiate the intricacies of the Irish property market, notably the difficulties presented by disputes over title. Such complexities defeated contemporaries with a greater understanding of Irish conditions. Nevertheless they reveal some of the characteristics that the same directors would exhibit when they shifted their focus to the slave trade with South America in their guise as directors of the South Sea Company, notably incomprehension of local conditions coupled with a talent for financial chicanery.

The Hollow Sword Blade Company's Irish experiences reveal much about the failure of the Williamite confiscation to generate sufficient funds to pay for the expense of the Irish war, let alone pay for the ongoing expenses of the Irish administration. The wholesale confiscation and redistribution of property no longer sufficed as a panacea for resolving Irish Treasury deficits. Solutions would need to be found elsewhere, which leads back to the importance of parliament as a catalyst for financial innovation in the aftermath of the Williamite revolution. As with its English counterpart, the Irish parliament gained a new prominence in the 1690s, as it made the transition from event to institution through regular meetings. Financial matters lay at the heart of this transition. The first postwar parliament although very short-lived – it sat for just one month – spent much of its only session engaged in constitutional wrangling over contentions by some of its members that it possessed the 'sole right' to initiate financial legislation.[50] This right was to a large extent conceded in a compromise agreement by the time the second Williamite parliament met in 1695 and it would have long-term significance for the development of Irish fiscal measures. From that point onward the three hundred members of the Irish Commons would decide the levels of taxation levied in Ireland and their duration, allowing the Irish parliament to extend its influence over Irish society.[51] As in post-revolution England, and indeed Scotland, parliament had secured a greater role for itself. This role would be exercised in two ways that are significant for the purposes of this chapter.

The first of these was through the sanctioning of additional taxation over and above the perpetual sums granted to the Irish administration by

---

49 Daniel Defoe, *The Anatomy of Exchange Alley* (London, 1719), pp. 38–9.

50 James McGuire, 'The Irish Parliament of 1692', in *Penal Era and Golden Age: Essays in Irish History, 1690–1800*, ed. Thomas Bartlett and D. W. Hayton (Belfast, 1979), pp. 1–31.

51 For these developments see C. I. McGrath, *The Making of the Eighteenth-Century Irish Constitution* (Dublin, 2000), esp. pp. 73–117.

the customs and excise legislation introduced to Ireland in 1662 following the restoration of Charles II. This legislation, which remained the basis of Irish taxation until the nineteenth century, was partly based on innovations introduced by the Cromwellian government in the 1650s. It codified Irish taxation and laid the foundations for the development of an efficient revenue-raising bureaucracy responsible not just for the collection of customs and excise duties, but also property taxes in the form of the hearth tax (a tax on every fireplace) and quit rents (taxes on properties previously forfeited to the crown).[52] Collectively these taxes paid for the costs of the Irish government until 1689, allowing successive administrations to avoid calling a parliament between 1666 and James II's 'patriot parliament' of 1689. The changed circumstances in the postwar period meant that new sources of income had to be found to cover first, the expenditure laid out on prosecuting the Irish war, and secondly, and much more significant in the long run, the great expansion in the Irish military establishment after the Peace of Ryswick in 1697 in order to accommodate William III's standing army.

Ireland's emergence as a garrison for the King's standing army offered a solution to the complex question of what to do with the greatly expanded military following the end of the Nine Years War. A compromise needed to be reached between two opposing positions: William III's belief that he needed to maintain a standing army and the longstanding English opposition to such a force. The eventual solution was to maintain a twelve-thousand-strong English standing army on the Irish establishment where they would be paid for by Irish taxpayers. These troops would also provide a degree of security to the Irish Protestant population who shared few of the English qualms about standing armies. Concerns about security rather than abstract ideas about liberty were to the forefront of the Irish Protestant elite's minds in the decades after the Williamite wars. Maintaining the army on the Irish establishment, and building the country-wide network of barracks to house them, in themselves a major innovation, necessitated maximizing the financial resources of the Irish state to meet the costs of this imperial contribution.[53]

This led to the expansion of the revenue bureaucracy to the point where it became the most 'pervasive agency of the state' in eighteenth-century Ireland, and the beginnings of parliamentarily sanctioned short-term taxation.[54] The first of these processes was already underway before the Williamite revolution and can be traced back to the end of the practice of

[52] 14 & 15 Car. II, c. 8, *An Act for Settling of the Excise* and c. 11, *An Act for Customs, Excise and New Impost*. See Sean Reamonn, *History of The Revenue Commissioners* (Dublin, 1981), pp. 13–16.
[53] McGrath, *Ireland and Empire*, pp. 133–42.
[54] Both this paragraph and the next draw extensively on Walsh, 'The Irish Fiscal State', pp. 635–7.

farming out the collection of government revenues to private individuals in 1681 and the consolidation of tax collection in the hands of the seven revenue commissioners. Under these commissioners around 600 subordinate officers, scattered across forty-three revenue districts covering the entire kingdom, were responsible for the collection of all Irish taxes. Regressive taxation in the form of customs duties and excises charged on alcohol and tobacco formed the bulk of Irish government income in this period, but they were supplemented by the hearth tax (which continued in Ireland after its abolition in England in 1689) and quit rents levied on property. From the 1690s onward, further sources of income were needed and three options presented themselves.

The first of these was to introduce a land tax along the lines of the English model. After a brief experiment in 1697–98, which served to plug an immediate shortfall in revenue, any attempt to introduce an Irish land tax was abandoned. The second option was to borrow money either from internal or external creditors. This, however, was not a viable option in the 1690s because, as will become apparent, Irish financial innovation lagged far behind that experienced in contemporary England and even that of Scotland, both of which witnessed expanding domestic capital markets in the same decade. The third and final option was to levy additional customs and excise taxation through short-term votes in parliament. This was the preferred option and instituted the practice of parliamentarily sanctioned 'additional' taxation, giving greater income-raising powers to the Dublin legislature and thereby increasing its significance. These additional duties, mostly charged on alcohol and tobacco, together with an expanding population and the return to relative domestic peace, led to increased levels of revenue, allowing the growing costs of the Irish military establishment to be met.[55]

These developments in taxation have been seen as highly significant both politically and financially. In financial terms they achieved greater importance in 1716 when the Dublin parliament voted to institute the Irish national debt, the second major financial intervention to originate in the Irish commons. A loan of £50,000 was raised to pay for thirteen new regiments in Ireland to replace the twelve regiments that had been dispatched to Scotland and northern England to put down the Jacobite rebellion during the previous year. As with the English national debt, the Irish debt therefore arose from the wartime demands of the fiscal-military state. Offering an attractive rate of interest of 8%, this first national loan quickly attracted subscribers, most of whom were drawn from the political and administrative elite. Interest payments were made out of the additional

---

[55]   C. I. McGrath, 'Money, Politics and Power: The Financial Legislation of the Irish Parliament', in *The Eighteenth-Century Composite State: Representative Institutions in Ireland and Europe, 1689–1800*, ed. D. W. Hayton, James Kelly and John Bergin (Basingstoke, 2010), pp. 21–43.

duties voted for by the Irish House of Commons, thus binding MPs and the public creditors (when they weren't one and the same) into a close and mutually beneficial relationship.[56] By the time a second loan of £150,000 was raised in 1729, particular additional duties were appropriated by parliament to meet the charge of interest payments on the debt. These developments in additional taxation, and then public credit, have been seen as cumulatively comprising the Irish financial revolution, although their pre-eminent historian has rightly stressed the evolutionary nature of these processes over the period 1662–1716.[57]

So far this chapter has shown how Ireland's particular version of the 1688 revolution, and subsequent constitutional and political settlement, influenced its experience of a wider British financial revolution. Whereas England and Scotland witnessed joint-stock booms as well as the development of national banks alongside revolutionary changes in public credit, Ireland's revolution was almost solely on the public credit side. Even then, its expansion was piecemeal, with the establishment of the national debt coming at a comparatively late stage in 1716 after the Hanoverian succession. The impact of the differing experiences of the Glorious Revolution as well as the legislative agenda of the Irish 'Protestant Interest' was important in this respect, but questions remain about the extent of the differences between Ireland and Britain.

III

It is expedient to briefly examine developments in England and Scotland in the period between the Glorious Revolution and the South Sea bubble. The English experience of the financial revolution is well known, and can be briefly summarized here.[58] The demands of war, coupled with the constitutional and political changes, which resulted in greater protection of individual property rights and the increased power of parliament, provided the context for the acceleration in financial innovation. Among the most important innovations were the establishment of the English national debt in 1692, the foundation of the Bank of England two years later, and the increased proliferation of joint-stock companies specializing in an ever-widening variety of commercial ventures. These developments had a huge impact on contemporary society and politics, and did not go uncontested.

---

[56] As well as nineteen MPs and seven peers, the subscribers included a number of parliamentary officials and clerks (*CJI*, vol. 3, Appendix, pp. cxiii–cxiv).
[57] C. I. McGrath, 'The Irish Experience of "Financial Revolution" 1660–1760', in McGrath and Fauske (eds), *Money, Power and Print*, pp. 157–88 (pp. 166–8).
[58] See Dickson, *Financial Revolution*; Roseveare, *Financial Revolution*; and Murphy, *Origins of English Financial Markets*, for the most useful accounts.

The growing influence of the coffee-house, the newspaper and the printed pamphlet – what some have called the emergence of a public sphere – meant that dissenting voices were more likely to be heard. Such dissenters and sceptics included not only writers and polemicists like Jonathan Swift and Daniel Defoe but also members of the 'country' interest in parliament.[59] They feared the rise of a moneyed 'city' interest, which would precipitate a shift in the balance of politics. Their concerns fed into the increasing levels of political partisanship evident in the growing tensions between the Whigs and Tories, with the former broadly representing the city and the latter, the country. Some scholars have made much of the entanglements visible between representatives of political factions and particular financial interests, while others have highlighted the circulation of critiques of financial innovations like the Bank, or joint-stock trading. In doing so they point to the divergent elements rather than the broader societal and political convergence on the adoption of the developments cumulatively seen as the financial revolution.[60]

This broad acceptance of so many elements of the financial revolution can be seen in the enthusiastic popular participation in the stock market as well as in the speed at which members of the English public were willing to subscribe to schemes of public credit. The 1690s saw the first English stock-market boom with over one hundred joint-stock companies floated during this decade. They ranged in size from large-scale international trading corporations like the New East India or Levant companies to smaller enterprises engaged in fisheries, mining or the paper trade. Most of these companies were quick to attract investors, and this significant numerical increase in the share-holding public led to the beginnings of an active secondary market and the appearance of the first Anglophone financial professionals. Both this market and the brokers/stockjobbers who populated it were physically based in the streets surrounding the Royal Exchange in the heart of the City of London. Much of this business was conducted in that other great innovation of late

---

[59] For useful studies of the literary and printed reactions to the financial revolution see J. A. Downie, 'Gulliver's Travels, The Contemporary Debate on the Financial Revolution and the Bourgeois Public Sphere', in McGrath and Fauske (eds), *Money, Power, and Print*, pp. 115–34; James Hartley, 'The Chameleon Daniel Defoe: Public Writing in the age before Economic Theory', in McGrath and Fauske (eds), *Money, Power, and Print*, pp. 26–50; Catherine Ingrassia, *Authorship, Commerce and Gender in Early Eighteenth-Century England: A Culture of Public Credit* (Cambridge, 2005); Colin Nicholson, *Writing and the Rise of Finance: Capital Satires of the Early Eighteenth Century* (Cambridge, 1994); and Sean D. Moore, *Swift, The Book, and the Irish Financial Revolution: Satire and Sovereignty in Colonial Ireland* (Baltimore, 2010).

[60] For example, Bruce C. Carruthers, *City of Capital: Politics and Markets in the English Financial Revolution* (Princeton, 1996). For accounts which stress convergence see Natasha Glaisyer, *The Culture of Commerce in England, 1660–1720* (Woodbridge, 2006) and Murphy, *Origins of English Financial Markets*.

seventeenth-century London, the coffee-house, with some establishments such as Lloyd's, Jonathan's and Garraway's quickly becoming known as centres of financial information and stock trading.[61] All of this expanding activity demonstrated the rising place of London within the global economy as well as the attraction of the new financial products that were being traded in the City.

These products included not just stock in private trading companies, but also stock in the state itself, as new methods were introduced to pay for the increased costs of William III's military interventions on the European continent. The first of these measures were the hugely popular tontine and lottery loans introduced in 1693 and 1694 respectively. Each raised £1 million for the exchequer, but carried high rates of return with the tontine promising short-term rates of up to 14%, imposing a significant burden on the state's resources.[62] The lottery was equally generous: each £10 ticket guaranteed its purchaser an annual prize, ranging from £1 to £1,000 for sixteen years.[63] Even more significant than these early steps at establishing new forms of government borrowing was the foundation of the Bank of England in 1694. The Bank was conceived as a crucial element of the new public credit infrastructure being developed by City financial and mercantile interests in partnership with senior Treasury officials. Established within the style of a joint-stock corporation, with a governor and twelve directors elected by the shareholders, it was granted a monopoly on the right to issue notes in return for a substantial loan of £1.2 million to the government.[64] These privileges would be jealously guarded over the succeeding decades. The Bank quickly established itself as a significant institution in English financial life, as can be seen in the rapid and positive response to its initial call for subscribers in 1694, when over 1,200 investors subscribed over £1 million in a period of just under two weeks.[65] The majority of these subscribers came from the greater London area suggesting that this was predominantly a metropolitan rather than an English affair. This was similarly reflected in the composition of the Bank's first board of directors, which was dominated by members of the Whig mercantile elite of London. It did also attract investors from beyond the metropole, however, with a tiny minority of subscribers listing their home address as outside London.[66]

Out of the 1,268 Bank subscribers, only twenty had addresses outside England. They included thirteen resident in the United Provinces (the

---

[61] Brian Cowan, *The Social Life of Coffee: The Emergence of the British Coffeehouse* (London, 2005); and Richard Dale, *The First Crash: Lessons from the South Sea Bubble* (Princeton, 2004), pp. 7–21.

[62] Roseveare, p. 35.

[63] Anne Murphy, 'Lotteries in the 1690s: Investment or Gamble?', *Financial History Review*, 12 (2005), 227–46.

[64] Dickson, *Financial Revolution*, pp. 54–6; and Roseveare, p. 35.

[65] Murphy, *Origins of English Financial Markets*, p. 151.

[66] List of Original Subscribers to the Bank of England, 1694 (BoE, M1/1).

modern Netherlands), four resident in Ireland, one in Hamburg, one in Fort St George in India, and one, Colonel Nathaniel Blakestone, who described himself as of the West Indies and Westminster.[67] To the four Irishmen can perhaps be added three men with the surname Butler, possibly members of the Ormonde/Butler dynasty based in counties Kilkenny and Tipperary. The four Irishmen positively identifiable are Robert Molesworth, the commonwealthman and recently returned Williamite diplomatic envoy to Denmark, Philip Savage, the chancellor of the Irish exchequer, the Revd Henry Scardeville, Dean of Cloyne, and Lord John Fitzharding, an Irish peer.[68] Their subscriptions to the Bank were among the very few known Irish forays into the London financial markets during the 1690s. This reflected less an Irish reluctance to participate in such schemes but more the general dominance of London residents within the city's early markets and their ability to fulfil the speculative and capital needs of both private corporations and the public 'funds'. This situation continued into the early eighteenth century with Londoners continuing to supply the bulk of the capital invested in the major joint-stock companies, and indeed the national debt.[69] This is despite the increased opportunities for investment in the Bank of England, East India Company and, after 1711, the South Sea Company.

IV

England, and London specifically, was the main locus of the British financial revolution, but Ireland, as we have seen, and Scotland both experienced their own versions of this revolution. The impact of the financial revolution in the northern British kingdom, particularly in the period before the 1707 Act of Union, is the focus of the final section of this chapter. As with Ireland, the Williamite revolution and settlement had important consequences for Scotland's post-revolutionary economic and financial development, and it is worth briefly outlining here. The Scottish experience of the 1688–89 revolution was different from that of its Irish and English counterparts. Unlike Ireland, neither king ventured north into Scotland during the tumultuous years of 1689–90. Despite this, William's arrival in England in 1688 was broadly welcomed by large swathes of lowland Scotland, while James' departure was equally greeted with enthusiasm by the same group, most of whom were Presbyterians and therefore politically as well as religiously hostile to the Stuart king's increasingly Catholic regime.[70]

The Jacobite administration in Edinburgh therefore quickly collapsed,

---

67 Murphy, *Origins of English Financial Markets*, table 6.6, p. 152.
68 This is probably John Berkeley, 4th Viscount Fitzharding of Berehaven (d.1712).
69 Dickson, *Financial Revolution*, pp. 276–9.
70 This account of the revolution in Scotland is largely based on D. W. Hayton, 'Contested

leaving a political vacuum that was filled by members of the pro-Williamite nobility and gentry. By the middle of 1689 when the Scottish estates met, the result of the English revolution was no longer in any doubt and the Presbyterian-dominated assembly in Edinburgh confirmed the abdication of James II as King of Scotland, where he had sat as James VII, offering the throne instead to William and Mary. In doing so they took control of their own constitutional destiny by stressing the separateness of their settlement. These constitutional changes did not go unchallenged, with opposition coming from both highlanders in the north, who were mostly motivated by dynastic and confessional loyalties, as well as from Episcopalians, who opposed the religious aspects of the Scottish revolution settlement. The most substantial armed resistance came from John Graham, Viscount Dundee, a Jacobite loyalist, who won a significant victory at Killiecrankie in July 1689. Unfortunately Dundee himself was killed, and his allies and supporters defeated in battle at Dunkeld a month later, with the final rebels succumbing to an English army at Cromdate on 1 May 1690, two months before William's defeat of James' Irish forces at the Boyne.

The military defeat of the opponents of the revolution was comparatively more easily achieved in Scotland than in Ireland, even if pockets of resistance remained despite the brutal methods used by Williamite forces at Glencoe and elsewhere.[71] It was also much cheaper than the Irish equivalent as there was much less wartime devastation wrought on either the local economy or on the physical landscape. Meanwhile, the constitutional settlement in Scotland ensured the continuation of a separate parliament in Edinburgh. All of these factors combined meant that the northern kingdom was a fertile ground for financial pioneers in the early 1690s. The most significant of these Scottish innovators was of course William Paterson, the leading light behind both the successful Bank of England in 1694, and the much less successful Company of Scotland founded in 1696.[72] The latter's infamous, and disastrous, Darien project has tended to dominate the historiography of Scottish financial enterprise in this period. Even then the focus of most attention has been on the folly of the Darien project, rather than what it can tell us about the contemporary Scottish investment community, although the work of Douglas Watt and W. Douglas Jones has offered an important corrective here.[73] Following their lead it is possible, however, to identify clear elements of a Scottish version of the financial revolution.

Kingdoms, 1688–1756', in *Short Oxford History of the British Isles: The Eighteenth Century*, ed. Paul Langford (Oxford, 2002), pp. 35–70, and Harris, pp. 364–421.

[71] For an account that emphasizes the violent dimension of the revolution not only in Scotland, but also in England, see Pincus, esp. pp. 276–7. For the 'Massacre of Glencoe' see Harris, p. 495.

[72] David Armitage, 'William Paterson, 1658–1719', in ODNB.

[73] Douglas Watt, *The Price of Scotland: Darien, Union and the Wealth of Nations*

The focus of Scottish innovation was less on the creation of forms of public credit, and more on corporate and mercantile initiatives.[74] Pre-Union Scotland, unlike England, or even Ireland, did not see the emergence of either an efficient revenue bureaucracy or a funded national debt. The northern kingdom's taxation administration was not reformed until the 1720s, and even then its annual per capita revenue yield remained below that witnessed elsewhere in Britain and Ireland.[75] Meanwhile the military contexts that created the need for government borrowing in England and Ireland were either absent or too politically complicated. It was only after the Act of Union in 1707 that Scottish revenues were used to contribute to the servicing of the British debt.[76] While Scotland experienced limited fiscal developments in the immediate post-revolution decades, it did see – like England, but unlike Ireland – the foundation of a national bank in 1695.

Founded just a year after its southern counterpart, the Bank of Scotland had a very different mission from that of the Bank of England. Unlike the London bank it was not established to provide credit to the government; indeed under the terms of its charter the bank was specifically forbidden to do so. Instead its focus was on providing credit and support for the growing Edinburgh and Glasgow mercantile interests.[77] This emphasis on private enterprise was a characteristic of the Scottish financial revolution, and it can be seen in the explosion in Scottish joint-stock activity noted by W. R. Scott in his seminal 1912 study, as well as in the widespread investor support secured for the Company of Scotland's trading adventure to Central America.[78] This venture failed due to a variety of factors including English intervention, a lack of understanding of the climatic, trading and political conditions on the Isthmus of Darien, and mismanagement on the part of the company's promoters.

The spectacular failure of the Darien adventure and its ruinous impact on the local investing public, both those of noble and mercantile background, has often been cited as evidence for the failure of the financial revolution in Scotland.[79] Within such a reading it becomes an inevitable prelude to Union, demonstrating once and for all that the Scots were incapable of managing their own affairs. Such views are misleading, failing as they do to understand the significance of the support for the investment mania that provided the

(Edinburgh, 2007); and W. Douglas Jones, '"The Bold Adventurers": A Quantitative Analysis of the Darien Subscription List (1696)', *Scottish Economic & Social History*, 21 (2001), 22–42.

74 Walsh, 'Bubble on the Periphery', p. 112.
75 For per capita revenue yield data see Walsh, 'The Irish Fiscal State', pp. 638–9.
76 Bruce Lenman, *An Economic History of Modern Scotland* (London, 1977), pp. 58–60.
77 Richard Saville, *Bank of Scotland, A History, 1695–1995* (Edinburgh, 1996).
78 Scott, vol. 3, pp. 128–9.
79 Lenman, p. 52; and Christopher A. Whatley, *Bought and Sold for English Gold? Explaining the Union of 1707*, 2nd edn (Edinburgh, 2001), p. 65.

company's capital. The ability of Paterson and his fellow promoters to raise over £400,000 in an ostensibly poor country like Scotland, together with the ease with which the Bank of Scotland first raised its initial capital and then withstood the Darien crisis, highlights just how much the Scottish public bought into the new financial opportunities already manifesting themselves in England.[80]

The collapse of the Darien scheme did not bring an end to Scottish experiments in high finance and speculative adventures. In 1705 and again in 1707, the projector John Breholt, 'a London shipmaster who specialised in get rich schemes', managed to enlist a number of prominent Scots, including directors of the Bank of Scotland and former directors of the Company of Scotland, in two daring schemes aimed at seizing the supposed pirate wealth of Madagascar.[81] Breholt's schemes failed to fully materialize but the willingness of prominent Scots to support them belies any notion that the Darien disaster made all Scots risk averse. Some other members of the Scottish political elite also remained interested in financial innovation. In 1705 John Law, the economist and financier, was encouraged to present his ideas for a land-bank to the Scottish parliament in a bid to remedy the perilous domestic fiscal and economic situation then apparent in the kingdom. Although Scotland's MPs failed to adopt his proposals, the same year saw the publication in Edinburgh of Law's seminal treatise, *Money and Trade Consider'd with a Proposal for Supplying the Nation with Money*, which contained many of the ideas that made him famous during the Mississippi bubble in 1719–20.[82] Law's proposals failed both because of parliamentary hostility to a land-bank (incidentally a trait shared by their Irish and English counterparts), and because of the increasing political uncertainty in Edinburgh, which would lead to the Anglo-Scottish Union two years later.

The impact of the Anglo-Scottish Union of 1707 on Scottish financial developments is a complex subject, particularly considering the persistent and ongoing debates about the impact of the Union on the local economy.[83] The Scots' continuing access to English colonial markets – something that marked out the Scottish situation as different from that of the Irish – allowed mercantile interests, notably in Glasgow, to realize great fortunes. This in turn created investment opportunities and a continued need for the banking facilities offered by the Bank of Scotland. The bank's survival post-Union, and indeed its resilience during the Jacobite rebellion of 1715 when it was

[80]   Jones, 'The Bold Adventurers', p. 38.
[81]   Arne Bialuschewski, 'Greed, Fraud, and Popular Culture: John Breholt's Madagascar Schemes of the Early Eighteenth Century', in McGrath and Fauske (eds), *Money, Power and Print*, pp. 104–14 (p. 105).
[82]   Antoin E. Murphy, *John Law: Economic Theorist and Policy Maker* (Oxford, 1997), pp. 71–5.
[83]   See Whatley, *Bought and Sold for English Gold*, *passim*, for this debate.

threatened with a run on its notes, confirmed the adaptation of large sections of the Scottish public to the new financial paradigms created in the 1690s. Indeed it might be argued that the particularly Scottish version of these innovations, with their emphasis on private entrepreneurial and investment activity, had penetrated local society sufficiently to withstand the twin shocks of union and rebellion. It is therefore not surprising that some Scots were active in the London markets in 1720, or that 'Scots projects' were also in vogue during 'South Sea Year'.[84]

V

This chapter has highlighted the different experiences of the financial revolution witnessed across Britain and Ireland in the three decades immediately after the Glorious Revolution. It has shown that while many of the innovations witnessed in Dublin, Edinburgh and London had longer roots, the political and constitutional convulsions of the years 1688–91 still had a major impact on subsequent developments. The various experiences of these years accelerated the process of change, while the differing postwar circumstances in each kingdom determined the scale and type of innovation. The emphasis here has been on Ireland and pre-Union Scotland, showing how developments in these two kingdoms increasingly converged with those in the metropolitan centre. In Ireland this was clearest in the establishment of the public credit structures, notably the beginning of a funded national debt in 1716. Meanwhile in Scotland, the success of joint-stock corporations and the foundation of a national bank indicated the spread of English financial influences, although the role of Scotsmen like William Paterson in London suggests that there was cross-fertilization of ideas. Similarly, perhaps the Hollow Sword Blade Company's Irish adventure warns of the need to see developments and events across the three kingdoms not in isolation, but as part of an integrated whole. This was particularly true of the nascent banking and investment sectors, which are the focus of the next chapter.

---

[84]   These points are developed at greater length in Walsh, 'Bubble on the Periphery'.

2

Banking and Investment on the Periphery: The Case of Ireland

The financial revolution encompassed more than just innovations in public credit and war financing. These developments coincided and were linked with innovations in banking, exchange and the stock market. For W. R. Scott writing at the beginning of the twentieth century, the period 1690–1720 was the era of the joint-stock company, while Larry Neal has described the same period as the 'age of financial capitalism'. Such synoptic descriptions, along with Natasha Glaisyer's uncovering of a burgeoning 'culture of commerce' in the same decades, capture something of the spirit of the age.[1] These years saw the growth of the English financial markets, the development and expansion of banking structures across the British Atlantic world, and greater acceptance of paper money and bills of exchange as mediums of exchange.[2] This period also saw the expansion of the London stock market as investors increasingly traded stocks and shares in private corporations as well as government debt. The extant print culture of the time clearly demonstrates that contemporaries understood that they were living during a period of great change and innovation.[3] Many participated enthusiastically in this revolution, becoming investors in joint-stock companies, speculating on the financial markets, remitting their rental income through banks, and by becoming more reliant on new mediums of exchange. Others became public creditors, purchasing lottery tickets or acquiring insurance policies. Historians have extensively charted these phenomena and their impact on contemporary society with close attention being paid to issues of geography, gender and political ideology, and demonstrating, as suggested in the previous chapter, how quickly they gained wide acceptance within contemporary English society.[4] What remains less clear, however, is how far the

---

[1]   W. R. Scott, *The Constitution and Finance of English, Scottish, and Irish Joint Stock Companies to 1720*, 3 vols (Cambridge, 1912); Larry Neal, *The Rise of Financial Capitalism: International Capital Markets in the Age of Reason* (Cambridge, 1990); and Natasha Glaisyer, *The Culture of Commerce in England, 1660–1720* (Woodbridge, 2006).
[2]   Anne Murphy, *The Origins of English Financial Markets: Investment and Speculation before the South Sea Bubble* (Cambridge, 2009), pp. 10–39.
[3]   In addition to the works cited in the previous chapter see J. A. Downie, *To Settle the Succession of the State: Literature and Politics, 1678–1750* (London, 1994).
[4]   Glaisyer, esp. pp. 143–84; Murphy, *Origins of English Financial Markets*, pp. 66–88 and

permeation of these innovations, and indeed acceptance of them, extended across Britain and Ireland. This chapter examines this question looking particularly at Ireland and Scotland, exploring their different histories of banking and investment, and comparing them to each other and to the experience in England.

I

The differing banking histories of the three kingdoms reflect their varied experiences of other elements of the financial revolution as broadly understood. Private deposit banking, for instance, had a longer history in London, where the first goldsmith bankers can be traced to at least the 1660s if not earlier.[5] Paper credit in the form of banker's notes and bills of exchange had also penetrated more deeply into the English provinces than in comparatively underdeveloped Scotland and Ireland during the same period. Already by the beginning of the 1690s 'a highly elaborate web of credit' connected vibrant regional economies with the metropolitan centre in London.[6] The providers of financial services, however, remained concentrated in the City, where recognizable banking interests were already visible. These included bankers like Sir Francis Child, Sir Robert Clayton and Richard Hoare, as well as the mercantile consortium behind the foundation of the Bank of England.[7] The establishment of the Bank in 1694 and its remarkable success in raising its foundational capital in just two weeks demonstrated the financial strength of the London mercantile and political elite.[8] Private banking partnerships continued to proliferate although they continued to be largely a City phenomenon with the first provincial banks only emerging at least a generation later.[9]

114–36; and Anne Laurence, Josephine Maltby and Jeanette Rutherford, 'Introduction', in *Women and Their Money, 1750–1950: Essays on Women and Finance*, ed. Anne Laurence, Josephine Maltby and Jeanette Rutherford (London, 2009), pp. 1–30.

[5] Frank T. Melton, *Sir Robert Clayton and the Origins of English Deposit Banking, 1658–1685* (Cambridge, 1986); and George Selgin, 'Those Dishonest Goldsmiths', *Financial History Review*, 19 (2012), 269–88.

[6] John Brewer, 'Commercialization and Politics', in *The Birth of a Consumer Society: The Commercialization of Eighteenth-Century England*, ed. John Brewer, J. H. Plumb and Neil McKendrick (London, 1982), pp. 203–60 (p. 205). See also Craig Muldrew, *The Economy of Obligation: The Culture of Credit and Social Relations in Early Modern England* (New York, 1998), *passim*.

[7] P. G. M. Dickson, *The Financial Revolution in England: A Study in the Development of Public Credit, 1688–1756* (London, 1967), pp. 253–60; and Anne Laurence, 'The Emergence of a Private Clientèle for Banks in the Early Eighteenth Century: Hoare's Bank and Some Women Customers', *Economic History Review*, 61 (2008), 565–86.

[8] Murphy, *Origins of English Financial Markets*, p. 152.

[9] Stephen P. Quinn, 'The Glorious Revolution's Effect on English Private Finance: A

If the Bank of England was the great symbol of the English financial revolution, its Scottish counterpart was the Bank of Scotland, which was established not to lend to the government but to stimulate the northern kingdom's domestic economy. Like its counterpart south of the border, the Bank of Scotland had no difficulty raising its initial capital of £100,000.[10] This initial success led to a near monopolization of the Scottish banking sector, at least until the foundation of the Royal Bank of Scotland in 1727. Smaller-scale Scottish banking partnerships, like those which appeared in England and Ireland, are conspicuous by their absence in this period, while early attempts to establish rival banks, including John Law's scheme for a land-bank, ended in failure. Nevertheless, the establishment of the Bank of Scotland can be seen as a revolutionary moment in the history of finance in the northern kingdom.[11] The bank's resilience and successful resistance to external shocks in 1696, 1707 and 1715 also suggests the adaptation of the Scottish commercial and political community to this particular financial innovation.

Dublin followed neither the London nor the Edinburgh model. Proposals for a national bank received short shrift from the Irish House of Commons in the mid-1690s, with a local scheme promoted by the city's merchants and one for a land-bank proffered by two Scottish projectors, Dr Hugh Chamberlain and Robert Murray, both being summarily rejected.[12] Instead the Irish banking revolution remained resolutely in the private sphere, with a number of banking partnerships emerging by the early years of the eighteenth century. The Irish banking scene in this period has been variously described as 'primitive', 'versatile' and 'highly innovative'.[13] These varying historiographical assessments reflect different perceptions of the role of the banks in the Irish economy, as well as the vantage points from which these

Microhistory, 1680–1705', *Journal of Economic History*, 61 (2001), 593–615; and Margaret Dawes and C. N. Ward-Perkins, *Country Banks of England and Wales: Private Provincial Banks and Bankers, 1688–1953* (Canterbury, 2000).

10 Richard Saville, *Bank of Scotland, A History, 1695–1995* (Edinburgh, 1996); and S. G. Checkland, *Scottish Banking: A History, 1695–1973* (Glasgow, 1975).

11 Scott, vol. 3, p. 269; and Saville, pp. 83–4.

12 For the Dublin merchant's proposal see Richard Holt, *Seasonable Proposals for a Perpetual Fund or Bank in Dublin* (Dublin, 1696) and Suzanne Forbes, 'Print, Politics and Public Opinion in Ireland, 1690–1715' (Ph.D., University College Dublin, 2012), pp. 204–5. For the second proposal see Hugh Chamberlain, *A Proposal and Considerations relating to an Office of Credit upon Land Security: Proposed to their Excellencies the Lords Justices: and to the Lords of the Privy Council; and the Parliament of Ireland* (London, 1697). For Chamberlain, a serial bank projector, see Helen King, 'Hugh Chamberlain the elder, (1630–after 1720)', in ODNB.

13 Malcolm Dillon, *The History and Development of Banking in Ireland from the Earliest Times to the Present Day* (Dublin, 1889), p. 16; David Dickson, *New Foundations: Ireland, 1660–1800* (Dublin, 2000), p. 135; and Padraig McGowan, *Money and Banking in Ireland: Origins, Development and Future* (Dublin, 1990), p. 8.

early developments were being viewed. Louis Cullen has shown how Irish developments could be viewed favourably when compared with the situation in the English provinces, and indeed in Scotland, the oft-cited cradle of modern banking.[14] Others have been more circumspect, with G. L. Barrow following Irish banking's nineteenth-century chronicler, Malcolm Dillon, in his judgement that the founding of the Bank of Ireland in 1783 marked the true beginning of banking in Ireland.[15] Certainly 1783 marked a new phase, but it would be a mistake to denigrate too far the achievements of earlier generations of Irish bankers. By 1720 there were at least six banks operating in the kingdom, each admittedly only on a rather small scale, but nevertheless it is arguable that their development marked a revolution in Irish finance.

The origins of Irish banking can be traced back to the 1660s when, as in contemporary England, paper money in the form of goldsmith's receipts and bills of exchange began to be used on a regular basis. Such bills were first employed by merchants engaging in foreign trade, but were gradually adopted for transactions inland, and then used by landlords who wished to transfer their country rents to Dublin, and increasingly to London.[16] The adoption of these forms of paper money allowed these groups to alleviate some of the worst effects of the chronic lack of specie or coin circulating in the Irish economy, a persistent problem with its roots in the turbulent military conflicts of the sixteenth and seventeenth centuries.[17] Goldsmith bankers like Sir Abel Ram and Thomas Parnell (both active in the 1660s and 1670s) offered new opportunities for creating credit, and in doing so they ushered in the beginning of the end of the statute staple, hitherto the dominant national credit network but one that was increasingly becoming unfit for purpose.[18]

The statute staple was a medieval relic. Originally conceived during the Middle Ages as a means to regulate trade between merchants in 'staple' or market towns, it had developed by the early seventeenth century into a regulated moneylending instrument whereby individuals could borrow and lend money on bond. These bonds were protected under the law and

---

[14] L. M. Cullen, 'Landlords, Bankers and Merchants: The Early Irish Banking World, 1700–1820', in *Economists and the Irish Economy from the Eighteenth Century to the Present Day*, ed. Antoin E. Murphy (Dublin, 1984), pp. 25–44 (pp. 26–7).

[15] G. L. Barrow, *The Emergence of the Irish Banking System, 1820–1845* (Dublin, 1975), p. 1; and Dillon, p. 16.

[16] The best account of this process is found in Cullen, 'Landlords, Bankers and Merchants'.

[17] R. G. Gillespie, *The Transformation of the Irish Economy, 1550–1700* (Dundalk, 1998), pp. 38 and 56; and Michael MacCarthy-Morrogh, 'Credit and Remittance: Monetary Problems in Early Seventeenth-Century Munster', *Irish Economic and Social History*, 14 (1987), 5–19.

[18] John Bergin and Patrick M. Geoghegan, 'Ram, Sir Abel (d. 1692)', in *DIB*.

enforced by a 'mayor of the staple' elected in each staple town, and proved to be a hugely popular method to get access to credit, or to lend at interest. The surviving records document over ten thousand transactions across the seventeenth century, with the majority coming from Dublin rather than the provincial staples although significant volumes of business also took place in other large urban areas like Cork, Drogheda, Limerick and Waterford. These debtors and creditors embraced every religious and ethnic group in Ireland, but the majority were drawn from the peerage and landed gentry. Families such as the Percevals in County Cork used the staple to build up their estates, while other prominent figures like the earls of Cork, Antrim and Ormond increased their fortunes through judicious moneylending.[19]

Access to the staple widened as interest rates fell from the punitive levels of 30–40% witnessed in the early decades of the seventeenth century. By the 1680s the legal rate was 10% but as Sir Robert Southwell, a leading government official and thriving landlord, noted: 'money is grown so plentiful and land so scarce that although the legal interest rate is ten per cent, yet everybody upon reasonable security is content with eight'.[20] The staple, however, diminished in importance from the 1680s onward, although the explanation offered by its historians, that 'economic, tenurial, and political instability totally undermined the mutual trust and economic interdependence that had sustained the operation of the staple as a national paper credit network', must be questioned in light of its survival through the wars of the 1640s.[21] Instead more weight should be given to the emergence of new forms of credit, notably the growth of private banking, itself partly a product of lower interest rates.

While some of the early Irish bankers like Ram and Parnell came from a goldsmith background, most of them were originally wholesale merchants.[22] The Hoare family in Cork, often described as operating one of the earliest Irish banks in the 1680s, established their banking venture as an adjunct to their successful naval provisions business. As the leading players in the growing Cork provisions trade they were in an excellent position to set up a banking concern, which exploited existing credit networks in the hinterland of the southern port, as well as links with London developed through their naval contacts.[23] Similarly, members of the Cairnes family were prominent merchants in Belfast, Dublin and London before they turned to banking,

[19] Jane Ohlmeyer and Éamonn Ó Ciardha (eds), *The Irish Statute Staple Books, 1596–1687* (Dublin, 1998), pp. 10–12 and 27.

[20] Quoted in Gillespie, *Transformation of the Irish Economy*, p. 57.

[21] Ohlmeyer and Ó Ciardha, p. 34.

[22] On the goldsmith bankers see C. M. Tenison, 'The Old Dublin Bankers', *Journal of the Cork Historical and Archaeological Society*, I (1893), 17–18, 36–8, 54–6, 102–6, 120–3, 143–6, 168–71, 193–7, 221–2, 241–3 and 256–60 (p. 17).

[23] John Bergin, 'Hoare, Edward (c.1620–1690) incl. Edward Hoare (1670–1709)', in *DIB*. David Dickson, *Old World Colony: Cork and South Munster 1630–1830* (Cork,

while other mercantile families involved in banking included the Normans in Derry, and the Fades, McGuires and Mitchells in Dublin.

Other early pioneers in the Dublin banking world enjoyed more shadowy antecedents. Some of the older histories of Irish banking identify Joseph Damer as the first Dublin banker.[24] He had come to Ireland during the Cromwellian period and quickly established himself as a moneylender and land agent. His success can be judged both by the almost £20,000 he bequeathed to his heir and nephew, John, and by the 'scurrilous' satirical attack published upon his demise in July 1720, allegedly by Jonathan Swift, which perpetuated his miserly reputation. Scurrilous or not, its existence indicates his prominence and status as a target worth attacking, even if only posthumously.[25] However, although a moneylender, dealer in mortgages and land agent, Damer probably does not deserve the epithet of 'banker'. Unlike other contemporary bankers, he possessed no business premises of his own, but instead carried out his moneylending transactions from a tavern in Fishamble Street in central Dublin.[26] He also does not seem to have been involved in the exchange business with London, nor the remittance of rural rents to Dublin, which were the mainstays of his contemporaries in the nascent Irish banking scene. Although goldsmith bankers like Ram, scriveners like Damer and proto-merchant bankers like the elder Edward Hoare were active in the 1680s, the real take-off in Irish banking only came after the Williamite wars. Gillespie has described the 'speedy' recovery of the economy after the 1689–91 war as 'remarkable', something that could be seen in the financial developments that characterized the period.[27] The failed attempts to establish a national bank in 1695 together with the establishment of the first major Dublin banking partnership, that of Burton & Harrison in the late 1690s, indicates the scale of the postwar recovery and the new-found confidence of the city's financial sector. It also echoed the rapid stabilization of the financial worlds in post-revolution Edinburgh and London.[28]

Burton & Harrison was not only the first but also the most important of the early banks in Dublin. Established by two Dublin merchants of landed background, Benjamin Burton and Francis Harrison, the bank's business model focused on providing financial services to members of the Irish landed

---

2005), pp. 80–1 and 163. Hoare was not related to the English banking family of the same name.

[24] Tenison, p. 104; and Dillon, pp. 17–19.

[25] Tom Tattler [J. Swift], *The Life and Character of Mr Joseph Damer* (Dublin, 1720).

[26] John Bergin, 'Damer, Joseph (c.1630–1720)', in *DIB*.

[27] Gillespie, *Transformation of the Irish Economy*, p. 49.

[28] For some comments on the rapid post-revolution developments in the Edinburgh financial world, see John Robertson, *The Case for Enlightenment: Scotland and Naples, 1680–1760* (Cambridge, 2005), pp. 90–1.

gentry.[29] They remitted rents from their clients' country estates to Dublin and London, while providing a regular line of credit at interest in antici-pation of expected rentals, an especially profitable business when the legal interest rate stood at 8%.[30] Facilitating the transfer of funds both within the country and abroad through the use of promissory notes or bills of exchange became the principal business of the early Irish banks. Their notes then began to circulate around the country helping to alleviate some of the problems caused by the lack of specie or coin within the domestic economy, a consequence of Ireland's having no mint and its reliance upon foreign currency, especially Portuguese moidors, to provide its circulating coin.[31] It was therefore not surprising that private banker's notes became ubiquitous, something that was recognized in law in 1709 when legislation passed by the Irish parliament declared that 'notes issued by any banker, goldsmith, merchant, or trader, whether made payable to bearer or order, should be assignable and transferable by delivery or endorsement'.[32]

Burton & Harrison were probably the most successful of the first generation of Irish bankers and enjoyed an excellent reputation among the Irish gentry. By 1706 a Belfast merchant, Isaac Macartney, was recommending them to James Lenox, a business associate in Derry, describing Burton as 'a substantial honest man' with a 'good interest with both nobility and gentry in that country'.[33] Other evidence suggests that their client list comprised a virtual Irish aristocratic and ecclesiastical roll-call, featuring names like the earls of Cavan, Kildare and Antrim, the archbishops of Armagh and Dublin, and the Bishop of Cloyne. Meanwhile the popular equation of Burton's name with the values of probity and solvency in the Dublin proverb 'as safe as Ben Burton' further indicates their early good standing, as does the entrance of both Burton and Harrison into the political elite as members of the Irish Commons in 1703.[34]

---

[29] For Burton and Harrison see their biographical entries in *HIP*, vol. 3, pp. 316–18 and vol. 4, p. 371.

[30] 2 Anne, c. 16 [Irish], *An Act for Reducing of Interest on Money to Eight per cent for the Future*.

[31] Joseph Johnston, 'Irish Currency in the Eighteenth Century', in *Bishop Berkeley's Querist in Historical Perspective*, ed. Joseph Johnston (Dundalk, 1970), pp. 52–71. See also L. M. Cullen, *An Economic History of Ireland since 1660* (London, 1972), pp. 31–3 and 41–3.

[32] 8 Anne, c. 1, s. 1 [Irish], *An Act for the Better Payment of Inland Bills of Exchange and For Making Promissory Notes More Obligatory*.

[33] Quoted by Jean Agnew in *Belfast Merchant Families in the Seventeenth Century* (Dublin, 1996), p. 167.

[34] For reference to Earls of Cavan see PRONI, D3000/27/1. For reference to Earls of Kildare see *The Case of the Appellants, The Surviving Trustees, in the Act of Parliament Above Mentioned* [Burton's Bank] (BL, Add MS 36161, fols 164–84). For reference to the Earls of Antrim see PRONI, D2977/2/7/1–19. I am indebted to Dr Rowena Dudley for these references.

Burton & Harrison's excellent reputation owed much to their expertise in transferring money not just within Ireland, but also across the Irish Sea. Upon their foundation they had quickly established links with the London banking and business community. By 1702 they were acting as the Dublin agents for the English lottery, selling tickets to their Dublin customers, while together with the Cork banker Edward Hoare they also acted as agents for the Hollow Sword Blade Company in Ireland.[35] These connections meant they were well placed to engage in the 'exchange business', a crucial component of the business model of all the early Irish banks.[36] This involved managing the transfer of funds across the Irish Sea to take best advantage of the fluctuating Anglo-Irish exchange rate, which tended to float either side of the par rate officially set in 1701 at thirteen Irish pence being equal to one English shilling. It was within these margins either side of the par rate that the Irish bankers could realize a profit especially where, like Burton & Harrison or their later rivals La Touche & Kane, they had access to a network of agents on both sides of the Irish Sea. Using these agents they were able to transfer bills for the use of the increasing number of Irish absentee landowners and politicians resident in London, as well as for merchants active in Anglo-Irish trade. The success of Burton & Harrison in establishing secure and efficient links with London correspondents can be judged by their employment as remitters of Irish government funds to the Treasury in London, itself an added mark of esteem.

Burton & Harrison, while the most prominent, were not the only banking house to appear during the first two decades of the eighteenth century. By 1716, there were at least three other banks active in Dublin, namely the partnership of James Mead and George Curtis (established around 1710), that of David La Touche and Nathaniel Kane and the bank of Hugh Henry, who was acting in conjunction with Sir Alexander Cairnes.[37] Meanwhile James Swift, later to achieve some notoriety in 1720 when his bank failed, was operating by at least 1719.[38] These were the most important bankers active in the city, although some merchants such as Richard McGuire, Joseph Fade and Joseph Nuttall intermittently described themselves as bankers.[39] This is not surprising since the majority of the Dublin bankers in this period either had mercantile roots, or else were closely connected with the city's trading community.

[35] *The Flying Post*, 6 Apr. 1702.
[36] L. M. Cullen, 'The Exchange Business of the Irish banks in the Eighteenth Century', *Economica*, 25 (1958), 326–38.
[37] Tenison, pp. 54–5, 120–1, 143–4 and 194–5.
[38] John Busteed, 'Irish Private Banks', *Journal of the Cork Historical and Archaeological Society*, 53 (1948), 31–7 (p. 32).
[39] See their entries in Subscription list for Forbes/Ponsonby bank, n.d. and Subscription list for the Bank of Ireland, 19–23 May 1720 (NLI, MS 2256, fols 39–41 and 65–6). See pp. 151–2 below.

Interestingly, most of these bankers were also members of religious minorities, particularly of the various Dissenting Protestant congregations present in Dublin. This reflected a trend elsewhere in Britain, and indeed the Continent, where religious minorities were disproportionately represented in the financial sphere.[40] Burton, Cairnes and Henry were all Presbyterians, while Fade was a Quaker and La Touche a Huguenot. Their background in often quite close-knit communities enabled them to build up relationships with potential customers, as well as to develop networks both across Ireland and abroad. This can be most clearly seen in the best documented case of La Touche & Kane, whose inland correspondents included Huguenot merchants in Waterford and Kilkenny, while their foreign correspondents included co-religionists in London and Rotterdam.[41] This latter connection extended their links to the Continent and marked them out as different from other Dublin bankers, at least in the early decades of the century. It reflected the Dutch upbringing of one of the principals, David La Touche, as well as his continued family ties among the Huguenot exile community there.[42] Their network of foreign correspondents was not, however, exclusively made up of Huguenots, and it would be misleading to categorize their bank as part of a wider 'Protestant International'.[43] La Touche & Kane's Bristol agent, James Hillhouse, for instance, was a Scot who enjoyed close links with a number of the leading Belfast mercantile families, most of whom were adherents of the Presbyterian religion.[44] Despite this connection La Touche & Kane's business was, however, strongest in the eastern and southern parts of Ireland. This is clear from the relatively modest balances in the hands of their Derry and Belfast correspondents.[45] Belfast was also still a comparatively small town well served by other rising banking interests, notably the Cairnes brothers, who had been active in the corporation's politics before the introduction of the sacramental test in 1704, and who still maintained strong personal and business connections there.

Sir Alexander Cairnes, together with his brothers William and Henry, and his sometime business partner Hugh Henry, was part of an identifiable

---

[40] On this see the nuanced discussion in Ole Peter Grell, *Brethren in Christ: A Calvinist Network in Reformation Europe* (Cambridge, 2011); and Francois Crouzet, 'The Huguenots and the English Financial Revolution', in *Favourites of Fortune: Technology, Growth and Economic Development since the Industrial Revolution*, ed. Patrice Higonnet, David S. Landes and Henry Rosovsky (Cambridge, MA, 1991), pp. 221–66.

[41] Abstract ledgers of La Touche & Kane, 1719–25 (NLI, MS 2785).

[42] David Dickson, 'Huguenots in the Urban Economy of Eighteenth-Century Dublin and Cork', in *The Huguenots and Ireland: Anatomy of an Emigration*, ed. C. E. J. Caldicott, Hugh Gough and J. P. Pittion (Dun Laoghaire, 1987), pp. 321–32 (p. 324).

[43] Crouzet, p. 258.

[44] Agnew, pp. 182 and 188.

[45] Balances in Belfast and Derry hands, 1719–25 (NLI, MS 2785, fols 7–8, 11–12 and 17–18).

Ulster interest in the Dublin financial sector. Both Cairnes and Henry, as well as Henry's occasional partner and eventual successor Henry Mitchell, were Ulster Presbyterians and they drew much of their business from their co-religionists who were active in the northern-dominated linen trade. In Dublin they remained connected to a northern interest who resided on the north side of the city, where the capital's linen trade was physically located.[46] Their customers included leading Ulster landlords, with Hugh Henry, together with Derry merchant and Dublin customs official Robert Norman, acting for the doyen of this identifiable northern interest, William Conolly, the speaker of the Irish House of Commons and Ireland's wealthiest resident landlord.[47] Sir Alexander Cairnes similarly acted for a number of families and individuals with Ulster connections, remitting their rents and official salaries across the Irish Sea to and from London, often acting in partnership with Hugh Henry, and then later Henry Mitchell.

Based on kinship, shared religion and a shared regional identity, such networks were common throughout the early modern financial world and could be extremely beneficial, especially in an era when transfers of information still relied upon 'primitive' communications systems. Family members were more likely to be in regular contact and were thus better able to share business as well as personal information. They were also less likely to default on obligations made to other members of the kinship group. These conclusions arrived at in a study of New England bankers in the early nineteenth century can be applied to the Irish case almost a hundred years earlier.[48] In the Irish situation, such networks of reliable personal and business correspondents could reduce the distance between the metropolitan centre in London and those customers on the periphery in Dublin and the Irish provinces. Such correspondents could not only transfer their money, they could also offer advice on investment opportunities and even on occasion act as financial brokers.

The emergence of an Irish banking community in the early eighteenth century constitutes an important aspect of the Irish financial revolution. Importantly, although clearly dominated by the capital, this was not exclusively a Dublin-based phenomenon. There were banks in Cork, Belfast and possibly Limerick, while most of the Dublin bankers had correspondents in many of the major trading towns.[49] These included leading mercantile interests such as the Bagwells in Clonmel, County Tipperary, who discounted

---

46 Agnew, p. 186.

47 Patrick Walsh, *The Making of the Irish Protestant Ascendancy: The Life of William Conolly, 1662–1729* (Woodbridge, 2010), p. 126.

48 Naomi Lamoreaux, *Insider Lending: Banks, Personal Connections and Economic Development in Industrial New England* (Cambridge, 1994), p. 26.

49 The Limerick bank was rumoured to have collapsed in 1720. It was connected to the Cairnes business empire.

bills drawn on Richard McGuire as well as La Touche & Kane.[50] Other local correspondents combined their remittance business with official employment as revenue officers, although this was in contravention of the policy laid down by the revenue commissioners in Dublin.[51] The growth of local banking activity, described by F. G. Hall as 'gigantic', can also be measured by the contemporary reports of the expanding circulation of paper money.[52] The value of the private banknotes in circulation has been the subject of some controversy. At the height of the pamphlet debate in 1721 over the proposed Bank of Ireland, a leading advocate of the scheme, the Irish MP Henry Maxwell, stressing the ubiquitous acceptance of paper money in Ireland, claimed there was up to £600,000 worth of banknotes in circulation. Louis Cullen, however, has rightly suggested that this figure is too high, citing the evidence of the extant La Touche & Kane bank ledgers. Their total notes in circulation in the years 1720–25 alone ranged only from £20,000 to £60,000, indicating that Maxwell's figures were almost certainly exaggerated.[53]

The expansion of paper credit and the existence of a greater number of providers of banking and financial services was an important development. Irish bankers' business interests, however, remained concentrated either on remitting inland balances or in transferring funds across the Irish Sea to the growing absentee community in London. Unlike the Bank of Scotland, Irish banks were not involved in creating mercantile credit. In this respect the Irish sector was less than innovative, and helped confirm the peripheral nature of the Irish financial world.[54] Bankers were concerned less with establishing a commercial and financial centre in Dublin than with providing easier access to either the local centre in Dublin, or more significantly the metropolitan centre in London. This emphasis on the London market opened up the Irish banks to the risks of external shocks, an issue that would become all too evident in 1720.

<hr />

[50] Abstract ledgers of La Touche & Kane, 1719–25 (NLI, MS 2785); and Accounts of Charles, Earl of Arran with Richard and William McGuire, 1721–22 (NLI, MS 2534, fols 3–4, 6 and 10–11).

[51] For the ban on revenue officers doing other business see Minute Book of the Revenue Commissioners, 27 January 1720 (TNA, CUST 1/15).

[52] F. G. Hall, The Bank of Ireland, 1783–1946 (Dublin, 1949), p. 3.

[53] Henry Maxwell, Mr Maxwell's Second Letter to Mr Rowley: Wherein the Objections Against the Bank are Answered (Dublin, 1721), p. 14; and L. M. Cullen, Anglo-Irish Trade 1660–1800 (Manchester, 1968), p. 199.

[54] For a comparative discussion of the Dublin and Edinburgh exchange business with London see L. M. Cullen, 'The Scottish Exchange on London, 1663–1778', in Conflict, Identity and Economic Development in Ireland and Scotland, 1600–1939, ed. S. J. Connolly, R. A. Houston and R. J. Morris (Preston, 1995), pp. 29–44.

II

If the business model of Irish banking confirmed Ireland's status as a dependent kingdom or province, so too did the failure of Irish joint-stock enterprise. The 1690s saw rapid growth in joint-stock activity across Britain, exemplified in the first London stock-market boom, as new forms of business organization were adopted to maximize capital resources. Scotland also witnessed a proliferation of joint-stock companies in the same decade including the Scots Linen Company founded in 1693, as well as mining, sugar refining and silk-making enterprises founded in the mid-1690s.[55] There would be no Irish equivalents. Contemporary attempts to establish an Irish Linen Company as well as an Irish Paper Company floundered with the primary reason ascribed to the lack of domestic capital.[56] Existing reserves were diverted into speculation in land, the Williamite land confiscation providing what turned out to be the last windfall of a turbulent century. Even here, the difficulties faced by the Trustees of Forfeited Estates and the intervention of the Hollow Sword Blade Company demonstrated the limited venture capital available. This situation was compounded by the capital flight, which accompanied the departure of the Jacobite Catholic elite into exile on the Continent, removing a further source of Irish investment funds. Difficulties with accessing capital certainly hindered Irish joint-stock investment, but also important were the legislative restrictions on Irish trade, which more than anything else confirmed Ireland's peripheral economic and financial status.

Foreign trade traditionally provided a significant focus for joint-stock investment as demonstrated by the listing of companies floated in Edinburgh, Glasgow and London. The long distances involved, and the need for substantial initial capital outlays meant that partnerships or corporations were the preferred method of business organization. Geographically Ireland was positioned perfectly to benefit from the expanding Atlantic markets lying on the major westward trade routes to the American colonies. Furthermore, the presence of competitive labour costs, safe ports, and historical trading links with the French and Spanish Atlantic ports all seemed to position the kingdom perfectly.[57] These same comparative advantages, however, also created jealousies among the English mercantile community. This led to the introduction of a number of legislative measures such as the Navigation Acts of the 1660s, which forbade direct exports to the American colonies, except from England. Of particular concern in the second half of the seventeenth

[55] Scott, vol. 2, pp. 128–9.
[56] Scott, vol. 1, pp. 341–2 and vol. 2, pp. 70–2.
[57] James Livesey, *Civil Society and Empire: Ireland and Scotland in the Eighteenth Century Atlantic World* (London, 2009), p. 64. For the persistence of trading links with France, even during wartime, see Siobhan Talbott, 'British Commercial Interests on the French Atlantic Coast, c.1560–1713', *Historical Research*, 85 (2012), 394–409.

century was the threat posed to English woollen and cattle trades by cheaper Irish competitors. The Cattle Acts of 1663 and 1671 first restricted and then banned the importation of Irish livestock and beef into Britain. This prohibition, however, led to the development of the provisions trade centred on the southern port of Cork, as Irish merchants and agricultural producers began to capitalize on the increased traffic crossing the Atlantic.[58] This unintended consequence shows that the legislative restrictions on Irish trade were designed primarily to appease the English mercantile and commercial community rather than deliberately halt Irish growth and prosperity, despite the claims of some contemporaries. This was especially true of the famous 1699 Woollen Act, introduced in Westminster at the instigation of West Country interests, to prevent the importation of cheaper Irish woollen goods.[59] Like the Cattle Acts, its influence on Irish economic growth was greatly exaggerated by an earlier generation of historians. Nevertheless, the commercial restrictions on Irish trade, particularly those governed by the Navigation Acts, would become a major grievance for Irish economic and political writers in the early decades of the eighteenth century.[60]

Crucially, these restrictions hindered Irish participation in the nascent Atlantic Empire and here the comparison with Scotland is instructive. The Navigation Acts similarly impeded Scottish trade with the English colonies in North America but, instead of resigning themselves to a subordinate role in the emerging British Empire, the Scots developed an audacious plan to establish their own colonies through the Company of Scotland. This was the famous Darien scheme, as previously discussed. Its failure is well known, the colonial enterprise was a disaster, and the company swallowed most of the available Scottish capital. Nevertheless the Company of Scotland's remarkable achievement in raising almost £400,000 in joint-stock investment should not be ignored. It demonstrated not only a belief that the commercial restrictions of English mercantile policy could be overcome, but also that Scots were prepared to subscribe large amounts of their own capital to try and make this happen. These attempts failed partly because of English opposition, motivated by fears of Scottish imperial expansion. Hereafter, Scottish trading ambitions would be incorporated into a new British imperial expansion, something that was reflected in the equal access to colonial markets granted to Scottish traders and merchants under the terms of the 1707 Act of Union. In the long run this would contribute to

---

58 Dickson, *New Foundations*, pp. 130–3.
59 P. H. Kelly, 'The Irish Woollen Export Prohibition Act of 1699: Kearney Revisited', *Irish Economic and Social History*, 7 (1980), 22–44.
60 Arthur Dobbs, *An Essay on the Trade and Improvement of Ireland* (Dublin, 1729).

the growth of Glasgow as an imperial entrepôt founded on the wealth of the Chesapeake tobacco trade.[61]

There would be no Irish Glasgow. Cork's significant eighteenth-century growth was dependent not on colonial ventures but on the provisions trade; Belfast's boom years came much later and were a product of the industrial revolution. Galway meanwhile stagnated, geographically located as a gateway to the Atlantic. Irish merchants continued to be constrained by the Navigation Acts until 1731.[62] This ongoing exclusion from colonial trade served to uphold Ireland's dependent political and economic status. Ireland remained neither a kingdom nor a colony and politically this situation would be copper-fastened by the passage of the Declaratory Act of April 1720, which confirmed the legislative superiority of the British parliament over Ireland.[63] This merely expressed the existing political reality in legislation, which in economic and financial terms had long been the case.

Irish men (and women), especially members of the Protestant elite, had long understood this dependent relationship, and acted accordingly. Dublin was recognized to be a provincial capital, while London was still regarded as the centre of taste, fashion, politics and business.[64] This could be seen in the increasing phenomenon of absenteeism among Irish landlords, with some becoming permanent residents of London, Bath or the English provinces. Others became Anglo-Irish in the truest sense, dividing their time between the two sides of the Irish Sea. Still others maintained close links with the English capital but travelled across much less frequently, if at all. In this regard, the Irish were much more successful than the Scots who, even after the Union in 1707, found it difficult to integrate into the commercial and social worlds of the British capital.[65] It has even been argued that post-Union Scottish investment in the London stock market was motivated by a desire to assimilate; similar arguments may perhaps be detected among wealthy members of the Irish community.

What is certainly true is that Irish investors with excess capital were increasingly looking to the London markets from the final decades of the seventeenth century onward. The absence of domestic investment

---

[61] T. M. Devine, 'The Scottish Merchant Community, 1680–1740', in *The Origins and Nature of the Scottish Enlightenment*, ed. R. H. Campbell and Andrew S. Skinner (Edinburgh, 1982), pp. 26–41 (pp. 31–2).

[62] Thomas Truxes, *Irish-American Trade, 1660–1783* (Cambridge, 1988), pp. 29–33.

[63] On the Declaratory Act see Isolde Victory, 'The Making of the 1720 Declaratory Act', in *Parliament, Politics and People: Essays in Eighteenth-Century Irish History*, ed. Gerard O'Brien (Dublin, 1989), pp. 9–29.

[64] Toby Barnard, '"Grand Metropolis" or "The Anus of the World"? The Cultural Life of Eighteenth-Century Dublin', in *Two Capitals, London and Dublin, 1500–1840*, ed. Peter Clark and R. G. Gillespie (Oxford, 2001), pp. 185–211.

[65] David Hancock, *Citizens of the World: London Merchants and the Integration of the British Atlantic Community, 1735–1785* (Cambridge, 1995), pp. 46 and 52.

opportunities combined with its proximity and improving communication networks, increased London's attraction. The development of an indigenous banking infrastructure rather than halting this process arguably hastened it, as Irish bankers introduced greater efficiencies into the Anglo-Irish money trade. They also offered little in terms of credit creation, unlike their London competitors. Crucially, Irish investors began to be attracted by the possibilities offered by the innovations in state finance. As noted earlier, Burton & Harrison were offering their Irish customers opportunities to purchase English lottery tickets in 1702.[66] This presumably reflected local enthusiasm for the English state-sponsored lotteries, which had no Irish equivalent. There were only much smaller private lotteries available in Dublin and even though they were heavily subscribed, the prizes were relatively modest, something that may have only further encouraged investment in London.[67] Irish participation in lottery loans can be traced further through individual examples. Alan Brodrick, 1st Viscount Midleton and a leading Irish lawyer and politician, for instance, managed lottery investments for one of his relatives, Martha Courthope, while Jane Bonnell, widow of a former Irish accountant-general then resident in London, purchased lottery tickets for her Irish relations and acquaintances.[68] Some of these Irish holdings of lottery tickets or 'orders' were later transmuted into South Sea stock as part of the company's debt conversion scheme.[69]

The lottery loans were not the only London destination for Irish capital. While there were only four Irish subscribers to the Bank of England upon its foundation in 1694, this number increased in the following decades.[70] Prominent Irish individuals connected with the Bank included Sir Alexander Cairnes, whose father-in-law, Nathaniel Gould, served as a director. The Bank of England was not the only London financial institution to attract Irish customers. They purchased East India Company stock albeit in small numbers, while the extant ledgers of Hoare's Bank, a leading London financial house, also included the earls of Bellamont, Mountrath and Orrery, members of the Bulkeley, Smyth and O'Brien families, as well as the Dublin banker Richard McGuire, further suggesting Irish engagement with the metropolitan financial world.[71] Irish participation in the capital's markets

---

66 On the lotteries see Anne Murphy, 'Lotteries in the 1690s: Investment or Gamble?', *Financial History Review*, 12 (2005), 227–46.
67 Rowena Dudley, *The Irish Lottery, 1780–1801* (Dublin, 2005), pp. 13–22. These local lotteries were suppressed in 1712 by legislation introduced in the Irish parliament, being regarded by the legislature as a nuisance.
68 Thomas Brodrick to Alan Brodrick, 1st Viscount Midleton, 13 Sep. 1720 (SHC, MS 1248/4, fols 318–19); and Samuel Holt to Jane Bonnell, 24 Apr. 1712 (NLI, MS 41,580/29).
69 Henry Ingoldsby to William Smyth, 30 July 1720 (NLI, MS 41,581/2).
70 Murphy, *Origins of English Financial Markets*, p. 152.
71 I am indebted to Anne Laurence for these references from Hoare's Bank ledgers.

was therefore visible before 1720, but the South Sea bubble greatly increased the outflow of Irish money to London. This would have, however, been much more difficult without the expertise and familiarity with the financial markets that had developed in the previous decades.

III

The South Sea scheme was only possible because of the impact that the financial revolution had on British society during the previous thirty years. Investors were willing to participate in the company's debt conversion scheme because they had developed a familiarity with the workings of the stock exchange and the securities market. This could be attributed to the growth in information networks, which in turn educated and enticed investors from an ever widening geographical area. The phenomenon would reach its high point in 1720 as investors from the periphery of the British state, from Ireland, Scotland and beyond, purchased South Sea stock in the expectation of what one Dublin commentator described as 'extravagant gain'.[72] Their ability and confidence to invest in the London markets reflected the great developments in the Irish and Scottish financial structures, both public and private, made in the previous decades. Paper money had become not just a familiar concept but a ubiquitous one, joint-stock investment especially in Scotland (and despite the Darien disaster) had become an acceptable use of capital, while banking in both kingdoms had developed in different but equally revolutionary ways. These dramatic changes, however, remained located within the periphery and these local innovations, like their political counterparts, remained dependent on London for inspiration and impetus. The possibilities offered by the South Sea Company's debt conversion scheme, as the next chapter illustrates, offered the opportunity for investors from the periphery to more fully engage with the financial world of the metropole.

---

[72] John Irwin, *To the Nobility, Gentry and Commonalty of this Kingdom of Ireland* (Dublin, 1720).

3

Investment from the Periphery: Irish Investors in the South Sea Company in Comparative and Transnational Perspective

The South Sea bubble was the great crisis of the financial revolution. The rapid rise of the South Sea Company's share price in late spring and early summer 1720, followed by its even more dramatic collapse in late August through to early September, instantly became the stuff of myth and legend. News of events in London quickly spread, not just across England and Wales, or even to Scotland and Ireland, but also across the Channel to the European continent and beyond. The reverberations of the London stock-market crash were felt in major and minor financial markets: in Amsterdam, Paris and Hamburg, as well as in Berne, Berlin, Dublin and Edinburgh. This transnational impact of the bubble reflected both the profile of investors in the South Sea Company and the organization's own global interests. From its incorporation in 1711 as a trading concern focusing on the Spanish colonies in South America, the company attracted investors from beyond the traditional financial heartland of the City. This was, of course, not unusual for British joint-stock enterprises during the age of the financial revolution, but during the 'year of the bubbles' the South Sea Company would become the most cosmopolitan of these corporations, eclipsing the more established Royal African and East India companies.[1] Indeed such was the range of its shareholders' origins during the bubble that it probably had one of the most internationally diverse investor bases of all the contemporary major European joint-stock companies. This is important because it points towards an often overlooked but crucial dimension of the bubble: its effect beyond London. Within this context, this chapter concentrates on the company's investors, looking particularly at those who came from outside England. While some attention is paid to those originating from mainland Europe, the primary focus in this chapter is on those investors from the British periphery, notably the Irish and the Scots. This group is largely excluded from existing accounts, apart from references to atypical figures such as the émigré bankers and speculators Richard Cantillon and

---

[1]   For some discussion of investment in the Royal African and East India companies in the period before the bubble see Anne Murphy, *The Origins of English Financial Markets: Investment and Speculation before the South Sea Bubble* (Cambridge, 2009), pp. 142–5.

John Law. The experience of their lesser-known compatriots rather than their own fascinating but exceptional speculations is, however, the subject of what follows.

I

Historians of the bubble, even if they have neglected Ireland and Scotland, have long noted the international dimension. Writing in the 1760s, Adam Anderson – a one-time clerk in the South Sea Company, and its first historian – recounted how investors came from far and wide. In particular, he highlighted the activities of the Canton of Berne who invested heavily and successfully in the London markets.[2] Later historians followed Anderson's account in describing the cosmopolitan nature of Exchange Alley during the spring and summer months of 1720. Other writers meanwhile have noted the linkages between the Paris and London markets, paying attention to the flight of capital and speculators across the English Channel that followed the collapse of John Law's Mississippi bubble in Paris in early 1720.[3] Until the 1960s such commentaries remained largely impressionistic and were primarily based either on anecdotal evidence, or on Anderson's late eighteenth-century writings. Nevertheless, they revealed the impact and influence of foreign investors on the London markets, demonstrating that the bubble was an event of international significance. It was, however, only with the magisterial work of P. G. M. Dickson that the full extent of foreign investment in the South Sea Company began to be revealed. Drawing upon a range of previously underexploited archival records, his 1967 study showed for the first time the number of foreign investors active in the English financial markets throughout the first six decades of the eighteenth century. As part of this analysis, he was able to provide estimates of the number of foreign investors who participated in the South Sea bubble.[4]

This was not a straightforward task. Many of the South Sea Company's own records, including their share registers and transfer books for the crucial bubble period in spring and summer 1720, were deliberately destroyed in the aftermath of the crash, creating problems for successive generations of historians.[5] Their absence has made it impossible to reconstruct a detailed picture of the company's shareholders in the same way that it is feasible

---

2   Adam Anderson, *An Historical and Chronological Deduction of the Origins of Commerce from the Earliest Accounts to the Present Time*, 2 vols (London, 1764), vol. 1, pp. 79–126.
3   Charles Mackay, *Extraordinary Popular Delusions and the Madness of Crowds* (Ware, 1995), pp. 1–38; and John Carswell, *The South Sea Bubble* (London, 1960), esp. pp. 77–97.
4   P. G. M. Dickson, *The Financial Revolution in England: A Study in the Development of Public Credit, 1688–1756* (London, 1967), pp. 249–337.
5   For an explanation of these difficulties see Anne Laurence, 'Women Investors, "That Nasty South Sea Affair" and the Rage to Speculate in Early Eighteenth-Century

to do for other joint-stock corporations such as the East India Company, or indeed for the Bank of England.[6] Dickson was able to overcome some of these archival complications by utilizing the records of the government-sponsored bailout of the South Sea Company. As part of Robert Walpole's successful post-bubble restructuring of the company and the British national debt, the company's stock was split in two with £16 million or half of the total stock being converted into perpetual annuities bearing 5% interest – the so-called South Sea Annuities – in 1723.[7] The ledgers recording this trans-action survive in the archives of the Bank of England, and they therefore provide a snapshot in time of the company's shareholders, most if not all of whom had held stock during the bubble. Naturally those investors who had sold their stock holdings before 1723 do not appear. Nevertheless, these records still provide valuable, and otherwise unavailable, evidence regarding the profile of the company's investors, giving not just their names, but also their addresses, as well as their stock holdings.[8] Using these address records Dickson was able to calculate that foreign residents held an estimated 7.6% of the company's stock. This was proportionally less than the contemporary figures for either the Bank of England or the East India Company, but the real number of foreign investors in the South Sea Company was much higher than that seen in either of the other two corporations.[9] Investors from the United Provinces (the modern-day Netherlands) were the single largest national group represented, holding approximately 60% of the foreign-held company stock. This was not surprising considering the pioneering role of Dutch financiers in developing the concepts and practices that underpinned the British financial revolution.[10] Dutch merchant capital was to be found elsewhere in the London markets as well as in other international exchanges,

England', *Accounting, Business & Financial History*, 16 (2006), 245; and Dickson, *Financial Revolution*, p. 133.

6   For the East India Company see H. V. Bowen, 'From Supranational to National: Changing patterns of investment in the British East India Company, 1750–1820', in *Colonial Empires Compared: Britain and the Netherlands, 1750–1850*, ed. Bob Moore and Henk Van Nierop (Aldershot, 2003), pp. 131–44, while for the Bank of England see Ann M. Carlos and Larry Neal, 'The Micro-Foundations of the Early London Capital Market: Bank of England Shareholders During and After the South Sea Bubble, 1720–25', *Economic History Review*, 59 (2006), 498–538.

7   On this restructuring process see Dickson, *Financial Revolution*, pp. 171–81; Carlos and Neal, 'Micro-Foundations of the Early London Capital Market', p. 502; and H. J. Paul, *The South Sea Bubble: An Economic History of its Origins and Consequences* (London, 2010), p. 104.

8   Stock Ledger: Old South Sea Annuities, 1723–51 (BoE, AC27/6437–80).

9   In 1723/24, 567 foreign domiciled investors held 14.2% of the Bank stock while 277 foreign residents held 15.9% of the East India Company's stock. See Dickson, *Financial Revolution*, p. 312.

10   Carswell, pp. 5–6; and Dickson, *Financial Revolution*, pp. 17–18. For some scepticism on the extent of Dutch influence see Murphy, *Origins of English Financial Markets*, p. 4.

indicating the transnational influence of traders from cities like Amsterdam, Rotterdam and The Hague.[11] Using exchange rate data, subsequent financial historians have shown the ways in which capital moved between London and Amsterdam during the middle months of 1720.[12] The impact of this investment from the United Provinces could also be seen in the satirical prints produced in Amsterdam commentating on the bubble, many of which were clearly designed for a domestic Dutch audience rather than for external consumption. Such images later helped to propagate the cultural memory of the bubble within a European context.[13]

Following the Dutch numerically came the Swiss whose investors included not just the well-documented case of the Canton of Berne, but also large numbers of Geneva merchants. Many of the latter were members of transnational Huguenot trading dynasties, often with connections in the United Provinces, and in Britain and Ireland.[14] The Irish, discussed in detail below, came next in Dickson's classification followed closely by the Germans. Most of those identified as German came from Berlin, with the local Huguenot émigré community again being especially prominent among them, but there were also investors from financial and trading centres like Danzig and Hamburg.[15] Dickson identified further minor groups including a small number of French investors and at least one from New England by the name of Captain Thomas Miller, as well as six investors from the West Indies.[16] His findings are summarized in table 3.1.

Dickson's pioneering work in the Bank of England archives brought

---

[11] Pit Dehing and Marjolhein 't Hart, 'Linking the Fortunes: Currency and Banking, 1500–1800', in *A Financial History of the Netherlands*, ed. Marjolhein 't Hart, Joost Jinker and Jan Luiten Van Zanden (Cambridge, 1997), pp. 37–61 (pp. 57–8).

[12] Larry Neal, *The Rise of Financial Capitalism: International Capital Markets in the Age of Reason* (Cambridge, 1990), pp. 65–8. See also Antoin E. Murphy, *Richard Cantillon: Entrepreneur and Economist* (Oxford, 1986), pp. 157–90.

[13] F. De Bruyn, 'Reading *Het Groote Tafereel der Dwaasheid*: An Emblem Book of the Folly of Speculation in the Bubble Year 1720', *Eighteenth-Century Life*, 24 (2000), 1–42; and Anne Goldgar, *Tulipmania: Money, Honor and Knowledge in the Dutch Golden Age* (Chicago, 2007), pp. 305–13.

[14] For Berne see Stefan Altdorfer, 'State Investment in Eighteenth-Century Berne', *History of European Ideas*, 33 (2007), 440–62. For the Huguenots see Francois Crouzet, 'The Huguenots and the English Financial Revolution', in *Favorites of Fortune: Technology, Growth and Economic Development since the Industrial Revolution*, ed. Patrice Higonnet, David S. Landes and Henry Rosovsky (Cambridge, MA, 1991), pp. 221–66.

[15] Dickson, *Financial Revolution*, p. 316.

[16] Dickson, *Financial Revolution*, p. 317. It is probable that these figures underrepresent the number of investors from the British colonies in North America, as many wealthy merchants and planters from the West Indies in this period also maintained London addresses, and were as a result quite active in the political, commercial and social life of the capital. See Julie Flavell, *When London was Capital of America* (London, 2010), pp. 22–3.

Table 3.1. Foreign investors in South Sea stock, 1723–24 (after Dickson).

Country	No. of investors	Value of investments (£)
United Provinces (Netherlands)	587	1,562,197
Switzerland	216	564,178
Ireland	100	81,988
Germany	79	121,847
Austrian Netherlands	30	70,189
Other	65	169,362
Total	1,077	2,569,761

Adapted from Dickson, *Financial Revolution*, p. 313, table 48.

a new, and arguably still unsurpassed, rigour to scholarly studies of the bubble. Subsequent historians have, however, built on his research, elucidating this subject still further. In particular, Ann Carlos and Larry Neal's studies of women investors and of the speculations of the international Jewish community have further emphasized the cosmopolitan nature of the London markets during the bubble.[17] Still other historians have used the ledgers of private London banks, such as Hoare's Bank, to further illuminate the investing community active in the City in 1720 and demonstrate its vibrancy and variety.[18] All of this research has added greater weight of evidence to the more impressionistic work of earlier writers and scholars on the subject, notably those whose interests were narrative rather than analysis driven.[19] Despite the ever-increasing scholarship on the bubble, and leaving aside the important exception that is Stefan Altdorfer's impressive study of the investment activities of the Berne mercantile and civic elite, we know very little about the foreign investors who came to London to invest and

[17] Ann M. Carlos and Larry Neal, 'Women Investors in Early Capital Markets, 1720–25', *Financial History Review*, 2 (2004), 197–224; and Ann M. Carlos, Larry Neal and Karen Maguire, '"A Knavish People …": London Jewry and the Stock Market during the South Sea Bubble', *Business History*, 50 (2008), 728–48.

[18] Anne Laurence, 'The Emergence of a Private Clientèle for Banks in the Early Eighteenth Century: Hoare's Bank and Some Women Customers', *Economic History Review*, 61 (2008), 565–86; and Peter Temin and H. J. Voth, 'Riding the South Sea Bubble', *American Economic Review*, 94 (2004), 1654–68.

[19] The best example of such an approach remains Carswell, *South Sea Bubble*, but see also Edward Chancellor, *Devil Take the Hindmost: A History of Financial Speculation* (London, 1999), esp. pp. 58–95; and Richard Dale, *The First Crash: Lessons from the South Sea Bubble* (Princeton, 2004).

speculate in the South Sea Company.[20] The remainder of this chapter, and the following one, will seek to illustrate this phenomenon through a study of investors from the British periphery with special emphasis on those from Ireland and Scotland.

II

The two previous chapters have shown how relatively limited domestic investment opportunities were in Ireland in the three decades before 1720. The same might be said for Scotland, and this is particularly true of the period after first, the Darien debacle, and then secondly, the Act of Union. As we have seen, the limited options available in either Dublin or Edinburgh did not, however, encourage large numbers to invest in the London markets. For instance, only a tiny number of Irish investors held stock in the Bank of England – they numbered nine in 1723–24 – while there were no Irish residents among the 277 foreign-domiciled holders of East India Company shares in the same year.[21] Even if the Irish presence in the great companies was nugatory, there was some Irish money laid out in English 'funds' in this period, for example in English lottery loans such as the 1694 Million Adventure and its successors. The lottery loans were attractive to investors because not only did they provide a regular dividend, but they also offered the possibility of winning significant sums in the regular draws held in London.[22] Evidence of the popularity of the state lottery with the Irish public can be seen in the advertisement of the Dublin bankers, Burton & Harrison, of their services as agents for the lottery, and in personal correspondence.[23] These buyers of lottery tickets and similarly Irish purchasers of government annuities were virtually invisible in the London markets in the first two decades of the eighteenth century. The Scots were, if possible, even less active, reflecting perhaps their more general struggles to assimilate into

---

[20] Altdorfer, 'State Investment'. For a brief discussion of the transnational dimensions see also Stephen Conway, *Britain, Ireland, & Continental Europe in the Eighteenth Century: Similarities, Connections, Identities* (Oxford, 2011), pp. 86–7, while for Scotland see Patrick Walsh, 'The Bubble on the Periphery: Scotland and the South Sea Bubble', *Scottish Historical Review*, 91 (2012), 106–24.

[21] Dickson, *Financial Revolution*, p. 313. Irishmen such as Col. James Waller, the deputy vice admiral for Munster, had however previously held East India stock in the 1690s. For his investments in the 1690s see Waller to Edward Southwell, 12 Jan. 1699 (BL, Add MS 38151, fol. 3).

[22] For investors in the lotteries see Murphy, *Origins of English Financial Markets*, pp. 156–8.

[23] See for example, Thomas Brodrick to Alan Brodrick, 1st Viscount Midleton, 13 Sep. 1720 (SHC, MS 1248/4, fols 318–19).

the commercial and financial life of the capital.[24] It would only be with the beginnings of the South Sea bubble in 1720 that these investors would have a more discernable presence in the London markets.

The question must therefore be asked as to why did Irish and Scottish investors speculate in the South Sea Company? Aside from the Hollow Sword Blade Company's Irish adventures, the South Sea Company had little if any connection with either Ireland or Scotland. This suggests the answer lies less in the specificities of the respective financial worlds of Dublin or Edinburgh, and more with the company and the attractions of its debt conversion scheme. Assessing the South Sea Company's success in quickly establishing its reputation more broadly, despite the geo-political hurdles it faced in the 1710s, Carl Wennerlind has stressed its skills as a master propagandist for its own cause.[25] It built up its initial reputation through the employment of skilled pamphleteers schooled in the partisan politics that characterized Queen Anne's reign. Among these writers was Jonathan Swift, who would later emerge as a savage critic of the company after the collapse of the bubble in 1720.[26] Such censure, however, lay in the future; in the early 1710s, Swift and his colleagues used their polemical and descriptive skills to convince a sceptical public to invest in the company, despite its uncertain trading prospects and the public's lack of knowledge of South America, from where its wealth was supposed to materialize.[27]

This skilled handling of the contemporary press resulted in drawing in some of the company's first investors and was again used during its negotiations with the government in 1719. It was particularly evident in February–March 1720, during the company's contest with the Bank of England for parliamentary approval for one of the two competing schemes to reduce the national debt. Contemporary newspapers reported on their ongoing rivalry, making a wider public aware of the competing interests and their contrasting proposals. These stories, like the earlier reports about the South American cornucopias, were read widely and helped to boost the company's share price. Crucially, they were carried not just in the London press, but in provincial

---

[24] David Hancock, *Citizens of the World: London Merchants and the Integration of the British Atlantic Community, 1735–1785* (Cambridge, 1995), pp. 46 and 52. Compare Hancock's description of the ill-at-ease Scots in early eighteenth-century London with Craig Bailey's *Irish London: Middle-Class Migration in the Global Eighteenth Century* (Liverpool, 2013).

[25] Carl Wennerlind, *Casualties of Credit: The English Financial Revolution 1620–1720* (Cambridge, MA, 2011), pp. 203–11.

[26] For Swift's complicated relationship with the company see Colin Nicholson, *Writing and the Rise of Finance: Capital Satires of the Early Eighteenth Century* (Cambridge, 1994), pp. 70–2.

[27] *The Examiner*, 7 June 1711, in Jonathan Swift, *Prose Works*, ed. Herbert Davis, 14 vols (Oxford, 1939–68), vol. 3, p. 170. See also *Some Remarks Upon A Pamphlet Entitled A Letter to the Seven Lords Etc.*, in *Prose Works*, vol. 3, p. 198; and *The History of the Last Four Years* (1714), in *Prose Works*, vol. 7, pp. 76–7.

newspapers including those published in Dublin.[28] Although undergoing a period of expansion at this time, the Dublin press remained somewhat derivative and published more on London events than on local news, and it was partly through such reports that Irish interest in the South Sea Company was first piqued.

The level of curiosity that was aroused is clear from the surviving correspondence of contemporaries, which is replete with references to the ongoing debates about the South Sea Company's proposals. What remains uncertain, however, is how well the public understood what they were reading in these reports. Even the Protestant Archbishop of Dublin, William King, normally a well-informed and intelligent observer of events, was confused by the machinations in parliament over the rival debt conversion schemes. He told Edward Southwell, the Irish secretary of state in London, 'I do not understand the contest between the South Sea Company and the Bank, but am told it makes a mighty commotion and divides the whole kingdom'.[29] Southwell had sought to assuage any fears King might have about the probity of the South Sea Company, telling him that its directors were 'honest men' rather than 'knaves'.[30] King does not seem to have been fully convinced. By May 1720 he was writing to friends telling them not to 'nonchalantly gamble' in what he termed 'the religion, policy, trade and business of England'.[31] At the same time he was preparing a draft memorandum, with James Hamilton, 6th Earl of Abercorn, warning prospective Irish investors of the risks involved in speculating in the South Sea Company.[32] Their concerns were not necessarily motivated by simple distrust of financial innovation or the stock market. Abercorn was, for instance, the most distinguished and prominent backer of the proposals for an Irish national bank. His correspondence with his relations and friends in May and June 1720 is full of advice both cautioning against investment in the South Sea Company, and encouraging support of his bank scheme.[33] It would, however, be too easy to see his opposition to Irish investment in London simply through the prism of his own financial projects in Dublin. Instead both he and King were simply sceptical of the South Sea Company's debt conversion proposals, with Abercorn attempting to explain

---

[28] See for example, *Harding's Impartial Newsletter*, 2, 16 Apr. 1720; and *Dublin Courant*, 22 Feb., 12 Mar., 2, 4 and 22 June 1720. For the circulation of ballads and prints from London see John, Lord Perceval to Philip Perceval, 14 Apr. 1720 (BL, Add MS 47029, fols 58–9).

[29] Archbishop William King to Edward Southwell, 6 Feb. 1720 (NLI, MS 2056).

[30] King to Southwell, 6 Feb. 1720.

[31] King to Robert, 1st Viscount Molesworth, 10 May 1720 (TCD, MS 750/6, fols 74–5).

[32] James Hamilton, 6th Earl of Abercorn, to King, 18 May 1720 (TCD, MS 1995–2008/1953); and King to Abercorn, 20 May 1720 (TCD, MS 750/6, fols 79–80).

[33] See for instance, Abercorn to Lord Perceval, 14 May 1720 (BL, Add MS 47029, fols 61–2).

his grounds for concern in a series of calculations sent to the archbishop.[34] Their proposed memorandum provisionally entitled 'A Queer Horn Book of ABC for the use of the South Sea Adventurers Without Compass' was, however, never published and does not seem to have survived even in draft form. The reason given for their failure to publish was a fear that it would be impolitic to be seen as an enemy of the British government, showing a clear association in their minds between the interests of the government and that of the company.[35] This suggests something of the company's perceived power and influence at the time, and might explain the relative paucity of critiques of their plans, even after the contemporaneous collapse of John Law's broadly similar Mississippi scheme in Paris.[36]

Abercorn and King were not the only Irishmen paying attention to events in London. In early May 1720, Jonathan Swift published his first significant Irish tract, A Proposal for the Universal Use of Irish Manufacture. Its immediate context was the passage of the Declaratory Act, incidentally on the same night as the South Sea Act received its final reading, which confirmed the constitutional dependence of Ireland on Britain.[37] His pamphlet contained a penetrating and grim analysis of the state of the Irish economy, highlighting the endemic weaknesses that were preventing growth. In its concluding pages, Swift poured scorn on the then current proposals for a national bank as a panacea for Irish economic (and political) ills.[38] This tract marked the beginning of Swift's serious engagement with Irish economic affairs and also showed an understanding of the problems affecting the local economy. Similar sentiments were also visible in his private correspondence. Writing in April 1720, he told Charles Ford that they could at least be thankful that Ireland could not have its own Mississippi or South Sea, as it was not a nation.[39] This prescient equation of the South Sea scheme with the recent stock-market bubble witnessed in Paris reveals something of Swift's ambivalent, if not negative, attitude to a company he had previously promoted in the London press.

[34] Abercorn to King, 18 May 1720 (TCD, MS 750/6, fols 79–80).

[35] Abercorn to King, 27 May 1720 (TCD, MSS 1995–2008/1954). King was at this point out of favour with the Irish administration because of his hostility to the passage of the Declaratory Act a month earlier.

[36] One interesting exception here is the series of pamphlets published by the Westminster MP Archibald Hutcheson, who was himself born in County Antrim, which critiqued with great mathematical detail the company's proposals. See Dale, pp. 82–90, but see also Paul, pp. 75–7, which questions the reliability of Hutcheson's analysis.

[37] Sean D. Moore, 'Satiric Norms, Swift's Financial Satires and the Bank of Ireland Controversy of 1720–1', Eighteenth-Century Ireland, 17 (2002), 26–56 (p. 32).

[38] Swift, Prose Works, vol. 9, pp. 21–2.

[39] Swift to Charles Ford, 4 Apr. 1720, in Williams, vol. 2, pp. 326–7; and Chris Fauske, 'Misunderstanding What Swift Misunderstood, or the Economy of a Province', in Money, Power and Print: Interdisciplinary Studies on the Financial Revolution in the British Isles, ed. C. I. McGrath and Chris Fauske (Newark, 2008), pp. 135–56 (pp. 137–8).

Another influential arbiter of elite Irish financial and political opinion, the London-based Lord Perceval, was, however, much more optimistic about the prospects of the company's debt conversion scheme.[40] Writing to his brother Philip in Dublin in early April 1720, he suggested that the South Sea Company was to be admired and should not be confused with some of the 'bubbles' then appearing in Exchange Alley. The company, according to Perceval, having survived 'the difficulties cast in the way by the bank and enemies of the government' was 'now fixed on so solid a foundation that it cannot possibly fail of answering the parliament's intentions of paying off the redeemable annuities, which come to above 30 million of our national debt'. This, he further explained, would happen without 'any manner of force or handicap on the annuitants', whose existing holdings of government debt were to be transmuted into company stock by the prodigious rise in price of that same stock.[41] Such positive reports undoubtedly influenced prospective investors, with several members of the extended Perceval family going on to purchase South Sea shares.

These Irish and Anglo-Irish discussions about the South Sea scheme are interesting not just because of the diversity of opinions displayed, warning perhaps with the benefit of hindsight of the danger of privileging those contemporaries who forecast doom and gloom, but also because they suggest that the company was successful in getting its message out through the press, and that once again its propaganda skills were effective. This interpretation can be further supported by reference to other contemporary Irish observers reporting an increased outflow of domestic capital to the London financial markets. At the beginning of May 1720, in the pamphlet that launched the scheme for an Irish national bank, its projector, John Irwin, described how Ireland's 'current cash' was being exhausted by those attracted by the prospects of 'extravagant gain' available in London and in Paris, where the Mississippi bubble had just burst.[42] Irwin's references to an exodus of Irish capital could be dismissed as a rhetorical trick, designed to encourage subscriptions to his own bank scheme, but his observations were echoed in other comments of the time. Letitia, Lady Molesworth, for instance, writing to her son John in late May, claimed that 'most of our money of this kingdom is gone over to the South Sea stock'.[43] Crucially, there were also gossipy reports of Irish success stories in both the London and Paris markets, not

[40] On Perceval's position in the London-Irish community see Patrick Walsh, 'Irish Money on the London Market: Ireland, the Anglo-Irish and the South Sea Bubble of 1720', *Eighteenth-Century Life*, 38 (forthcoming, 2014).

[41] Lord Perceval to Philip Perceval, 14 Apr. 1720 (BL, Add MS 47029, fols 58–9).

[42] John Irwin, *To the Nobility, Gentry and Commonalty of this Kingdom of Ireland* (Dublin, 1720).

[43] Letitia, Lady Molesworth to John Molesworth, 17 May 1720, in HMC, *Report on Manuscripts in Various Collections, vol. 8 The Hon. Frederick Lindley Wood; M. L. S. Clements, Esq.; S. Philip Unwin, Esq.* (London, 1913), p. 287.

only fuelling anxieties about the perceived capital flight phenomenon, but also encouraging others to venture their wealth in Exchange Alley.[44]

There is no doubt that prospective Irish investors were encouraged by reports of the fortunes gained by successful speculators, and also that on occasion they acted on these reports. This was of course not unique to Ireland and was instead a feature, and indeed a cause, of the bubble in the company's stock price. Investors from the British periphery, however, were potentially disadvantaged by their physical distance from the locus of the stock market in London's financial district. News travelled slowly with the postal service dependent on the weather, the tides and the condition of the roads. Letters sent from Dublin could reach London in four days, but they could also take a month, subject to the vagaries of the packet boat service that sailed between South Wales and Dublin Port.[45] Edinburgh was closer to the capital, with it not being uncommon for it to take up to twelve days for letters and newspapers to travel between the two cities. Delays in the relay of information from the capital meant that these investors from the periphery were more likely to enter the markets later than their London contemporaries. This could then lead to a greater exposure to potential losses as the price of stock rose between the writing and receipt of letters of instruction. This phenomenon was recognized by contemporaries: looking back on the events of the previous year in April 1721, the London Mercury reported that the gentlemen of Ireland 'went late into the stocks [and] bought dear'.[46] Similarly, some Scottish investors who only ventured into the South Sea markets late in summer 1720 bemoaned their own tardiness: Lewis Grant, for example, wished that he 'had bargained sooner for the stocks have risen near one hundred since my arrival and the game is now turned to drop so there is no meddling without a large fund of money or friends'.[47]

III

Reading such correspondence and commentary, it is clear that contemporaries believed that significant numbers of Irish and Scots invested in the South Sea bubble. They saw it as having potentially damaging consequences for the

[44] See for example, Madame Catherine da Cunha to Valentine Browne, 3rd Viscount Kenmare, 22 Feb. 1720, in The Kenmare Manuscripts, ed. Edward MacLysaght (Dublin, 1942), p. 108. For reports of Irish Mississippians in their gilded berlins see Robert Arbuthnot to Matthew Prior, 28 Sep. 1719, quoted in Murphy, Richard Cantillon, p. 76.
[45] See G. W. Place, 'Parkgate and the Royal Yachts: Passenger Traffic between the North-West and Dublin in the Eighteenth Century', Transactions of the Historic Society of Lancashire and Cheshire, 138 (1988), 67–83 (pp. 73–4); and Bailey, Irish London, pp. 42–3.
[46] London Mercury, 29 Apr. 1721.
[47] Lewis Grant to Sir James Grant, 12 July 1720 (NRS, GD248/170/3/79). See Walsh, 'Bubble on the Periphery', p. 120.

domestic economy as investors drained specie, precious metals and credit out of circulation. These problems, as we have seen, were also exaggerated by the comparatively late arrival into the London market of these speculators from Ireland and Scotland. If these were the assessments at the time, how accurate were they and how do they change our understanding of both the investing public and the consequences of their activities in 1720?

Writing in June 1720, James Graham, Duke of Montrose, claimed that the Scots alone had invested £1.5 million in the South Sea Company.[48] It is impossible, based on the evidence available, to assess the accuracy of such a calculation, but it does suggest substantial levels of investment from north of the border, at least relative to the available local capital. This figure is, after all, four times the capital subscribed to the Company of Scotland, the architects of the ill-fated Darien adventure in the 1690s, indicating a remarkable recovery in the confidence of the Scottish investing public in the intervening two decades.[49] Such apparently precise yet in all probability misleading calculations do not exist for Ireland. Instead contemporary observers were content to make reference to the 'the exhaustion of the current cash in the kingdom' and other such generalized descriptions of what was perceived as significant capital flight across the Irish Sea.[50]

Modern scholars have often been content to rely on selected quotations from contemporary sources, frequently treating them with a certain degree of scepticism.[51] In doing so they have downplayed the numbers of investors concerned, with the exception being Dickson's work on the 1723–24 annuity registers discussed previously. Although his conclusions are the most authoritative figures available, careful scrutiny of the surviving records in the Bank of England's archives suggests that his numbers for both Ireland and Scotland should be revised upwards.[52] In turn, such modifications to Dickson's findings offer a slightly different profile of the investors from the periphery, and suggest that they were even more significant than has

---

[48] Montrose to Mungo Graham of Gorthie, 2 June 1720 (NRS, GD220/5/833/1).

[49] Walsh, 'Bubble on the Periphery', p. 108.

[50] Aside from the observations of William King, John Irwin and Lady Molesworth previously cited, see William Conolly to Charles FitzRoy, 2nd Duke of Grafton, 9 Jan. 1721 (IAA, MS 97/84 A3/21); and Bishop William Nicolson to Archbishop William Wake, 21 Oct. 1721 (BL, Add MS 6116, fol. 114).

[51] Julian Hoppit, 'The Myths of the South Sea Bubble', *Transactions of the Royal Historical Society*, 6th ser., 12 (2002), 141–65 (p. 158).

[52] Old South Sea Annuities, 1723–28 (BoE, AC27/6437–52). For similar revisions of Dickson's figures regarding levels of English Huguenot investment in the Bank of England see Robin Gwynn, 'The Huguenots in Britain, the "Protestant International" and the defeat of Louis XIV', in *From Strangers to Citizens: The Integration of Immigrant Communities in Britain, Ireland and Colonial America, 1550–1750*, ed. Randolph Vigne and Charles Littleton (Brighton, 2001), pp. 412–26 (p. 417). I am grateful to Ann Carlos and Anne Laurence for advice on using these records.

previously been allowed. 'Significance' is of course a difficult concept to measure and the interpretation given here focuses not only on the contribution of such investors to the company's total share capital, but also upon the impact of such investment on both the economies and also the financial systems on the periphery.[53] This latter element is crucial in understanding the importance of these findings to the history of the bubble, emphasizing as it does the transnational dimension.

Re-examining the Bank of England's ledgers from 1723–24 and looking particularly for investors from the periphery, shows that there were at least 136 Irish holders of South Sea stock who had half of their holding converted into South Sea annuities as part of the British government's resolution of the post-bubble crisis. This figure is almost one third higher than the hundred Irish men and women identified by Dickson and can be partly explained by a different methodological approach, specifically in terms of categorization. Where Dickson just counted those individuals with identifiable Irish addresses, I have included some with no address who can be positively identified as Irish from other sources, as well as those who might be classified as the London-Irish. This fluid category contained Irish absentee landlords, such as the Irish secretary of state Edward Southwell, but the inclusion of such potentially problematic hybrid individuals does not solely account for discrepancies between the two sets of figures. The revised total for Irish investors is interesting for several reasons: it increases the known number of Irish holders of South Sea stock, while the details of these individuals alter our understanding of their profile notably in terms of geography and background.

Looking more closely at these 136 Irish investors, perhaps the most striking element is the preponderance of Huguenot names, with eighty-three of the Irish resident holders of South Sea stock appearing to be from a Huguenot background. This is perhaps not all that surprising: they made up a sizeable proportion of South Sea Company investors from across Europe. Huguenots resident in Berlin, for example, accounted for the majority of German investors, while they were also prominent among those investors resident in Geneva and Amsterdam.[54] They were often capital rich and drew their income largely from military and mercantile activities. The revocation of the Edict of Nantes by Louis XIV in October 1685 had led to their final expulsion from France and dispersal across Europe, and it was in the 1680s that they began to increase their presence in Dublin, with approximately four thousand Huguenots resident there by the 1720s.[55] Many Huguenots fought

---

[53] Here I have been influenced by my reading of Crouzet, esp. pp. 241 and 249.

[54] Dickson, *Financial Revolution*, pp. 315–16. For some discussion of the Huguenot contribution to the financial revolution see Murphy, *Origins of English Financial Markets*, p. 18; and Crouzet, *passim*.

[55] Raymond Hylton, *Ireland's Huguenots and their Refuge 1662–1745* (Brighton, 2005), p. 112.

in William III's armies in Ireland and on the Continent, and a good number of these 'French Pensioners' either remained as half-pay officers in Ireland or enjoyed pensions on the Irish military establishment. Such military pensions provided investment capital and it is therefore not surprising that names such Captains Paul Blosset, Solomon De Blosset and Gabriel Lamotte, as well as Major Anthony Delamaria, appear among the Irish investors.[56] Similarly, it was far from coincidental that one of the earliest Irish Huguenot agents, David La Touche, became a leading Dublin banker. He, like other Huguenot financiers and merchants, was able to exploit an extensive kinship network, including relations in London and Amsterdam, where he had completed his own education.[57] At least one of the Irish Huguenot military agents at the time of the bubble, Captain Theophilus Debrisay, can also be found among the South Sea Company investors. This was a role that might have allowed him access to extensive funds, as a common strategy employed during the bubble was for military agents to invest their client's money before remitting it back to them.[58] Unfortunately, in Debrisay's case we can only speculate due to the fragmentary evidence available.

Huguenots made up a significant component of Ireland's trading community, with mercantile members active in most Irish cities.[59] It is not surprising, therefore, that Huguenot merchants from Cork and Waterford, such as John Allanet, John Vestier and John Galtier, are included among the Irish names holding South Sea stock in 1723.[60] These merchants enjoyed not only close connections with merchants in Dublin, but may also have been part of wider transnational kinship groups, which were reinforced by religion, trade and mutual financial interests.[61] These were important networks in the early European financial markets, and have been clearly identified among investors active in London in 1720. The Dublin Huguenots were not just the largest element within the Irish investment community, they were also

[56] South Sea transfer annuities, 1723 (BoE, AC27/6438, 6440 and 6445). For Blosset and De Blosset see Hylton, pp. 126 and 129.
[57] On this point see David Dickson and Richard English, 'The Latouche Dynasty', in *The Gorgeous Mask: Dublin 1750–1850*, ed. David Dickson (Dublin, 1987), pp. 17–30; and David Dickson, 'Huguenots in the Urban Economy of Eighteenth-Century Dublin and Cork', in *The Huguenots and Ireland: Anatomy of an Emigration*, ed. C. E. J. Caldicott, Hugh Gough and J. P. Pittion (Dun Laoghaire, 1987), pp. 321–32 (pp. 323–6).
[58] For Debrisay see A. P. W. Malcomson, *Nathaniel Clements: Government and the Governing Elite in Ireland, 1725–75* (Dublin, 2005), pp. 145–6.
[59] Dickson, 'Huguenots in the Urban Economy', *passim*. There was a significant Huguenot presence among Dublin goldsmiths but, perhaps surprisingly, none of the known goldsmiths appear in the list of Irish investors. See Jessica Cunningham, 'Dublin's Huguenot Goldsmiths, 1690–1750: Assimilation and divergence', *Irish Architectural and Decorative Studies*, 12 (2009), 159–85.
[60] South Sea Annuity Ledgers, 1723 (BoE, AC27/6437 and 6442).
[61] For continuing trading links with the Continent among Irish Huguenots see the examples cited by Dickson, 'Huguenots in the Urban Economy', p. 324.

part of a wider international Huguenot phenomenon.[62] In this regard they were comparable to the Sephardic Jews who made up an influential and financially significant grouping within the London stock market.[63] Like them too, they could receive unwarranted attacks in the press from those who were fearful of the pernicious influence of such moneyed 'foreign' interests.[64] Similar attacks, including those notably and infamously by Jonathan Swift against the Dublin Huguenots, betrayed both their opponents' prejudices and the Huguenots' own growing authority.[65]

Swift's assaults on what he saw as the dangerous Huguenot influence on the Dublin financial sector bring us to another element within the Irish investing public: the clergy, and particularly ministers in the established Protestant Church of Ireland. Swift's own investments in the South Sea Company remain something of a puzzle, with the evidence proving inconclusive. Certainly, if he held shares in the company in 1720, he had divested himself of these holdings by the time of the 1723 conversion.[66] It is clear that he had made some investments in the London markets earlier in his career, and that he also encouraged others to invest in the South Sea Company, both as an agent for Robert Harley in 1710–11 and in his private correspondence. Swift's complicated and often hypocritical relationship with the innovations of the financial revolution has been documented elsewhere.[67] However, it is worth considering the wider investing role of the Irish Anglican clergy, a number of whom had holdings in the South Sea Company. This is not surprising as the clergy, alongside widows and urban merchants, were among the groups most commonly found in 'the funds' across early modern Europe. They had a ready access to capital through the profits arising from their benefices and living, while the higher clergy, notably bishops but also deans, could draw on diocesan and deanery revenues. Many clergy, including Swift, acted as moneylenders, offering a useful low-cost credit service.[68] Clearly, unlike the members of the Catholic clergy in Ireland, they had few scruples

---

[62] See L. M. Cullen, 'The Huguenots from the Perspective of the Merchant Networks of W. Europe (1680–1790): The Example of the Brandy Trade', in Caldicott, Gough and Pittion (eds), *The Huguenots and Ireland*, pp. 129–50 (p. 131).

[63] Carlos, Neal and Maguire, *passim*.

[64] Paul, pp. 94–5.

[65] Vivien Costelloe, '"Pensioners, Barbers, Valets or Markees"?: Jonathan Swift and Huguenot Bank Investors in Ireland, 1721', *Proceedings of the Huguenot Society of Great Britain and Ireland*, 29 (2008), 62–92.

[66] Nicholson, pp. 70–2; and Moore, 'Satiric Norms', pp. 45–6.

[67] On this subject see Sean D. Moore, *Swift, The Book, and the Irish Financial Revolution: Satire and Sovereignty in Colonial Ireland* (Baltimore, 2010).

[68] Sean D. Moore, '"Vested" Interests and Debt Bondage: Credit as Confessional Coercion in Colonial Ireland', in *The Empire of Credit: The Financial Revolution in Britain, Ireland and America, 1688–1815*, ed. Daniel Carey and Christopher Finlay (Dublin, 2011), pp. 209–28.

about lending at interest, or indeed about benefiting from interest accrued on their investments. The need to support their families – concerns about this subject abound in the extant correspondence of both prelates and lower clergy – might also explain their propensity to engage in the various forms of financial innovation available.

Among the Irish Protestant clerics to venture into the South Seas were some of the leading lights of the Irish episcopal bench, including the bishops of Derry, Down and Kilmore. William Nicolson, the Bishop of Derry, was a passive participant, having seen a government annuity he had previously purchased being converted into company stock. Meanwhile Francis Hutchinson, Bishop of Down, a keen supporter of the Bank of Ireland proposals and an enthusiastic advocate of economic improvement, had very deliberately purchased South Sea stock to the value of £560 early in 1720 and retained his holdings throughout the summer. By 1723 his shares were worth four times the original purchase price and by the time he disposed of the remaining stock in 1728, he had enjoyed a healthy annual dividend income for over eight years.[69] He attributed his success to his early entry into the market, and blamed the disproportionate losses suffered by Irish investors on their late realization of the opportunities available and, therefore, their purchases of stock at much higher prices.[70] This contemporary analysis is borne out by Larry Neal's empirical analysis of share price data, and confirms Hutchinson's contemporary reputation as an astute economic commentator.

The clergy and members of the armed forces, including at least one naval captain operating on the 'Irish station', are the easiest professions to identity among those listed as holders of South Sea stock.[71] Other entries in the Bank ledgers include the appellation 'merchant', and what is notable is that not all of these so described were based in Dublin, pointing towards another important element within the Irish investor profile: their geographic dispersal throughout the island. The majority of investors were resident in the capital, but there were others who listed their addresses in provincial cities and towns as well as members of the country gentry. These included merchants, some of them Huguenots, in Cork, Galway and Waterford, as well as military personnel in Kinsale, a leading naval port. Moving beyond the investors listed in the 1723 transfer books, it is possible to find those members of the Irish gentry who speculated in the bubble similarly widely dispersed. The geographical concentration of Irish investors in Dublin, however, is probably more akin to the trend witnessed in England rather

---

[69] Andrew Sneddon, *Witchcraft and Whigs: The Life of Bishop Francis Hutchinson* (Manchester, 2008), p. 186.

[70] Francis Hutchinson, *A Letter to the Gentlemen of the Landed Interest in Ireland Relating to a Bank* (Dublin, 1721), p. 22; and Neal, *Rise of Financial Capitalism*, pp. 111–12.

[71] Captain Thomas Lawrence of the *Aldborough*. See Lawrence to Josiah Burchett, 15 Jan. 1721 (TNA, ADM 1/2037).

than that seen in Scotland, where at the time of the Darien scheme Scottish 'proto-venture capitalists' were spread across the northern kingdom.[72] In England, the majority of investors still came from London and its environs, although analysis of the 1723 annuity registers does illustrate that English investors did come from virtually all counties in the kingdom.[73]

Complicating the picture are those investors who enjoyed a hybrid Anglo-Irish, or Anglo-Scottish identity, dividing their time between London and Ireland or Scotland. The London-Irish have been included in the figures presented here because many of them either drew the majority of their revenues, or spent significant amounts of time, in the western kingdom. Their inclusion points to some of the problematic aspects of dealing both with Ireland's relationship with Britain and with the question of the diaspora especially in terms of situating Ireland, or indeed Scotland, or for that matter the French Huguenots, within a transnational framework. Many of those included here – and the numbers are small – generally regarded themselves, and were regarded by contemporaries, as Irish. It is possible, for instance, to describe an 'Irish interest' at court or within the wider London mercantile community.[74] Among these investors were absentee Irish peers like Charles Boyle, 4th Earl of Orrery, lords Gowran and Lanesborough, as well as Irish officeholders such as Edward Southwell and Sir Gilbert Dolben, a judge in Ireland.[75] Other prominent London-Irish investors included the merchant George Fitzgerald, whose address at Basinghall Street placed him at the heart of the Irish mercantile community in London.[76]

Many London-Irish networks flourished through the exploitation of business and official connections, but at least as important, if not more so, were family ties. Many Irish families were Anglo-Irish in the truest sense of the phrase in that they maintained a presence on both sides of the Irish Sea.[77] Some of the more interesting and noteworthy examples, such as the

---

[72] W. Douglas Jones, '"The Bold Adventurers": A Quantitative Analysis of the Darien Subscription List (1696)', *Scottish Economic & Social History*, 21 (2001), 22–42.

[73] This assessment is based on an analysis of the address records in the 'A' Ledger of the 1723 South Sea Annuity Ledgers (BoE, AC27/6437).

[74] Craig Bailey, 'Metropole and Colony: Irish Networks and Patronage in the Eighteenth-Century Empire', *Immigrants and Minorities*, 23 (2005), 161–81; F. G. James, 'The Irish Lobby in the Early Eighteenth Century', *English Historical Review*, 81 (1966), 543–57; Thomas Truxes, 'London's Irish Merchant Community and North Atlantic Commerce in the Mid-Eighteenth Century', in *Irish and Scottish Mercantile Networks in Europe and Overseas in the Seventeenth and Eighteenth Centuries*, ed. David Dickson, Jan Parmentier and Jane Ohlmeyer (Gent, 2007), pp. 271–300; and Bailey, *Irish London*.

[75] For Dolben's investments see F. E. Ball, *The Judges in Ireland, 1221–1921*, 2 vols (London, 1926), vol. 2, pp. 66 and 93.

[76] L. M. Cullen, 'The Two George Fitzgeralds of London, 1718–59', in Dickson, Parmentier and Ohlmeyer (eds), *Irish and Scottish Mercantile Networks*, pp. 251–70 (p. 266).

[77] James, 'Irish Lobby', p. 556.

Molesworths, Percevals and Brodricks, are discussed in the next chapter, but there were many more. In financial and speculative matters, family members could act as intermediaries with brokers, pass on information and generally act for familial interests as well as for their own. This role was taken up by family patriarchs such as Lord Perceval or Robert, 1st Viscount Molesworth, but it could also be fulfilled by women, especially widows and spinsters, as recent research has shown. Possibly the best known was Mrs Jane Bonnell, the widow of an Irish accountant-general, who acted as a conduit of news and financial information for her family and personal connections in both Ireland and the English provinces.[78] Her story is detailed in the next chapter, but it is important to note here that she was just one of a number of Irish female investors in the South Sea Company. Such women included Martha Courthope, the widowed sister-in-law of Alan Brodrick, 1st Viscount Midleton, the Irish Hanoverian lord chancellor, and Frances Talbot, Duchess of Tyrconnell, the widow of Ireland's last Catholic chief governor, as well as a number from other Irish gentry families. They were joined by at least twenty female members of the Dublin and Cork Huguenot communities. Of the 136 Irish names in the 1723–24 ledgers, twenty-six were women. Proportionately these figures conform to the best estimates of total female participation in the bubble. In this regard, Irish female investors therefore belonged to a wider pattern, one that is only now being fully uncovered by historians, whereby women were beginning to emerge as active investors during the period of the bubble. Their participation in the financial markets of Paris, and especially London, drew no shortage of contemporary commentary – much of it hostile – although detailed research suggests that women were no more inclined to be foolhardy investors than their male counterparts. Indeed women, like the aforementioned Jane Bonnell or the Scottish Jacobite countess Margaret, Lady Panmure, were skilled financial strategists, while at least one female broker, Johanna Cock, has been identified as having operated quite success-fully in Exchange Alley.[79]

The Duchess of Tyrconnell stands out among the Irish investors for two reasons: first, because she was a woman and furthermore, because she was a Catholic. Following the death of her husband, Richard Talbot, the Duke of Tyrconnell, in 1691, and the confiscation of the family estates, she lived a life of relative penury until the accession of Queen Anne in 1702. Thereafter and thanks to the influence of her sister, the queen's 'favourite' Sarah Churchill, the Duchess of Marlborough, she regained some of her former fortune and status.[80] In this regard she was atypical of the dispossessed

---

[78] See also Laurence, 'Women Investors', *passim*.

[79] For Margaret, Lady Panmure see Walsh, 'Bubble on the Periphery', pp. 119–20, while for Johanna Cock, see Carlos and Neal, 'Women Investors in Early Capital Markets', pp. 205–8.

[80] Deirdre Bryan, 'Talbot, Frances (c.1649–1731)', in *DIB*.

Catholic elite, many of whom had fled to France in 1690–91 taking their liquid capital with them, even while their Irish estates were confiscated by the victorious Williamite regime.[81] There, some appear to have speculated in Law's Mississippi bubble, facilitated by the presence of émigré bankers like Sir Daniel Arthur and Richard Cantillon. Few Irish Catholics are immediately visible within the ranks of Irish investors in the bubble, although there were notable exceptions, such as Madame da Cunha, a sister of Nicholas Browne, 2nd Viscount Kenmare and estranged wife of a former Portuguese ambassador to London, and Thomas Butler of Kilcash, a prosperous Catholic landowner with close family links to the exiled Jacobite Duke of Ormonde.[82] Butler of Kilcash was an unusual case among the Irish investors in the bubble. He was, however, wealthier than most of the small number of his Catholic co-religionists who survived within the Irish gentry after 1691.[83]

Unsurprisingly, the majority of Irish investors were drawn from the various elements within Irish Protestantism, notably the Huguenots and other members of the established Church of Ireland. There were also a small number of Irish Protestant Dissenter investors, notably Presbyterians, including the banker Sir Alexander Cairnes, who was well connected to leading City interests through his father-in-law Sir Nathaniel Gould, a director of the Bank of England. Cairnes was an active speculator in the London stock market in 1720 investing not only in the South Sea Company, but also in a company trading with Germany which was prescribed by the Bubble Act in July 1720, and for whom he was the leading promoter.[84] However, his London speculations were seen in Dublin as injurious to his reputation, leading some to view Cairnes' involvement with one of the three schemes for a national bank as a black mark against the project.[85] This turned out to be a rather astute judgement as Cairnes suffered heavy losses as a result of not only his own investments in the South Sea Company, but also where he had acted on behalf of his Irish customers. This led to reverberations on

---

[81] Up to ten thousand Irish women may have accompanied the twelve thousand men who departed for France in 1691: see Mary Ann Lyons, "*Digne de Compassion*": Female Dependents of Irish Jacobite Soldiers in France, c.1692–c.1730', *Eighteenth-Century Ireland*, 23 (2008), 55–75, which details the limits of the capital they took with them.

[82] Madame Catherine da Cunha to Lord Kenmare, 30 June 1720, in MacLysaght, p. 113. For some evidence that the exiled Duke of Ormonde maintained a personal, even financial, interest in the repercussions of the fall of the South Sea Company, see Ormonde to Richard Butler, 9 Dec. 1720 (Staffordshire Record Office, D641/2/K/2/5/H). I am indebted to Dr John Bergin for this reference.

[83] For the surviving Catholic gentry, see Kevin Whelan, 'An Underground Gentry: Catholic Middlemen in Eighteenth-Century Ireland', *Eighteenth-Century Ireland*, 10 (1995), 7–68.

[84] Carswell, p. 166.

[85] Thomas Brodrick to Midleton, 13 Aug. 1720 (SHC, MS 1248/4, fols 263a–b).

both sides of the Irish Sea.[86] His business nonetheless survived, although the Limerick bank that was supposed to have closed in the aftermath of the crash was connected to the wider Cairnes business empire.[87]

Cairnes was the not only Ulster Presbyterian banker to suffer losses in this manner. Robert Gardner, a previously successful Carrickfergus merchant who also acted as an agent and broker in London, was reported to have become so involved in the bubble, 'losing then most of all he had, that he died in low circumstances and his affairs were very much encumbered'.[88] Cairnes and Gardner were, however, rare examples of Irish Protestant Dissenter investors, despite their co-religionists' preponderance in the Irish banking sector and their mercantile influence in cities like Belfast and Derry. Their comparative lack of investment activity as a group appears somewhat anomalous when viewed within a transnational or British perspective, where religious dissenters were known for their particular involvement in the capital markets even while they still suffered civil and religious discrimination.[89] The most likely answer to this conundrum is that many Irish Dissenters had not yet acquired significant capital resources to enable investment beyond the island; neither Belfast nor Derry, where greatest numbers of them lived, had fully taken off economically, as would occur later in the century. This was also, more generally, a fallow period for the Ulster economy, and many capital-rich Presbyterians were choosing to migrate to the North American colonies, thus participating in the first great wave of Irish transatlantic emigration.[90] As such, some prospective investors may have been looking to the west rather than directing their gaze, and their money, southward and eastward towards London.

IV

The analysis so far in this chapter has largely focused on those 136 Irish investors who still held South Sea stock in 1723. These individuals do not, however, represent the totality of Irish investors in the South Sea Company during the bubble period. Among those excluded are the investors who sold

[86] For some of the knock-on effects of Cairnes' losses see Jane Bulkeley to Jane Bonnell, 23 June 1721 (NLI, MS 41,580/3).
[87] L. M. Cullen, 'Landlords, Bankers and Merchants: The Early Irish Banking World, 1700–1820', in *Economists and the Irish Economy from the Eighteenth Century to the Present Day*, ed. Antoin E. Murphy (Dublin, 1984), pp. 25–44 (p. 32).
[88] Jean Agnew, *Belfast Merchant Families in the Seventeenth Century* (Dublin, 1996), pp. 154 and 186.
[89] Bruce C. Carruthers, *City of Capital: Politics and Markets in the English Financial Revolution* (Princeton, 1996), pp. 156–7.
[90] Patrick Griffin, *The People With No Name: Ireland's Ulster Scots, America's Scots Irish and the Creation of the British Atlantic World* (Princeton, 2001), pp. 67–9.

their stock during the year of the boom or shortly afterwards, encompassing both those who made considerable profits, and also some who suffered heavy losses. Nevertheless, using these 136 investors, it has been possible to extract information about religion, gender, geographical dispersal and professional standing, allowing a sketch of their collective profile to be developed. Missing so far, however, has been any discussion of the scale of their specu-lation? How much did they invest? And how did this compare with the sums invested by other national and regional groups? The final section of this chapter provides some answers to these questions.

Quantifying levels of investment in the South Sea Company during the bubble presents particular challenges for the historian. The absence, as discussed earlier, of the company's share registers and transfer books, where purchases and sales of stock were recorded, is the most important obstacle. These archival problems are further complicated by the complexities of the South Sea debt conversion scheme, which allowed for a number of different categories of shareholders.

Not all investors in the South Sea Company purchased stock during the heady days of May and June 1720, when crowds flocked to Exchange Alley to participate in scenes often described as a form of mania. Some had purchased their interests in the months and years following the estab-lishment of the corporation in 1710. Still more had held other forms of government debt, such as long-term annuities, which were converted into company stock either in 1719 or even in late 1720 as part of the company's privatization of the national debt.[91] Finally, a select few, including a number of politicians and courtiers, were gifted stock by the company's directors who were eager to curry favour with those in power. Irish men and women can be found in all of these different categories. William Conolly, speaker of the Irish House of Commons, received a subscription for £2,000 worth of stock through the goodwill of Charles Spencer, 3rd Earl of Sunderland, a leading British minister and former lord lieutenant of Ireland.[92] Among those whose annuities were converted into company stock were the Irishwomen Martha Courthope and Esther Van Homrigh, while Robert, 1st Viscount Molesworth, his sons John and Richard, and Sir Oliver St George were among those Irishmen who purchased stock in the London secondary market during the spring and summer of 1720.[93]

These examples illustrate some of the different means and methods by

91   Dickson, *Financial Revolution*, pp. 93–105; and Paul, pp. 44–5.

92   William Conolly to Charles Delafaye, 27 Dec. 1720 (TNA, SP 63/379, fol. 87); and Patrick Walsh, *The Making of the Irish Protestant Ascendancy: The Life of William Conolly, 1662–1729* (Woodbridge, 2010), p. 167.

93   For Van Homrigh's and the Molesworth family's investments see chapter 4. For Sir Oliver St George see his correspondence with the London banker Nathaniel Gould, 1720–24 (TNA, C 110/46/248–300).

Table 3.2. Revised figures for foreign investment in the South Sea Company, 1723–24.

Country	No. of investors	% of total	Value of investments (£)	% of total	Average investment/ investor
United Provinces (Netherlands)	587	52	1,562,197	57	2,661
Switzerland	216	19	564,178	20	2,612
Ireland	136	12	184,651	7	1,358
Germany	79	7	121,847	5	1,542
Austrian Netherlands	30	3	70,189	3	2,340
Scotland	19	2	55,504	2	2,921
North American colonies	1	0	25	0	25
Other foreign investors	64	6	169,337	6	2,646
Total	1,132	100	2,727,928	100	2,410

Source: South Sea Annuity Ledgers (BoE, AC27/6437–6452) and Dickson, *Financial Revolution*, p. 313, table 48.

which Irish men and women became involved in the bubble, but what still remains elusive is the scale of their investments. The best information we have regarding the monetary value is the sums recorded in the 1723 annuity ledgers. Doubling the figures for individual holdings listed in the ledgers provides a snapshot of these investments at the time of the conversion of half of the company's stock into long-term annuities and reveals that Irish investors held shares valued at £184,651 as shown in table 3.2.

Examining this in a comparative context, it appears that Ireland's total investment figure, perhaps unsurprisingly, reflected the trend described earlier whereby Ireland came third behind the United Provinces and Switzerland in the league table of total foreign investor numbers. More interesting, however, are the figures describing the average holdings of investors at this juncture. Irish investors held proportionally less South Sea stock than any other group with an average figure of £1,358, just over half the Dutch and Swiss average holding. Only the Germans, interestingly those most comparatively similar in terms of gross numbers of investors, had a similarly low average investment level. There are a number of possibilities why the Irish figure is so low. First, both the average and aggregate national figures seem to broadly correlate with known patterns of financial and economic development, something that would explain the Dutch and Swiss cases. The Scottish figures for total

Table 3.3. Irish investors by holding (£), 1723–24.

Stock holdings (£)	No. of investors
£1–£100	15
£100–£250	29
£250–£500	28
£500–£1,000	29
£1,000–£2,000	12
£2,000–£5,000	12
£5,000–£10,000	9
> £10,000	2
Total	136

investment value, however, seem suspiciously low, and should be treated with caution, especially as it is quite likely that many Scots dually resident in London and the northern kingdom have escaped capture within this data series. What is striking, however, about these Scottish individuals is the profile of investors: most were landed or gentry rather than coming from mercantile backgrounds, suggesting that it was the latter group who were most reluctant to risk their fortunes in the aftermath of the Darien debacle.

The second point worth noting about the average Irish figure is that it is, if anything, artificially high. This becomes clear when the individual component figures are examined more closely, as shown in table 3.3. Just over half the total number of Irish investors held shareholdings of less than £500 in 1723. Only two individuals had stock valued at more than £10,000, namely Sir John Molesworth, British ambassador to the court of Savoy at Turin and scion of a prominent Dublin landed family, and Henry Boyle, Lord Carleton, a member of the wealthy Anglo-Irish Boyle dynasty whose estates and revenues straddled the Irish Sea. Molesworth's holdings were reckoned at a not insubstantial £10,878 in 1723, but he was supposed to have had a 'paper fortune' of around £100,000 in midsummer 1720 when friends and acquaintances were urging him to sell his stock at a great profit.[94] Carleton, meanwhile, was not the only member of the extended Boyle clan to speculate in the bubble though he was probably the most successful. His cousin William Boyle, writing to his brother Henry, the future speaker of the Irish House of Commons, reckoned his losses to be the equivalent of £500 per annum and told his brother that he was not 'one of those to

[94] Daniel Pulteney to John Molesworth, 12 June 1720 (HMC, *Various Collections*, vol. 8, p. 287).

remain sanguine'.[95] He consoled himself, however, with the thought that his family were provided for. Other Irish investors who had ventured more modestly into the markets could also be confident of making provision for their families. At a time when the average Church of Ireland living was worth approximately £60 per annum, clerics like the Revd Arthur Duff of Belfast or the Revd Peter Maturin of Dublin were still doing very well with their stock holdings of £206 and £840 respectively. This pattern could be repeated for other professionals, such as military officers, who continued to retain an interest in the company.[96] Even after half of these holdings were converted into annuities they continued to accrue interest for their owners. Investments in South Sea stock even after the bubble, and in relatively small quantities, could therefore continue to be an important supplement to other sources of income.

The comparatively low average Irish balances in 1723 still require some consideration. It is possible that they reflect the low levels of capital and credit available in the Irish economy, a subject much commented upon and bemoaned in contemporary pamphlet literature. The ease with which the Irish government had filled the subscription for the first national loan in 1716 and the large sums promised to the various national bank schemes in 1720 (discussed in chapter 6), however, raise some questions about the veracity of these contemporary claims, although it is important not to overstate this point.[97] The bank subscriptions, as we shall see, may have been based on expectation and patriotic sentiment rather than realistic assessments of available capital. They do, however, point towards another way of interpreting the apparent low levels of Irish investment: the attractiveness of more locally based investment opportunities such as the proposed bank and also other contemporary plans for a fire insurance scheme. Here it is possible to see some parallels with Scotland where enthusiasm for specific 'Scots projects' like the North Sea Fishery and the Edinburgh Society for Insuring Houses Against Loss by Fire attracted local capital in preference to the more distant London markets.[98]

It is also possible that the low Irish balances in 1723 indicate the heavy losses supposed to have been suffered by Irish investors who came late to Exchange Alley. While there is some anecdotal evidence to confirm their late arrival into the London markets, it is difficult to know how much Irish

95 William Boyle to Henry Boyle, 13 June 1721 (PRONI, D2707/A1/2/8B).

96 For clerical incomes see Toby Barnard, *A New Anatomy of Ireland: The Irish Protestants, 1649–1770* (London, 2003), pp. 82–5.

97 For a detailed analysis of the Irish public creditors see C. I. McGrath, '"The Public Wealth is the Sinew, the Life, of Every Public Measure": The Creation and Maintenance of a National Debt in Ireland, 1716–45', in Carey and Finlay (eds), *The Empire of Credit*, pp. 171–208.

98 Walsh, 'Bubble on the Periphery', pp. 122–3.

investors differed from others caught up in the speculative mania described by so many contemporary and later writers.[99] Debates continue to rage within the scholarly literature about the irrationality of investors and how much of the investment in the South Sea Company can be termed 'speculation' or attributed to the influence of the majority, the so-called 'wisdom of crowds' effect. These arguments are likely to continue without reaching any definite conclusions in the absence of greater evidence about the timing and amount of individual investments.[100] Similar problems hamper the study of the Irish investors in particular. It is impossible to know, for instance, when each of these 136 investors purchased their stock and at what terms, or indeed how many were holders of long or short-term government annuities which were converted into South Sea stock in 1720, a process only completed in December of that same year and therefore after the bursting of the bubble.[101] Without more definitive answers to these questions, all conclusions about the value of these holdings and the reasons for their apparent low value must remain somewhat speculative.

V

This chapter has examined the participation of investors from the periphery in the South Sea bubble through an analysis of some of the most important statistical evidence. The primary focus has been on investors from Ireland, although their experiences have been situated within two broader contexts. The first of these, comparative in nature, is the experience of Scottish investors, while the second has been a wider transnational one. This dual approach reflects the complicated status of Ireland as both an integral and separate component part of the British polity. Questions about Ireland's constitutional status relative to, and economic relationship with, the rest of Britain preoccupied some contemporaries and, it could be argued, played at least some role in their investment choices. Investment from the British periphery was significant at least in terms of the outflow from Ireland and Scotland, if not in terms of the inflow into London. The overall contri-bution of transnational or international investors was, however, important within the metropolitan core, and investment from the periphery played a part in this. The profile of these investors was, as has been shown, cosmo-politan, politically and religiously diverse, and also mixed in terms of gender

---

[99] The classic work here is Mackay, *Extraordinary Popular Delusions*, but see also Carswell, esp. pp. 154–73.

[100] The rationality of the South Sea scheme is emphasized in Peter Garber, *Famous First Bubbles: The Fundamentals of Early Manias* (Cambridge, MA, 2000), esp. pp. 121–2. See also Paul, pp. 102–3.

[101] Laurence, 'Women Investors', p. 247.

and professional background. In these ways it was not dissimilar to that of investors from London. The difference was that many of these investors from the periphery were participating in the London markets for the first time, thus helping in the creation of London's status as the emerging international capital of finance.

4

'Most of Our Money of This Kingdom
is gone over to the South Sea':
Irish Investors and the South Sea Company

In 1723 George Berkeley, then a fellow of Trinity College Dublin and already a renowned philosophical thinker, received an unexpected bequest from a woman he had never met. It was for the not insubstantial sum of £2,000 and was partly derived from the profits of a successful investment in the South Sea Company during 1720.[1] Berkeley may not have been acquainted with his benefactor but she is well known to posterity. She was Esther Van Homrigh, the daughter of a prominent Dublin merchant and politician of Dutch origin. She is, however, better remembered as Jonathan Swift's 'Vanessa' in which capacity she served as both correspondent of, and muse to, the dean. Swift's dislike of the South Sea Company, as expressed in his public and private writings, is common knowledge, but Van Homrigh, despite Swift's scepticism, converted a government annuity she held into company stock and realized a small profit.[2] Her bequest to Berkeley is proof of this, even if her motives for leaving this sum to him remain somewhat opaque.

The philosopher would later use these funds to part-finance his famous project to establish a college in Bermuda. That scheme may have failed but Berkeley's time in the American colonies, specifically Rhode Island, would prove important when he came to develop his theories on money and banking in *The Querist*, possibly the most influential Irish economic text of the eighteenth century.[3] Within its pages, Berkeley explored the ideas on finance that he had first considered in the aftermath of the South Sea bubble in his *Essay upon the Ruin of Great Britain* (1721), and also in his private correspondence with John, Viscount Perceval, later 1st Earl

---

[1]   George Berkeley to John, Viscount Perceval, 4 June and 19 Sep. 1723, in *The Works of George Berkeley*, ed. A. A. Luce and T. E. Jessop, 9 vols (London, 1948–57), vol. 8, p. 130.

[2]   Swift to Esther Van Homrigh, 15 Oct. 1720, in *The Correspondence of Jonathan Swift*, ed. Harold Williams, 5 vols (Oxford, 1963–65), vol. 2, pp. 359–60. For details of her life see Andrew Carpenter, 'Van Homrigh, Esther (Hester) (1688–1723)', in *DIB*.

[3]   George Berkeley, *The Querist: Containing Several Queries, Proposed to the Consideration of the Public*, 3 vols (Dublin, 1735–37). See Joseph Johnston, *Bishop Berkeley's Querist in Historical Perspective* (Dundalk, 1970) for what still remains an informative guide to its political and economic contexts.

of Egmont.[4] Ironically, therefore, Esther Van Homrigh's bequest would indirectly influence one of the most seminal economic texts of the period, and one that is greatly critical of the events and methods by which this legacy was earned. Adding of course to the irony was the fact that one of her initial financial advisers, Jonathan Swift, was the author of *The Bubble*, one of the most important literary texts produced in the aftermath of the South Sea crash and a poem that has been described as providing a significant contribution to the fashioning of the popular myth of the bubble.[5] But what does this tale about an Irish woman and two clergymen tell us about the South Sea bubble?

First, it gives us information about one of the many thousands of investors in the company. It shows what happened to her investment and to what use it was subsequently put, moving beyond the slightly reductionist comments of one modern historian who has suggested that the transfer of wealth occasioned by the bubble from the country squires to city traders was a universally positive outcome.[6] In this case it is especially interesting because of the connection with two well-known critics of the bubble, particularly because their writings have had such an influence on later accounts, especially those by literary scholars and the more popular chroniclers of the episode. Such accounts, which often draw both consciously and unconsciously on Swift and his literary contemporaries, have propagated a view of the bubble that gives much weight to its ruinous effects and the great losses suffered by easily led and manipulated speculators.[7] Some contemporary reports went further and singled out female investors for special scorn, while also employing feminized language to depict the impact of the crash, using gendered terms such as 'hysteria'.[8] The case of Esther Van Homrigh, despite its links with Swift as one of the most influential of these polemicists, is therefore especially

---

[4]   See P. H. Kelly, '"Industry and Virtue Versus Luxury and Corruption": Berkeley, Walpole and the South Sea Bubble Crisis', *Eighteenth-Century Ireland*, 7 (1992), 57–74.
[5]   Pat Rogers, 'Plunging in the Southern Waves: Swift's Poem on the Bubble', *The Yearbook of English Studies*, 18 (1988), 41–50 (p. 41).
[6]   H. J. Paul, *The South Sea Bubble: An Economic History of its Origins and Consequences* (London, 2010), p. 103.
[7]   Julian Hoppit, 'The Myths of the South Sea Bubble', *Transactions of the Royal Historical Society*, 6th ser., 12 (2002), 141–65 (pp. 159–62). For the problems of relying on Swift as an economic commentator see Chris Fauske, 'Misunderstanding What Swift Misunderstood, or the Economy of a Province', in *Money, Power and Print: Interdisciplinary Studies on the Financial Revolution in the British Isles*, ed. C. I. McGrath and Chris Fauske (Newark, 2008), pp. 135–56 (p. 135); and J. A. Downie, 'Gulliver's Travels, The Contemporary Debate on the Financial Revolution and the Bourgeois Public Sphere', in McGrath and Fauske (eds), *Money, Power, and Print*, pp. 115–34.
[8]   See for example, Archibald Hutcheson, *Four Treatises Related to the South Sea Scheme* (London, 1721). For modern critiques of this gendered literature see among others Catherine Ingrassia, *Authorship, Commerce and Gender in Early Eighteenth-Century England: A Culture of Public Credit* (Cambridge, 2005), pp. 17–40; and M. De Goede,

interesting as it highlights an example of a woman investor who gained from her South Sea venture, an outcome that recent scholarship has demonstrated was much more common than traditional accounts allowed. Added to this is the fact that she was a female investor from the periphery, another group that has begun to gain some attention from scholars, notably through the work of Anne Laurence.[9] Our information about Esther Van Homrigh comes not from stock ledgers, though her name does appear there, but from personal correspondence and family papers. Historians of the bubble rarely consult such sources, at least outside the political and financial correspondence of the main players, but they are extremely valuable for uncovering the stories of ordinary investors. In turn, these individual experiences can help provide a better understanding of the fascinating and complex events of 1720.

This chapter expands on the more analytical and statistical investor profile developed in chapter 3. The approach used there, while essential in terms of identifying general trends and conclusions, concentrated on aggregate figures. In contrast, this chapter starts from a different point of view and emphasizes the role of individual agency, drawing on the personal experience of known investors. It also employs different types of historical source materials, using personal correspondence and accounts to explore the trajectories of individual investors through the sometimes uncharted waters in which they found themselves during 'South Sea Year'. The use of such personal records raises some methodological questions, but the bank ledgers used in the previous chapter, and employed to good effect by other financial historians, are not unproblematic sources themselves. In particular, the 1723 ledgers, while the best source we have in terms of quantifying and identifying shareholders in the South Sea Company, only provide a snapshot of a particular moment that came three years after the height of the bubble in midsummer 1720. As a result, many investors and speculators in South Sea stock are not included, having sold their holdings during the periods of greatest market activity. Conversely, those South Sea shareholders enumerated in the 1723 records include many whose holdings of government debt were only finally transferred to the South Sea Company's books in late 1720 after the bubble burst.[10] Absent from these records, however, is any indication of the motivations that led individual investors to purchase their stock. These are important issues for those who want to better understand this crucial period in the history of financial capitalism, and they are central to what follows.[11]

'Mastering "Lady Credit": Discourses of Financial Crisis in Historical Perspective', *International Feminist Journal of Politics*, 2 (2000), 58–81.

9   Anne Laurence, 'Lady Betty Hastings, Her Half-sisters, and the South Sea Bubble: Family Fortunes and Strategies', *Women's History Review*, 15 (2006), 533–40.

10   Hoppit, 'Myths of the South Sea Bubble', p. 148.

11   For some recent attempts by more avowedly econometric scholars of the bubble to

Using personal correspondence and papers gives us an opportunity to understand better the mentalities of some of the many thousands of investors caught up in the bubble. These sources give us insight into their motivations, their learning experiences and the results of their investments. We are able to learn more about the function of networks, both those used for passing information, and those used to manage and encourage investments. These are some of the benefits of this approach, but there are of course important issues that need to be borne in mind. While this chapter builds on a methodology first suggested but not pursued by John Carswell, to examine the effects of the bubble on individual pockets through wide-ranging reading and archival research, it is dependent upon the quality of surviving evidence.[12] This leads to questions about sample selection and representation. Is it possible, for instance, that more commentary on the impact of the bubble has survived in the letters of those who suffered heavy losses rather than those who profited greatly from their speculations and investments? Such people were perhaps, in Henry Roseveare's words, more likely to 'bleat' in the aftermath and in doing so, give credence to theories prevailing then and now about 'the madness of crowds' and 'herd movement'.[13] Even so, taking the evidence from private correspondence presented here together with the more statistical approach laid out in the preceding chapter, it is possible to get a clearer picture of events in 1720.

The methodology employed in these chapters using these two complementary rather than necessarily opposing approaches, provides the opportunity to place greater emphasis on 'context and environment', elements that have recently been identified as 'crucial factors in understanding market behaviour'.[14] Analysing individual investor case studies as well as profiles of some of the wider networks operating in the London stock market helps us to understand the impact of the impetus to invest in Exchange Alley. In doing so it builds on the fascinating and insightful work of other scholars on surviving bank ledgers, and private bank and stock accounts. In its elaboration of individual narratives this chapter goes further and argues that it is possible, as David Hancock states, 'to mediate between the mass and

---

understand the role of individual agency see Larry Neal, *'I Am Not Master of Events':* *The Speculation of John Law and Lord Londonderry in the Mississippi and South Sea Bubbles* (London, 2012); and Gary S. Shea, 'Sir George Caswall vs. the Duke of Portland: Financial Contracts and Litigation in the Wake of the South Sea Bubble', in *The Origins and Development of Financial Markets and Institutions from the Seventeenth Century to the Present*, ed. Jeremy Attack and Larry Neal (Cambridge, 2009), pp. 121–60.

[12] John Carswell, *The South Sea Bubble* (London, 1960), p. vi. See also Laurence, 'Lady Betty Hastings', pp. 533–40.

[13] Henry Roseveare, *The Financial Revolution, 1660–1760* (London, 1991), p. 58; Paul, p. 103, makes a similar point referring to the same people as 'noise traders'.

[14] Jane Humphries and Steve Hindle, 'Editors' Introduction', *Economic History Review*, 62, *Special Issue: Finance, Investment and Risk* (2009), 1–7 (p. 7).

the individual, as well as between impersonal forces and human reactions, statistics and biographies', in order to extrapolate wider trends from the analysis of individual networks and narratives.[15]

The geographical focus is again on investors from the periphery, notably those from Ireland, but also including some comparative discussion drawing on Scottish examples. These are, as shown in the previous chapter, but a small proportion of the total number of investors. Nevertheless, they provide interesting and illuminating case studies that have relevance beyond Ireland or Scotland. Investors from the periphery who travelled to London, in the same way as those from the English provinces, or indeed some from the European continent, were probably more likely to commit their thoughts to paper than those who were ordinarily resident in the metropolitan centre. Either they were acting on behalf of others who remained geographically distant from the markets or they just wished to pass on their experiences and stories to relatives and friends eager for news from the capital. This last dimension is important when we consider that London was still their metropolitan capital and the source of ideas, consumption patterns, luxury products and, increasingly, financial opportunities.[16] It is not surprising therefore that so many of the surviving collections of contemporary correspondence feature news from London, and more specifically information and gossip about the South Sea Company and its activities. In this regard they mirrored the contemporary newspapers, which were full first of accounts of John Law's Mississippi bubble and then, as its fortunes declined and interest in it waned, the South Sea scheme.

The case studies discussed here highlight a number of interesting issues, but they are also often typical of some of the groups of investors as determined in the previous chapter. Significantly they, together with other research carried out in surviving manuscript and printed collections from the period, make it possible to identify a number of investors who do not appear in the Bank of England ledgers, and were not hitherto known to have been linked with the South Sea Company. Such individuals included representatives of some of the most powerful families in Ireland and Scotland. Uncovering their investments adds further detail and opens up new fields of enquiry regarding the financial activities of the Irish and Scottish elites, as well as providing greater material for comparative and transnational studies of the landed and moneyed interests active in this period.

---

[15] David Hancock, *Citizens of the World: London merchants and the integration of the British Atlantic community, 1735–1785* (Cambridge, 1995), p. 8. See also Nini Rodgers, *Ireland, Slavery and Anti-Slavery: 1612–1865* (Basingstoke, 2009), pp. 197–229 for a similar approach.

[16] For the idea of London as a metropolitan capital in this context see Julie Flavell, *When London was Capital of America* (London, 2010); while for the Irish context see Martyn J. Powell, *The Politics of Consumption in Eighteenth-Century Ireland* (Basingstoke, 2005).

I

The investors chosen for closer attention have been selected largely on the basis of surviving evidence. Preference has been given to those for whom documentation is available covering the whole time-span of the bubble, that is from the passage of the South Sea Act in March 1720 through to the final collapse of the company's share price during the following October. Not all of the case studies discussed below cover this period in its totality, but they are otherwise representative of the different groups of investors from the periphery at this point. As explored briefly in the previous chapter, determining who should be included within the category of Irish investor is more difficult than might be immediately apparent. This was a time after all when identities were particularly fluid and when it was possible to be both Irish and English or even British.[17] Individuals could, depending on their circumstances and position, define themselves differently at particular times and in particular places, leading on some occasions to episodes of self-doubt and confusion. It is important to note, however, that this was a position not unique to Ireland, as Scots and North American colonists suffered from similar crises of identity. Such dilemmas make it more difficult for historians to construct rigid categories. Nevertheless, using contemporary sources, it is possible to devise a wide, yet still meaningful, category of Irish investors that includes more than just those wholly resident in Ireland.

Irish-born peers and politicians resident in London, like Lord Perceval and Thomas Brodrick, could describe themselves as Irish yet they spent most of their careers in England, owned English as well as Irish estates and were members of the Westminster parliament. On both sides of the Irish Sea, however, they were seen as part of the 'Irish interest' in London. They encompassed more than just the political lobby active at Westminster, although this group – among the longest established, best integrated and most successful lobbies operating in this period – comprise an important subcategory.[18] Beyond the political sphere there were active Irish banking, legal and mercantile concerns. Compared with the London-Scottish interest, the Irish were much more subsumed into the political, societal, commercial and financial worlds of the capital, reflecting a longer history of integration, which crossed political, social and even religious divides.[19] As F. G. James

---

[17] On the complexities of Anglo-Irish identity in this period see D. W. Hayton, *The Anglo-Irish Experience, 1680–1730: Religion, Identity and Patriotism* (Woodbridge, 2012), esp. pp. 25–49. See also Craig Bailey, *Irish London: Middle-Class Migration in the Global Eighteenth Century* (Liverpool, 2013), esp. pp. 15–16.

[18] F. G. James, 'The Irish Lobby in the Early Eighteenth Century', *English Historical Review*, 81 (1966), 543–57 (p. 556).

[19] See John Bergin, 'The Irish Catholic Interest at the London Inns of Court, 1674–1800', *Eighteenth-Century Ireland*, 24 (2009), 36–61; and Craig Bailey, 'The Nesbitts of London and their Networks, 1747–1817', in *Irish and Scottish Mercantile Networks in Europe and*

has noted in his analysis of their political activities, economic self-interest rather than patriotism united an often disparate group. Their investments in 1720 were made with Irish capital, and they were as concerned with the ready availability of Irish credit as their counterparts who remained in Ireland, something that could be seen in the absentee enthusiasm for the national bank projects launched in the same year, one of which was chiefly promoted by the largely absentee Lord Forbes.[20] Similarly, their gains and losses during the bubble were likely to, and did have, an impact on the Irish economy. As absentee landowners, much of their income was drawn from Irish estates, and their investments could, and should, be seen as part of the outflow of capital to the metropolitan markets. Contemporaries regarded them as Irish, much in the same manner that the 'Scottish interest' in London was treated collectively.[21] The travails of both groups during the bubble were referred to in national terms, suggesting a level of homogeneity that potentially simplified individual experiences too much.

Secondly, there were those who divided their time and money on both sides of the Irish Sea, perhaps those who could be truly defined as Anglo-Irish. Among this group were Alan Brodrick, 1st Viscount Midleton and Robert, 1st Viscount Molesworth, both of whom enjoyed significant careers and incomes in Ireland and England. Like their counterparts among the English provincial landowners and the Scottish lairds, who divided their time between the centre and the periphery, many of the Anglo-Irish were drawn to invest in South Sea stock. Indeed as is suggested below, their motivations for investment were often similar to those Scottish and provincial investors who sought to raise sufficient capital to support their metropolitan lifestyles in London.[22] Often co-existing in this category were those Englishmen who had made a career in Ireland, but still were regarded as part of an 'English interest'. These included judges in the Dublin courts as well as a number of bishops of Irish dioceses.[23] Their investments were funded from the profits

---

Overseas in the Seventeenth and Eighteenth Centuries, ed. David Dickson, Jan Parmentier and Jane Ohlmeyer (Gent, 2007), pp. 231–50.

[20] For Forbes' presence within the Irish absentee milieu see Polly Molesworth to John Molesworth, 13 Oct. 1719, and Robert, 1st Viscount Molesworth to Letitia, Lady Molesworth, 29 July 1721, in HMC, *Report on Manuscripts in Various Collections, vol. 8 The Hon. Frederick Lindley Wood; M. L. S. Clements, Esq.; S. Philip Unwin, Esq.* (London, 1913), pp. 281 and 318. More generally see A. P. W. Malcomson, 'Absenteeism in Eighteenth-Century Ireland', *Irish Economic and Social History*, 1 (1974), 15–35.

[21] Alan Brodrick, 1st Viscount Midleton to Thomas Brodrick, 8 Oct. 1720 (SHC, MS 1248/4, fols 326–7); and James, Duke of Montrose to Mungo Graham, 2 June 1720 (NRS, GD220/5/833/1).

[22] Carswell, p. 144.

[23] Patrick McNally, '"Irish and English Interests". National Conflict within the Church of Ireland Episcopate in the Reign of George I', *Irish Historical Studies*, 29 (1995), 295–314.

of Irish benefices and offices, and therefore Irish revenues, and should be counted among the Irish capital exported to Exchange Alley.

Finally, there were those Irish men, and women, whose income and lives were largely Irish based. Many members of this last category relied on investment intermediaries, often drawn from the other groups identified here. They included Irish soldiers, merchants and clergy, as well as landowners. The majority were also members of the Church of Ireland, although there were interesting exceptions from the Dissenting and Catholic communities. As in the other categories identified, these individuals were mostly drawn from either the property-owning elite or the rising mercantile classes. The impact of their investments did, however, extend beyond the confines of their own social strata, especially following the crash as access to credit diminished and pressures grew to extract rents and call in debts.

While members of the Anglo-Irish including the Bonnell, Brodrick, Molesworth and Perceval families were recognizably Irish, other ostensibly 'Irish' investors are harder to classify. Where for example does the County Kerry-born and French-domiciled Richard Cantillon fit? He was one of the greatest and most successful speculators active in Paris, London and Amsterdam during 1720, but though Irish born, Cantillon maintained little contact with the land of his birth. His fortune may have owed its origins to the exodus of Irish Catholic capital that followed the defeat of the Jacobite interest in 1691, but by the second decade of the eighteenth century the Anglo-French nexus was more important than the Anglo-Irish or even Franco-Irish for Cantillon. Even his closest Irish associates were either fellow émigrés in Paris such as his cousin, the banker Daniel Arthur, or members of the Catholic London-Irish community such as his lawyer Francis Garvan.[24] Like Cantillon, their financial interests focused on London and Paris, not Ireland. Cantillon's inclusion among the Irish investors is therefore problematic: a truly transnational figure, he should perhaps be counted with the French investors, if he can be said to belong to any international grouping at all. Thomas Pitt, Lord Londonderry, is another who might tenuously be considered Irish, his peerage being of Irish rather than British provenance. However, as with many holders of Irish peerages, his connection with Ireland was nominal at best: he never took up his seat in the Irish House of Lords, nor visited his Irish estates, which like his title were a product of his marriage. Instead his greatest significance in terms of Irish investment in the South Sea Company was the role he played as an expert adviser and broker for his Irish relations, notably members of the St Leger family of Doneraile, County Cork.[25] The examples of Cantillon

---

[24] I am indebted to John Bergin for helpful discussions on this point. See also Bergin, p. 57.

[25] Arthur St Leger to Thomas Pitt, Lord Londonderry, 27 June, 5 Aug. and 7 Oct. 1720 (PRONI, T3425/2/22, 25 and 30).

and Londonderry, like the analogous case of John Law as a representative Scottish investor, highlight the difficulties in devising watertight categories. Despite these caveats it is still possible to focus in on individual narratives, which it is hoped will illuminate a wider experience.

II

Many Irish investors in the South Sea Company were absentee landlords, equally at home in London or Bath as they were in Dublin or on their Irish country estates. They were often part of the London political establishment, sitting at Westminster, or active at court, but they maintained an Irish identity. Significantly they drew the majority of their income from Irish estates and offices. Edward Southwell, a former chief secretary in Ireland and owner of extensive estates in County Cork, reckoned that by 1718 he had remitted £60,000 across the Irish Sea since 'the revolution'.[26] Much of this was official income drawn from his Irish offices, as well as the rental income from his Irish properties. Like other members of the Irish elite resident in London he invested in the South Sea Company, though unfortunately his otherwise voluminous correspondence is silent on the amount and fate of his investments. No such problem arises, however, with the case of his cousin John, Lord Perceval, one of the most active and well-documented Irish investors.

Although the owner of 22,000 acres in counties Cork and Tipperary and the possessor of an Irish peerage, Perceval spent most of his career in England, especially after the Hanoverian succession in late 1714.[27] In London, having become a leading authority on, and lobbyist for, Irish affairs, he also attached himself to the rising political interest of Sir Robert Walpole. In this context he was especially active in spring 1720 in organizing the unsuccessful absentee campaign in opposition to the Declaratory Act.[28] Perceval's role as a recognized voice for Irish parliamentary and political interests was confirmed in June 1720 when he was one of a select band of Irishmen resident in London approached by the promoters of a putative Bank of Ireland to promote their interest at Westminster and at court.[29]

[26] Edward Southwell to William King, 23 Dec 1718 (NLI, MS 2056). For his offices, see his entry in *HIP*, vol. 6, pp. 306–7.
[27] See Betty Wood, 'John Perceval, first Earl of Egmont (1683–1748)', in *ODNB*.
[28] This link between the South Sea and Declaratory acts is noted by Sean D. Moore in his 'Satiric Norms, Swift's Financial Satires and the Bank of Ireland Controversy of 1720–1', *Eighteenth-Century Ireland*, 17 (2002), 26–56 (p. 32), where he suggests, convincingly, that it may have contributed to the paucity of parliamentary debate on the Irish legislation.
[29] D. W. Hayton, 'The Stanhope/Sunderland Ministry and the Repudiation of Irish Parliamentary Independence', *English Historical Review*, 113 (1998), 610–36 (pp. 613–14).

His correspondence on this subject with Lord Abercorn, the leading figure behind the bank, suggests he possessed a keen financial, as well as political, mind.[30] This impression is confirmed by his growing interest in the stock market, and more specifically in the South Sea Company.

He seems to have first taken notice of the company during what he termed its 'war' with the Bank of England over the rights to the lucrative contract to manage the national debt in February 1720.[31] It was only in April, however, that he began to take serious notice of the company's prospects and to consider their debt conversion scheme in some detail. In a letter to his Irish-based brother Philip, an MP in Dublin, he gives a fascinating account of proceedings in Exchange Alley. Enclosing two songs 'much in vogue', including a 'humorous' one about bubbles, he proceeds to define the term: 'You can't be ignorant what the word bubble means in Exchange Alley, an airy project set up by designing men to cheat ignorant subscribers'.[32]

The South Sea Company in Perceval's view was different. It was, he explained, 'fixed upon so solid a foundation' that it could not fail. Acknowledging the similarities with John Law's Mississippi Company, which had just experienced its final collapse, he insisted that though the South Sea Company was built on the Mississippian plan, it was done with 'more justice and concern for the security of men's property'. To illustrate the company's success, Perceval described how if one had purchased stock to the value of £1,000 a year previously, that same holding would be now worth £3,500, and that this was likely to rise over the course of the following months. Relating the general to the specific, he also informed his brother that their cousin Daniel Dering had been prudent in postponing his marriage to that summer as both he and his intended wife, a Ms Parker, were 'in a fair way of getting by South Sea what will make them easy during their lives'.[33] By the end of June, John Perceval was able to report that Dering had gained £30,000 in Exchange Alley, leading Philip Perceval to comment that considering his recent marriage, Dering had confounded 'the old proverb which says one must not expect to wive and thrive in one year'.[34]

Reading his brother's reports of the successes enjoyed by his relations and others in Exchange Alley, as well as John's confident protestations that the South Sea was no bubble, must have served only to whet Philip Perceval's appetite. Writing to his brother in late April he complained that he had

---

[30] James Hamilton, 6th Earl of Abercorn to John, Lord Perceval, 14 May 1720, and Perceval to Abercorn, 26 May 1720 (BL, Add MS 47029, fols 61–3).

[31] Lord Perceval to Charles Dering, 2 Feb. 1720 (BL, Add MS 47029, fols 9–10). On this 'war' see Hoppit, 'Myths of the South Sea Bubble', pp. 146–7.

[32] Lord Perceval to Philip Perceval, 14 Apr. 1720 (BL, Add MS 47029, fols 58–9).

[33] Lord Perceval to Philip Perceval, 14 Apr. 1720.

[34] Lord Perceval to Philip Perceval, 16 June 1720, and Philip Perceval to Lord Perceval, 30 June 1720 (BL, Add MS 47029, fols 69–70).

not received sufficient advice about the company's prospects to benefit from its rising share price. John Perceval's response is particularly illustrative of the problems of investing from afar and deserves some consideration here. Referring to the complaint that he had not encouraged Philip to purchase South Sea stock before its price began to rise, John explained that like many others he had initially expected the Bank of England to triumph in the parliamentary contests over the two conversion schemes. He therefore, again like many others, had purchased Bank stock. Once South Sea shares first 'came to a great height' he 'bought in' but, as he told Philip, the share price then fell by 50%. Would Philip have been happy in this instance, he asked, or would he have been 'very angry after that fall and imagined I gave you very sorry advice'? The reality of the situation during this volatile period, as described by John, was that prices were liable to change rapidly, rising or falling by as much as 10–20% during the course of an hour making it 'impossible at the distance you are to tell you what to do, or [for] you to be certain of success were my advice ever so good for the time'. Bearing this in mind, John, like many of his acquaintances, was reluctant to give advice.[35] He was, however, quite willing to pursue his brother's directions if he so desired, and did later promise to purchase shares in the proposed Dublin fire insurance company, which was being floated in London in June 1720.[36]

John Perceval's pragmatic approach towards giving advice to others about investing in the stocks was reflected in the way he managed his own investments. Initially he seems to have been somewhat cautious, telling one correspondent that he had not 'ventured deep' into the 'scramble', unlike some of his friends and relations. Despite this both he and his wife stood to make considerable profits by the end of June. Writing to his brother, John told how his wife had gained 'about a thousand pound, but has not yet realised it as we say when we withdraw our money and make sure of it'.[37] Indeed at this time, realizing his fortune seems to have been far from Perceval's mind. Writing to his friend Lord Abercorn, he rejected the latter's advice to withdraw from the market, reporting instead with some excitement the projections for the company's share price:

> Ill news from abroad or a war would undoubtedly sink the stock, but God be thanked, we were never under less apprehensions of those evils than now, and in the meantime it rises so fast, that a man can scarce justify his selling out, for it is at present near 500, and it is said there will be a dividend in money of 3% over above the 10% in stock, and that the second dividend will in a little time be declared as great as the first. There will likewise be a new Subscription taken in at 7 or 800 and the Company lend money on their stock, which with

---

[35] Lord Perceval to Philip Perceval, 7 May 1720 (BL, Add MS 47029, fols 59–60).
[36] Lord Perceval to Philip Perceval, 16 June 1720 (BL, Add MS 47029, fol. 69).
[37] Lord Perceval to Philip Perceval, 16 June 1720.

exchequer notes that are speedily to issue will supply the market with money, and consequently increase the number of buyers; all this must necessarily raise the stock to a far greater value than it is at present and people offer freely £50 for the refusal of a £1,000 stock at a thousand at the opening, which will be some time in August next.[38]

This passage provides a classic illustration of an investor who despite his earlier pragmatism had got caught up in what some at the time, and many later commentators too, described as a speculative mania. In the same letter, Perceval anticipated selling out before August when, with remarkable prescience, he foresaw greater risks arising if a new subscription of £1,000 per share was to be announced by the company. It seems that he did not follow the logic of his own analysis and instead continued to hold stock through to the winter of 1720. His losses during the bubble would later be estimated as amounting to over £10,500.[39] This was a substantial amount but it did not entirely turn him against the possibilities offered by such investments. He remained to the end a strong supporter of the Irish bank scheme, although he became more cautious about investing in the London stock market. When his brother purchased two tickets in the York Buildings Lottery in 1721, Perceval described it as 'the plainest cheat that I have known if that which is plain can be at the same time a deceit', suggesting he had learned his lesson from his experiences during the previous year.[40] His losses during the bubble also led to some retrenchment on his Irish estates, as he struggled to collect his County Cork rents following the impact of the crash on the Irish economy.[41] This in turn had an adverse effect on Perceval's already diminished personal income, although the bubble did not ruin him.

The Percevals were not the only Anglo-Irish family to invest in the bubble. Indeed a number of their County Cork neighbours were also active in the London money markets, including several members of the influential Boyle family, whose investments were discussed in the previous chapter. More successful than William Boyle, who described his losses as being equivalent of £500 per annum, was Arthur St Leger, 1st Viscount Doneraile, who benefited from the expert advice of his relation Thomas Pitt, Lord Londonderry. St Leger's newly improved fortune, which he used to purchase an estate in

---

[38] Lord Perceval to Abercorn, 26 May 1720 (BL, Add MS 47029, fol. 63).

[39] Andrew Sneddon, *Witchcraft and Whigs: The Life of Bishop Francis Hutchinson* (Manchester, 2008), p. 188.

[40] Lord Perceval to Philip Perceval, 30 Aug. 1721 (BL, Add MS 47029, fol. 136). For the York Buildings Company see A. J. G. Cummings, 'Industry and Investment in the Eighteenth-Century Highlands: The York Buildings Company of London', in *Industry, Business and Society*, ed. A. J. G. Cummings and T. M. Devine (Edinburgh, 1994), pp. 24–42.

[41] On the impact of the bubble on the Munster region see David Dickson, *Old World Colony: Cork and South Munster, 1630–1830* (Cork, 2005), p. 124.

England and clear some of his inherited debts, led him to seek an elevation in the peerage.[42] He was, however, neither successful in his pursuit of an earldom nor able to pass his own investing acumen onto his son, also named Arthur. The younger St Leger had, thanks to the influence of Lord Londonderry and St Leger's mother, converted a lottery annuity into South Sea stock in autumn 1720 just as the share price was collapsing, an occurance to which he seems to have been oblivious. Instead he told Londonderry that 'I hope it will turn to a considerable account for I hear that about the middle of October stocks will rise even till it comes up to 1500. If so I would advise that it should not be sold till the latter end of February next.'[43]

Such confidence in the ability of the markets to bounce back was misplaced, but it was also not uncommon. Another Irish absentee, Madame Catherine da Cunha, encouraged her nephew Valentine Browne, 3rd Viscount Kenmare, based in County Kerry, to purchase South Sea shares in October 1720, telling him that 'nobody doubts that the stock will come to five if not six [hundred], and now is a very good time to buy'.[44] Similar advice was current in Scotland where it was rumoured that ministers would intervene to raise the price of the company's stock.[45] Perhaps luckily Lord Kenmare did not follow this advice, and thus unlike his aunt was not 'disappointed'.

Kenmare's cautious response to his aunt's encouragement to lay out his fortune in London shows that it was possible for those on the periphery not to be seduced by the reports of spectacular gains emanating from the capital.[46] In Kenmare's case these included the news that his future father-in-law, Thomas Butler of Kilcash, had made a substantial fortune thanks to his speculation in South Sea stock.[47] Butler was one of a small number of British and Irish Catholics who took the opportunity to increase their wealth in this way. The penal legislation then in force in both kingdoms restricted their ability to build capital through property ownership making investment in the 'funds' a viable alternative. The supposed scale of Catholic investment was so great that some contemporaries even saw it has having potential political consequences. Purchasing stock, it was thought, would bind Catholics closer to the state, and push them further away from supporting a restoration of the exiled Stuart monarchs. This viewpoint, based on an exaggerated perception of Catholic investment, was ably expressed with some clarity by John Perceval when he commented: 'that all the papists who had money are

42   St Leger to Londonderry, 5 Aug, 7 Oct. 1720 (PRONI, T3425/2/25 and 30).
43   St Leger to Londonderry, 7 Oct. 1720 (PRONI, T3425/2/30).
44   Madame da Cunha to Lord Kenmare, 8 Oct. 1720, in *The Kenmare Manuscripts*, ed. Edward MacLysaght (Dublin, 1942), p. 114. The current price of stock on this date was £265: John Castaing, *Course of the Exchange* (London, 1720).
45   William Aikman to John Clerk, 25 Oct. 1720 (NRS, GD18/4578). See also Archibald Douglas of Cavers to John Clerk, n.d. [October] 1720 (NRS, GD18/5319/10).
46   Da Cunha to Kenmare, 19 June, 18 July 1720 (PRONI, D4151/F2, fols 55–6).
47   Da Cunha to Kenmare, 30 June 1720 (PRONI, D4151/F2, fol. 144).

deep in the stock, so that were the pretender to attempt a new invasion he would be surprised to find that numbers of his old friends would wish him at the bottom of the sea'.[48] This may have been the position of Jacobite investors during the early months of summer 1720, but by the autumn the Pretender was trying to capitalize on the changed circumstances following the crash by issuing a proclamation damning the South Sea Company and the government.[49]

As Irish Catholics, Madame da Cunha and Thomas Butler were unusual within the broader mass of investors from Ireland; in other respects they were not atypical. They both seem to have operated within wider family networks that used the expertise of relatives then resident in London to benefit those living further afield. In this manner they were like the Percevals, but also like the other family networks considered below, namely the Molesworths and Brodricks, and also the wider kinship group surrounding Jane Bonnell, who was particularly active in the London markets both for herself as well as on behalf of others.[50] These sorts of family networks could be crucial in helping to negotiate the complexities of the stock market, though some individuals like Madame da Cunha, the former Catherine Browne, could proffer some questionable advice. Her enthusiasm for the opportunities available in Exchange Alley probably owed something to the precarious financial situation in which she personally, and the Kenmare family more broadly, found themselves. Through a combination of careful legal strategy and good fortune, the Brownes of Kenmare had managed to retain their estates following the Williamite wars, despite the departure into French exile of Nicholas Browne, the 2nd Viscount. His sister Catherine had married the Portuguese ambassador to London, Don Luis da Cunha, though by the late 1710s they were estranged and she was living alone in London, surviving predominantly on an allowance from the family's Irish estates.[51] These had become increasingly indebted during the first two decades of the eighteenth century when they passed into the hands of a trust controlled by a Protestant relation John Asgill, a former land-bank promoter and Irish agent for the Hollow Sword Blade Company,[52] and only reverted to Kenmare control when Valentine Browne inherited them in early 1720 following his father's death in exile in Brussels. It was in these uncertain financial circumstances that Madame da Cunha encouraged her nephew to speculate in order to

[48] Lord Perceval to Charles Dering, 23 June 1720 (BL, Add MS 47029, fol. 67).
[49] Proclamation of the pretender about the South Sea scheme, 10 Oct. 1720 (NRS, GD45/1/217).
[50] See also Michael Ward to John Hamilton, 27 Aug. 1720 (PRONI, D2092/1/2, fol. 35), where he asks a cousin in London to invest on his behalf.
[51] For biographical details see Ruth Musielak, 'Madame da Cunha Prefers Her Own "Dunghill" to a Palace: City Lodging and Country Visiting in Early Eighteenth-Century London', *Irish Architectural and Decorative Studies*, 14 (2011), 56–77.
[52] Patrick A. Walsh, 'Asgill, John (1659–1738)', in *DIB*.

rebuild the patrimony and procure a wife worthy of the family.[53] Her desire to assist was no doubt motivated by good intentions, but Lord Kenmare's reluctance to follow her into the markets, where she herself had been unsuccessful, turned out to be a sensible decision.

If Catherine da Cunha failed to persuade her relations to take advantage of the possibilities for social and financial advancement on offer in London in 1720, Jane Bonnell was perhaps better placed to do so. The widow of an Irish accountant-general she had lived in London since 1704, and during that time had established herself as a conduit for news, financial information and consumer goods.[54] Ably assisted by her banker Edward Hoare, she quickly became familiar with the investment opportunities available in the city, purchasing lottery tickets as a means to supplement her limited inherited income.[55] Lottery tickets were more akin to modern premium bonds, and therefore posed no risk for the purchaser, offering instead the possibility of great rewards through the regular public draws. They were also frequently used as an entry point into the London financial markets, although of course many purchasers of lottery tickets never invested in other forms of public credit. Mrs Bonnell was one of those who did, purchasing shares in the South Sea Company in March and April 1720, possibly with money borrowed from Hoare's Bank.[56] She later purchased South Sea bonds, another short-term investment option available from the company in August that same year.[57] Her motivations for investing in the South Sea Company are impossible to discern with certainty, but they were most likely connected to her difficulties in extracting her other source of income – interest on an Irish mortgage – from her dissolute and unreliable nephew, Williams Conyngham, after his coming of age in 1719.[58] It was probably in connection with this family dispute that a connection through marriage, the Dublin MP Thomas Pearson, wrote to her in March 1720 enquiring whether she desired some money he owed her as part of an annuity to be paid promptly so she could 'put' it into 'the South Sea', though he left this decision to her.[59] This annuity may in turn have been the source of the capital for one of her purchases of South

53   Da Cunha to Kenmare, 9 Apr. 1720 (PRONI, D4151/F2, fol. 28).
54   Toby Barnard, 'A Tale of Three Sisters: Katherine Conolly of Castletown', in *Irish Protestant Ascents and Descents, 1641–1770*, ed. Toby Barnard (Dublin, 2004), pp. 266–89; and Anne Laurence, 'Women Investors, "That Nasty South Sea Affair" and the Rage to Speculate in Early Eighteenth-Century England', *Accounting, Business & Financial History*, 16 (2006), 245–64 (pp. 252–9).
55   Laurence, 'Women Investors', p. 247.
56   Laurence, 'Women Investors', p. 256.
57   For South Sea bonds, see P. G. M. Dickson, *The Financial Revolution in England: A Study in the Development of Public Credit, 1688–1756* (London, 1967), p. 185.
58   Barnard, 'A Tale of Three Sisters', p. 277.
59   Thomas Pearson to Jane Bonnell, 12 Mar. 1720 (NLI, MS 41,580/24).

Sea stock; purchases that she later claimed made her a 'great sufferer by the South Sea and other bubbles'.[60]

Mrs Bonnell, while providing a well-documented individual example of female investor activity in the early stock market, is also interesting because of her various financial activities on behalf of others. Her letters, as Anne Laurence has shown, make it clear that she was trusted as a source of reliable information and as an intermediary who could introduce correspondents to her bankers and financial advisers in London.[61] She acted in both of these capacities for a number of Irish friends and relations as well as for the Yorkshire-based Hastings sisters. In September 1720, for instance, Ann and Frances Hastings asked for her assistance to arrange the purchase of some South Sea stock. They also enquired of her about the then current reports of the falling company share price.[62] Mrs Bonnell reassured them about the continuing good prospects of the company, and the sisters purchased South Sea shares at a high price. The relative small size of their investment, however, combined with their decision to hold on to it, resulted in regular dividends for some years after the crash, which meant that their losses were minimal.[63] In this instance, Mrs Bonnell might have been better off remembering the perceptive advice she was given earlier in the summer, when she arranged for the sale of some of Lady Betty Hastings' South Sea portfolio. On that occasion Mrs Bonnell was warned that 'all the knotty heads had already sold out'.[64]

It seems that this advice was also unheeded when it came to her dealings with an Irish relation Edward Worth, though at least he bore his losses with great equanimity:

> I find by all accounts the stocks are fallen and several persons are great losers, amongst whom I cannot think but we are a little; for which I would not have you in the least disturbed; believe me I am not, being well satisfied my true friend has done the best that was in your power ... and I don't doubt but providence in his own time will make it all up to us.[65]

Despite these setbacks and her own South Sea losses, Mrs Bonnell continues to stand out as an excellent example of an independent women acting rationally in the stock market in the age of the bubble. She was, of course, far from alone. The statistical analysis in the previous chapter suggests that approximately one fifth of Irish investors were women, while

60   Bonnell to Francis Dickens, 15 Sep. 1720 (NLI, MS 41,580/31).
61   Laurence, 'Lady Betty Hastings', *passim*.
62   Frances Hastings to Bonnell, 7 and 14 Sep. 1720 (NLI, MS 41,580/10).
63   Laurence, 'Women Investors', p. 255.
64   Charlotte Fox to Bonnell, 30 July 1720 (NLI, MS 41,580/36–9).
65   Edward Worth to Bonnell, 6 Oct. 1720 (NLI, MS 41,580/27). This Worth was not the famous Dublin doctor and philanthropist of the same name.

this pattern was replicated more broadly across all of the holders of South Sea stock during the bubble. Among the better documented Scottish investors, for instance, was Margaret, Lady Panmure who held stock in the York Buildings Company as well as the South Sea Company. Unlike most prominent women investors she was still married, but her husband was in exile at the Jacobite court at St Germain, leaving her in control of the family estates and income in Scotland.[66]

The cases of Madame da Cunha, Jane Bonnell and Lady Panmure provide some insight into the role played by female investors in the early capital markets. Investment in the South Sea Company was clearly a socially acceptable activity for wealthy women of independent means. These women, whether through their widowhood or their particular political circumstances as in the case of Lady Panmure, also enjoyed independent incomes, giving them greater opportunities to invest. Mrs Bonnell, through her long association with Hoare's Bank and her extensive circle of correspondents both in Ireland and England, also build up a reputation as a shrewd observer of the London financial markets. This meant that she was much in demand in 1720 as others sought to benefit both from her experience and from her contacts in the capital.

III

Female members of the Molesworth and Brodrick families were also active investors. Both families were seventeenth-century arrivals in Ireland and the seeds of their respective fortunes were sown during the Cromwellian and especially the Restoration periods. However, it was only after 1690 that the leading members of each family came to national prominence in both Britain and Ireland. Robert, 1st Viscount Molesworth made his reputation following his term of office as William III's ambassador in Copenhagen and the publication of his controversial critique of the Danish state, the *Account of Denmark* (1692). Elected to the Irish parliament in 1692, he enjoyed a political career in both Dublin and Westminster, where he established himself as a leading exponent of the 'commonwealth Whig' tradition.[67] He was also a substantial landowner with Irish estates at Swords, County Dublin,

66 Patrick Walsh, 'The Bubble on the Periphery: Scotland and the South Sea Bubble', *Scottish Historical Review*, 91 (2012), 106–24 (pp. 119–20).
67 Caroline Robbins, *The Eighteenth-Century Commonwealthman: Studies in the Transmission, Development, and Circumstance of English Liberal Thought from the Restoration of Charles II until the War with the Thirteen Colonies* (Cambridge, MA, 1959), pp. 385–6. For Molesworth see also Justin Champion, '"Mysterious Politicks": Land, Credit and Commonwealth Political Economy, 1656–1722', in *Money and Political Economy in the Age of Enlightenment*, ed. Daniel Carey (Oxford, 2014), pp. 117–62. I am grateful to Justin Champion and Daniel Carey for allowing me to see an advance copy of this essay.

and in King's County as well as some property in Yorkshire. The Brodricks, meanwhile, divided their time between County Cork and Surrey. The family patriarch at the time of the revolution was Sir St John Brodrick, but it was his two sons, Thomas and Alan, who made the greatest mark on Irish and British politics over the next thirty years.[68] Thomas Brodrick was largely based in England, sitting at Westminster where he gained a reputation as an independent-thinking Whig. As such he was a popular choice in 1721 after the crash to chair the parliamentary committee of investigation into the South Sea Company's activities. His brother Alan Brodrick, 1st Viscount Midleton, was one of the most significant Irish politicians of his generation, rising to become lord chancellor of Ireland in 1714, a position he held until 1725. An often difficult and cantankerous figure, he was also an active parliamentarian at Westminster, although his primary theatre of action was in College Green.[69]

The years 1720–21 would turn out to be turbulent for Midleton. He had fallen foul of the English ministries in Dublin and London over his opposition to the Earl of Sunderland's peerage bill and the Declaratory Act at Westminster, and was convinced that he was going to lose the lord chancellorship and his position as one of the Irish lords justices.[70] Thrice married and with a number of dependants, his concerns for his political survival were motivated not just by pride and the fear of a loss of prestige but also by financial considerations. These would also influence both his own and his family's investments in the South Sea Company. Molesworth too was the head of a large family, and his venturing into the South Sea should be seen as partly driven by dynastic concerns, in the same way that his contemporaneous improvement projects at his country house, Breckdenstown, in north County Dublin were designed as much for posterity as for the present.[71] The speculative activities of a number of members of both families reflected a wider desire to achieve lasting financial security. This was also particularly true for the Scottish and Anglo-Irish elites who were trying to cope with the increased pressures of maintaining a presence in London in the decades after 1689.[72]

Such pressures are clearly visible in the surviving correspondence of the Molesworth family. Writing to his wife in December 1719 Robert, 1st Viscount Molesworth described how 'the government neglected the whole

---

68 Hayton, *Anglo-Irish Experience*, pp. 76–103, offers the best account of the Brodricks and their milieu.

69 For details of the parliamentary careers of Thomas and Alan Brodrick, see their entries in *HIP*, vol. 3, pp. 266–9 and 272–3.

70 Hayton, *Anglo-Irish Experience*, p. 98.

71 Viscount Molesworth to Lady Molesworth, 1 Dec. 1719 (HMC, *Various Collections*, vol. 8, p. 283). On these developments see Finola O'Kane, *Landscape Design in Eighteenth-Century Ireland: Mixing Foreign Trees with the Natives* (Cork, 2004), pp. 9–46.

72 Carswell, p. 144; and Walsh, 'The Bubble on the Periphery', p. 116.

family', and recommended 'sparing and good economy'.[73] This 'neglect' was probably somewhat exaggerated, but reflected his real concern for the continued employment prospects of his adult sons in the civil and military arms of the government. The younger generation of Molesworths – seven sons and four daughters survived into adulthood – could not all be supported by the family landed patrimony, and therefore pursued careers in the military, the diplomatic service and the law. In 1720 John Molesworth, Robert's eldest son, was British ambassador to the court of Savoy at Turin in 1720, while John's younger brother Richard was a half-pay colonel in the British Army seeking preferment. Three of their younger brothers, Edward, Walter and William, were also army officers, while the fourth, Coote, was studying law in London in 1720, and the fifth, Bysse, was employed in the revenue in Dublin.[74] At least two, possibly three, of the Molesworth sons along with one of their sisters and their father, Robert, invested in the South Sea Company, and their correspondence suggests they saw it as a potential panacea for their respective financial problems.

In October 1719, in a letter to John from London, Walter wrote enviously of a friend's success in 'the Mississippi stock', commenting 'would to God we had all of us had the money and luck to have done the same'.[75] In the same letter he reported both his and his wife's investments in the latest lottery, indicating some familiarity with contemporary financial innovations. Like Mrs Bonnell, it seems he was concerned to supplement his other income, in this case his half-pay captain's salary, with returns from investment.[76] John and Richard Molesworth sought to improve their fortunes by purchasing South Sea stock. By the middle of June 1720 John Molesworth was rumoured to possess a paper fortune of £100,000, drawing envious comment from a Paris-based relation Daniel Pulteney, who reckoned that 'the cake would be all eaten up before he got a crumb'. This realization that the window for such successes was likely to be short-lived, perhaps borne out by his first-hand experience of the Mississippi bubble, led Pulteney to advise John 'to be moderate in his desires and be contented with a hundred thousand pounds'. John Molesworth's brother Richard, however, as a younger son and 'soldier of fortune', was advised not to 'complete' at this juncture.[77] John

[73] Viscount Molesworth to Lady Molesworth, 1 Dec. 1719 (HMC, *Various Collections*, vol. 8, p. 283).

[74] For worries about the financial burden of Coote's legal studies see Viscount Molesworth to Lady Molesworth, 7 Apr. 1720 (HMC, *Various Collections*, vol. 8, p. 286).

[75] Walter Molesworth to John Molesworth, 5 Oct. 1719 (HMC, *Various Collections*, vol. 8, p. 281).

[76] For concerns about his military position see Walter Molesworth to John Molesworth, 17 Sep. 1719, in which letter he also reports the birth of his son (HMC, *Various Collections*, vol. 8, p. 280).

[77] Daniel Pulteney to John Molesworth, 12 June 1720 (HMC, *Various Collections*, vol. 8, p. 287).

however did not take Pulteney's advice and neither he nor Richard realized their expected 'imaginary riches'.

Complicating matters further, their anticipated inheritance was also diminished. Their father, Robert, although later to achieve some fame as a savage parliamentary critic of the company, had also purchased South Sea stock. In late summer of 1720 he borrowed £2,000 from a relation in Dublin, Nancy Forster, to invest in the final subscription raised that August. Writing two years after the crash, he was at pains to explain that he entered the market not for political reasons but instead 'purely in hopes of the stock's further rise and in order to cheat some other buyer, fancying it would not die in my hands'.[78] Instead the stock price fell two days later and Molesworth lost two-thirds of his original investment. The subscription he arranged for his protégé, the political writer John Toland, also came to nothing, leaving the latter almost completely destitute by his death in 1722.[79] Molesworth's personal losses compounded his animosity towards the company and its directors but it would be mistaken to see his later criticisms as solely motivated by personal grievance.[80] However, the extent of his South Sea losses led to further financial retrenchment and the decision to settle his Irish estates on his wife in 1722 in exchange for a monthly allowance.[81]

At least one member of the Molesworth family, Viscount Molesworth's daughter Charlotte Tichborne, was more fortunate in her investments. Writing to her mother in October 1720 she declared explicitly that her motivation for first borrowing money, and then investing it in South Sea stock was driven by a desire to provide for her children. After initially fearing that she was not going to be in a position to repay the sums she had borrowed to purchase her 'subscriptions', she was able to inform Lady Molesworth that not only was she 'not ruined' but she was 'rather a gainer', albeit on a very small scale, estimating that her profits would be insufficient to buy the 'little plate and furniture' she badly wanted.[82] Her modest success shows that not all family members suffered by what one of their extended family, Henry Tichborne, 1st Baron Ferrard, called 'the plaguy South Sea'.[83]

The surviving Molesworth correspondence for the period of the bubble

---

78 Viscount Molesworth to John Molesworth, 20 Oct. 1722 (HMC, *Various Collections*, vol. 8, pp. 349–50). For the risky phenomenon of investors borrowing to raise their initial capital see Carswell, pp. 152–63.

79 Justin Champion, *Republican Learning: John Toland and the Crisis of Christian Culture, 1696–1722* (Manchester, 2003), p. 1.

80 Viscount Molesworth to John Molesworth, 9 Jan. 1721 (HMC, *Various Collections*, vol. 8, pp. 293–4). On this see Champion, 'Mysterious Politicks'.

81 O'Kane, p. 44.

82 Charlotte Tichborne to Lady Molesworth, 5 Oct. 1720 (HMC, *Various Collections*, vol. 8, p. 288).

83 Henry Tichborne, 1st Baron Ferrard to Viscount Molesworth, 14 June 1721 (HMC, *Various Collections*, vol. 8, p. 316).

and especially its aftermath is, however, largely a catalogue of financial woe. John Molesworth, for instance, found it extremely difficult to get either his rental or official income remitted to him in Turin after the crash, a situation that only compounded his stock-market losses. When in January 1721 he expressed his frustration at this turn of events, his London agent told him it would be very difficult to raise the necessary funds thanks to the loss of credit, and that though he was then 'in the country of miracles ... miracles are very scarce'.[84] Meanwhile his brothers, Richard and Coote, were continuing to struggle in London with Coote, the youngest Molesworth, telling his mother that he would rather join his elder brother in Savoy than remain in England:

> I should live better there, and pass my time with more satisfaction with them, under the character of chaplain, secretary, page or anything than I do here under the ample title of Lord Molesworth's son, living upon two meals a day, and one of them the residue of my bread at dinner, with a draught of my water bottle.[85]

Richard meanwhile was still seeking to exchange his position on the half-pay list for an active commission in the army. This was proving a challenge, and he complained to John of the indifference of his friends to his difficulties, while a 'project' he had to go abroad was hindered by his lack of funds, and possibly also by his father's outspoken critiques of the government and the South Sea Company in the British House of Commons.[86] It would not be until 1725 that he would return to active military service, and in time he would retire having achieved the rank of field marshal. While counting his losses in the bubble in late 1720 and early 1721, however, such a prospect must have seemed improbable.[87]

There are many similarities between the investing experiences of the cosmopolitan Molesworth family and those of the equally transnational Brodrick family. While the Molesworths looked to Europe for careers, the Brodricks looked to the West Indies. The British and Irish political careers of Thomas and Alan Brodrick are well known, but that of William, the third Brodrick brother, is much more obscure. Like his elder siblings he was a lawyer and politician, but instead of setting up practice in Dublin or London he went to Jamaica where he became attorney general and then speaker of the colonial assembly, mirroring his brother Alan's career progression in the Dublin parliament.[88] Returning to Ireland sometime after 1716, he invested

---

[84] J. Eckershall to John Molesworth, 19 Jan. 1721 (NLI, P3752). This section of the letter is not included in HMC, *Various Collections*, vol. 8, p. 294.

[85] Coote Molesworth to Lady Molesworth, n.d., 1720 (HMC, *Various Collections*, vol. 8, p. 292).

[86] Richard Molesworth to John Molesworth, 27 Jan., 14 Feb. and 5 Mar. 1720 (HMC, *Various Collections*, vol. 8, pp. 296, 299 and 300).

[87] For his later career see David Murphy, 'Molesworth, Richard (1680–1758)', in *DIB*.

[88] See the entry for William Brodrick in *HIP*, vol. 3, pp. 274–5.

£1,000 of borrowed money in the South Sea Company's fourth subscription in August 1720. Like Viscount Molesworth, and those other 'gentlemen of Ireland who came late to the stocks', he failed to profit from this investment, later selling his share to a London apothecary for £120.[89] His losses served only to confirm the views of his eldest brother Thomas, an implacable sceptic of the company both in public and in private from the very beginning of its conversion scheme in early 1720.

Viscount Midleton, the former Alan Brodrick, had initially shared his elder brother's scepticism but by July he too had abandoned his earlier reservations, writing to Thomas that, since 'your South Sea frenzy continues to rage … I wish while such sums are got I could turn a little of my money'. He cited two reasons why he had changed his mind, both of which echoed the motivations behind Viscount Molesworth's investments described above. First, he had come under pressure from family members, notably his niece who seemed to think, mistakenly as it turned out, that he had influence with the company directors who controlled initial access to the money subscriptions.[90] She had apparently told him that it was possible to get a subscription of £1,000, which could then be sold for £1,500. Midleton, confessing he knew little of such things, declared, 'I wish something of this kind could be done for Ally or my namesake', giving an insight into his second motivation to provide for his family; notably his younger son Allan, later 2nd Viscount Midleton.[91] The elder Midleton was too late to profit from his proposed venture in the South Sea, and he seems to have listened to the advice of his brother, Thomas, who told him that 'when the cloud will burst I know not, but that it must do so, everybody sees, who are not wilfully blind'.[92] Even as Midleton failed to secure this subscription, other family members continued to hold stock. These included a female relation, Martha Courthope, whose interests were managed by both Thomas Brodrick and Viscount Midleton between them, with Thomas attending company general courts in London on her behalf.[93]

Viscount Midleton's brief flirtation with the South Sea Company, though it caused him little personal damage, is however interesting because it shows how a figure generally hostile to the moneyed interest could be swayed by the all-pervading sense of optimism that engulfed so many members of the British and Irish elites. Like Molesworth, his correspondence also betrays a belief that he saw the South Sea as a potential remedy to the financial

---

89 Bargain and sale with bond by William Brodrick, one of HM's serjeants-at-law for Ireland, to Thomas Barrow, citizen and apothecary of London (SHC, MS 1248/1, fol. 343).
90 Hoppit, 'Myths of the South Sea Bubble', p. 150.
91 Midleton to Thomas Brodrick, 12 July 1720 (SHC, MS 1248/4, fols 287–9).
92 Thomas Brodrick to Midleton, 22 July 1720 (SHC, MS 1248/4, fols 290–1).
93 Thomas Brodrick to Midleton, 13 Sep. 1720 (SHC, MS 1248/4, fols 318–19).

problems caused by a large and growing number of dependants. In both these cases and in so many others, real knowledge of the company or the machinations of the stock market was less important than the seemingly endless prospects of fortunes to be made. Thomas Brodrick on the other hand was one of the many individuals who understood the problems inherent in the company's schemes. Some like him remained distant from the stock market, while other 'knotty heads' played it carefully and successfully.[94]

Such considerations motivated many of the individuals discussed in this chapter. They were, of course, not the only Irish investors, merely some of the better documented. Among the other Irish gentry who invested in the bubble were at least three of the promoters of the project for an Irish national bank: Michael Ward, Arthur Hill and Sir Oliver St George. Both Ward and St George incurred losses through their investments in London, but these seem to have had little effect on the prospects of their bank, or indeed their enthusiasm for it. Less fortunate was John Maxwell, 1st Baron Farnham, who was forced to sell his Dublin house following the failure of his South Sea speculations, while among the successful were the Irish judge Sir Gilbert Dolben, who was able to retire to England in 1721, and Francis Hutchinson, Bishop of Down.

IV

Most of the investors discussed so far were members of the aristocracy and gentry, and a disproportionate amount of them seem to have lost out financially due to their investments. Questions of typicality therefore naturally arise and can be answered by considering these case studies within the context of the more analytical research into the Bank of England ledgers featured in the previous chapter. The evidence contained in the ledgers demonstrated that Irish investors came from a wide variety of backgrounds, not just from the aristocratic and gentry classes. Unfortunately, it is the latter group who have left the best records especially in terms of personal correspondence and papers, the type of materials utilized in this chapter. Uncovering the lives and experiences of the mercantile and professional classes, notably members of the Huguenot community, is very difficult due to a paucity of suitable sources. Occasional glimpses of their investing activities can however be traced, including the group of Irish army officers who allowed their agent William Leathes to purchase South Sea stock with their pay before he remitted their balances home.[95] Such practices were not uncommon among

---

94 See Hoppit, 'Myths of the South Sea Bubble', p. 148 for examples of such 'cautious' investors.

95 For William Leathes see Toby Barnard, A New Anatomy of Ireland: The Irish Protestants, 1649–1770 (London, 2003), p. 196.

the military, with Scottish army officers stationed both at home and abroad engaging in similar strategies. However, others such as George Berkeley on the Grand Tour in Italy, and Robert Cowan, an Irish officer in the East India Company in Bombay, bemoaned the effects of their remoteness in time and space from London, which prevented them from profiting in London.[96]

Moving further away from the gentry, it is possible to uncover some of the investing and speculative activities of a small number from the Dublin banking and commercial communities, though again it is hard to generalize from what are probably exceptional examples. For instance, some of the financial difficulties that caused Sir John Eccles, the revenue collector of Dublin Port, to be dismissed for reasons of malfeasance from his lucrative office in late 1720 were caused by bad investments in the South Sea Company made either by him or by his clerk.[97] Other members of the Dublin business establishment who were known to have invested in the South Sea Company included the Huguenot banker David La Touche. He purchased stock not only in the South Sea Company, but also in an insurance company in London as well as one in Rotterdam, indicating that even at this early stage, four years after its foundation, La Touche & Kane's banking business operated at a transnational level. His Dutch investment was made through the offices of a cousin, John Delamotte, who acted as his Amsterdam agent, while John Hillhouse and John Puget, who acted as La Touche's Bristol and London agents respectively, managed the investments made in London.[98] Hillhouse purchased two shares in the South Sea Company at £810 each in late June 1720.[99] By October 1721, however, the bank was recording holdings of £3,991 in South Sea stock, suggesting they had made further purchases and that they had successfully ridden the bubble.[100] Certainly they had divested their stock by 1723, as they do not appear among the lists of shareholders who transferred their holdings to the Bank of England. La Touche's investments may be contrasted with those of the banker Sir Alexander Cairnes, whose losses, discussed in the previous chapter, were the subject of negative contemporary comment about his reputation.

---

[96] Berkeley to Lord Perceval, 20 July 1720 [from Florence], in Luce and Jessop, vol. 8, pp. 114–15; and Robert Cowan to his father, 19 Nov. 1721 [from Bombay] and Cowan to Henry Cairnes, 19 Nov. 1721 (PRONI, D654/B/1/1AA, fols 100–1).

[97] Report of the Commissioners of the Revenue, Ireland on John Eccles 14 Jan. 1721, in *Calendar of Treasury Papers Volume 6: 1720–28*, ed. Joseph Redington (London, 1889), pp. 41–2. On the Eccles affair see Patrick Walsh, *The Making of the Irish Protestant Ascendancy: The Life of William Conolly, 1662–1729* (Woodbridge, 2010), pp. 137–42.

[98] La Touche & Kane, abstract of account 1720–21 (NLI, MS 2785, fols 13–14). Puget was a prominent London Huguenot banker. See Bailey, *Irish London*, p. 173.

[99] La Touche & Kane, abstract of account 1720–21 (NLI, MS 2785, fol. 14).

[100] La Touche & Kane, abstract of account 1 July to 1 Oct. 1721 (NLI, MS 2785, fols 19–20). For a discussion of the concept of 'riding the bubble' see Peter Temin and H. J. Voth, 'Riding the South Sea Bubble', *American Economic Review*, 94 (2004), 1654–68.

V

The focus in this chapter has been on the experiences of individual investors, rather than on the aggregate experience explored in chapter 3. The case studies discussed here illuminate not just the faces behind some of the names listed in the South Sea Company's ledgers, but also some of the motivations that encouraged them to invest in Exchange Alley in 1720. Their stories, whether of fathers trying to provide for their offspring, military officers trying to improve their prospects from the precarious vantage point of the half-pay list, or widows trying to supplement an irregular income because jointures had been entrusted to unreliable relations, show that investment in the South Sea Company was not all about participating in a collective 'frenzy' or mania. It was also about improving one's place in life, whether through securing a fortune or just a regular dividend income from a financial product that promised much. These individual cases therefore warn against simple narratives of the bubble, but they also provide exemplars of those who were prepared to take great risks in anticipation of great rewards. Not all of them could be satisfied, and the result of their investments, both positive and negative, was felt beyond their own pockets. This wider impact will be the subject of the next chapter.

5

'Nothing here but Misery'?
The Economic Impact of the
South Sea Bubble on Ireland

In autumn 1720 the South Sea bubble burst. The company's share price tumbled, falling from a high of £950 per share in mid-July to £200 by the end of September. This dramatic collapse caught the imagination of contemporaries who were eager to understand and discuss both the reasons for the rapid crash, and its impact. Such debates were, of course, heard in the coffee-houses and 'walks' of Exchange Alley and the Royal Exchange in London, but they were also heard elsewhere across Britain, Ireland and even further afield, as word of the stock-market crash spread. The news circulated in many ways, whether through newspapers, prints and even playing cards, or the more traditional means of private correspondence and gossip. All of these media helped to create an enduring image of the bubble as a particularly calamitous event, with William Hogarth's famous print 'The South Sea Scheme' with its visual echoes of the seventeenth-century plague perhaps the best known graphic portrayal. Squibs of verse meanwhile quickly appeared from the Grub Street presses, some of which came from the same pens that had previously celebrated the inflation of the bubble during the previous spring.[1]

Like the bubble itself, these written and graphic representations were not just a London phenomenon. Prints quickly appeared in Amsterdam following the crash, while in Edinburgh the poet Allan Ramsay followed up his perceptive June 1720 poem, *Wealth or the Woody: A Poem on the South Sea* with two post-crash compositions, *The South Sea Sang* and *The Rise and Fall of the Stocks*.[2] These verses have been seen as part of the already emerging tradition of anti-Union writings, and featured ferocious attacks on the English financiers who, it was alleged, had led Scottish investors astray.[3]

---

[1]   On the influence of the plague see Pat Rogers, '"This Calamitous Year": *A Journal of the Plague Year* and the South Sea Bubble', in *Eighteenth Century Encounters* (Brighton 1986), pp. 151–69. More generally see Silke Stratmann, *Myths of Speculation: The South Sea Bubble and 18th Century English Literature* (Munich, 2000); and J. A. Downie, *To Settle the Succession of the State: Literature and Politics, 1678–1750* (London, 1994), pp. 98–110.

[2]   Allan Ramsay, *Poems by Allan Ramsay* (Edinburgh, 1721), pp. 237–45.

[3]   Murray Pittock, *Scottish and Irish Romanticism* (Oxford 2008), p. 47. See also Steve

Meanwhile in Dublin, Jonathan Swift – himself no stranger to controversy – was directing his pen towards the impact of the crash both in its local and wider British contexts. In the last three months of 1720 he would produce two important poems inspired by the London crash, *The Run upon the Bankers* (October 1720) and *The Bubble* (December 1720).[4] The first of these attacked the Dublin bankers, some of whom had lost heavily as a result of the ripple effects of the London crash. Its verses reveal Swift's contempt for the mercantile interests – 'Quakers and aldermen in state' – who dominated the Dublin banking sector, as well as the contagious effect of the London crash on the availability of credit in the Irish economy:

> Money, the life-blood of the nation,
> Corrupts and stagnates in the veins,
> Unless a proper circulation
> Its motion and its heat maintains.
>
> Because 'tis lordly not to pay,
> Quakers and aldermen in state,
> Like peers, have levees every day
> Of duns attending at their gate.[5]

Swift's second and more famous work has been described as one of the most significant contributions to the fashioning of the popular myth of the bubble.[6] Extracts from *The Bubble* were included as elements within some of the satirical prints produced in response to the crisis, with Swift's words being surrounded by images of the famous bubble playing cards, which mocked the supposed gambling instincts that had encouraged the flight of speculators to Exchange Alley.[7]

Just as important as the sentiments that Swift was expressing was the location from where he was actually physically writing these poems. Swift was in Dublin: *The Run upon the Bankers* focused on the impact on the local economy and the financial world outside the gates of his deanery, while *The Bubble* was written from an outside perspective far removed

Newman, 'Second Sighted Scot: Allan Ramsay and the South Sea Bubble', *Scottish Literary Review*, 4 (2012), 15–33.

4   Jonathan Swift, *Poems*, ed. Harold Williams, 3 vols (Oxford, 1958), vol. 1, pp. 238–41 and 248–59.

5   Extract from Jonathan Swift, *The Run upon the Bankers* (1720) in Swift, *Poems*, vol. 1, pp. 239–40.

6   Pat Rogers, 'Plunging in the Southern Waves: Swift's Poem on the Bubble', *The Yearbook of English Studies*, 18 (1988), 41–50 (p. 41).

7   The most commonly reproduced print featuring Swift's poem was entitled *The Bubblers Medley or a Sketch of the Times Being Europe's Memorial for the Year 1720*. See Ross B. Emmett (ed.), *Great Bubbles*, 3 vols (London, 2000), vol. 1, p. 178.

from London's Exchange Alley.[8] In the latter poem, Swift's savage condemnation of the company's directors echoed his earlier criticism of the Dublin bankers, as well as the scepticism about the South Sea scheme expressed in his correspondence of earlier in the year. Writing from Dublin, Swift, like most Irishmen, was dependent on news reports and correspondence for information on the progress of the South Sea Company's debt conversion scheme. If perhaps there were deficiencies in the quality of information he was receiving, then this might raise some questions about his reliability as a witness of the bubble. Meanwhile other scholars have issued warnings about his more general understanding of economics and finance.[9] These would be valid criticisms if we were primarily interested in his writings as a source on events in Exchange Alley or South Sea House. Instead this book is concerned with the impact of the bubble on people and places far from the City of London.

As such the observations and commentaries of Swift and his Irish, Scottish and even North American contemporaries are of particular interest for the insights they give into the perception at the time of the wider effects of the London crash. From Derry, Bishop William Nicolson, himself a shareholder in the South Sea Company, wrote to an episcopal colleague in England describing the impact of the crash on local credit structures, bemoaning how difficult it was to get even bills of £100 paid where once it was possible to get their equivalents for £1,000 paid on sight.[10] His colleague in the Church of Ireland, Edward Synge, Archbishop of Tuam, in a similar vein claimed that the calamity had especially affected the province of Connacht.[11] In Dublin, reports were current of a falling balance of trade, a shortage of specie and, perhaps even more seriously, of a run on the city banks.[12]

Such observations were echoed across the British world. In Scotland it was claimed that those 'who never had much faith in stocks have been

---

[8] For the writing and publishing history of *The Bubble* see Swift, *Poems*, vol. 1, pp. 248–50.

[9] See Chris Fauske, 'Misunderstanding What Swift Misunderstood, or the Economy of a Province', in *Money, Power and Print: Interdisciplinary Studies on the Financial Revolution in the British Isles*, ed. C. I. McGrath and Chris Fauske (Newark, 2008), pp. 135–56.

[10] Bishop William Nicolson to Archbishop William Wake, 6 Dec. 1720 (BL, Add MS 6116, fol. 102).

[11] Archbishop Edward Synge to William Wake, 22 Mar. 1722, cited in Mary-Lou Legg, 'Money and Reputations: The Effects of the Banking Crises of 1755 and 1760', *Eighteenth-Century Ireland*, 11 (1996), 74–87 (p. 76).

[12] William Conolly to Charles FitzRoy, 2nd Duke of Grafton, 9 Jan. 1721 (IAA, MS 97/84 A3/21); Robert, 1st Viscount Molesworth to John Molesworth, 9 Jan. 1721 (HMC, *Report on Manuscripts in Various Collections*, vol. 8 *The Hon. Frederick Lindley Wood; M. L. S. Clements, Esq.; S. Philip Unwin, Esq.* (London, 1913), p. 293); and Nicolson to Wake, 21 Oct. 1720 (BL, Add MS 6116, fol. 114).

of late unfortunately drawn in to be pretty concerned in England',[13] while significant individual losses were also detailed in contemporary correspondence. In Edinburgh, the Bank of Scotland was forced to restrict its lending activities, reflecting the tightening in the availability of credit in the local economy.[14] Around England investors felt the effects of the crash and contemporary publications described the ruin of many families.[15] Across the Atlantic in New England, a Boston newspaper reported an increase in emigrant numbers from Ireland, something it attributed to the impact of the London crash.[16] This contrasted with the scenes witnessed earlier in the summer when transatlantic traders were spotted rushing directly from their ships to invest their commercial profits in London, before beginning their return voyage to the American colonies.[17] Even further afield in India, an Irish officer in the East India Company, Robert Cowan, having heard of the 'late confusions in England about the South Sea', made several enquiries about the fate of his friends and relations in the stocks.[18]

Cowan's letters home show both how the bursting of the bubble was perceived half way around the globe, as well as the more immediate personal and familial impact of the crash. His letters, together with the other commentaries described above, provide an insight into the contemporary perception of the crash. It is clear that everywhere talk was dominated by the South Sea but it is less clear whether this was just 'talk' rather than accurate descriptions of the effects of the crash.[19] Many historians are quite sceptical about the value of such contemporary testimonies, seeing them as exaggerated, with one twenty-first-century scholar of the bubble viewing much of the immediate post-bubble literature as an example of the 'Georgians pontificating on the themes of vanitas and folly', while the economy around them was reviving.[20] Historians and economists have also questioned the dominance of a narrative that favours the experiences of those who suffered

---

[13] Hugh Dalrymple quoted in Douglas Watt, *The Price of Scotland: Darien, Union and the Wealth of Nations* (Edinburgh, 2007), p. 43.

[14] Patrick Walsh, 'The Bubble on the Periphery: Scotland and the South Sea Bubble', *Scottish Historical Review*, 91 (2012), 106–24 (p. 121).

[15] Daniel Defoe, *A Tour thro' the Whole Island of Great Britain*, 3 vols (London, 1724–26), vol. 1, pp. 37, 90, 169 and 346. See also Pat Rogers, 'Literary Art in Defoe's Tour: The Rhetoric of Growth and Decay', *Eighteenth-Century Studies*, 6 (1972–73), 153–85 (pp. 183–4).

[16] *New England Courant*, 6 Nov. 1721.

[17] Sir John Clerk to John Clerk, 15 Aug. 1720 (NRS, GD18/5294/20).

[18] Robert Cowan to [his father], 19 Nov. 1721 (PRONI, D654/B/1/1AA, fol. 100).

[19] Jonathan Swift to Esther Van Homrigh, 15 Oct. 1720, in *The Correspondence of Jonathan Swift*, ed. Harold Williams, 5 vols (Oxford, 1963–65), vol. 2, pp. 359–60.

[20] H. J. Paul, *The South Sea Bubble: An Economic History of its Origins and Consequences* (London, 2010), p. 102. For a more measured view see Julian Hoppit, 'The Myths of the South Sea Bubble', *Transactions of the Royal Historical Society*, 6th ser., 12 (2002), 141–65 (pp. 159–62).

financial losses – they were more likely to write about their misfortunes than the 'winners' were to document their successes – in the literature on the bubble.[21] Such historiographical assessments have contributed to a depiction of the bubble as a London-centric event, which had little effect outside the metropole. This chapter explores the impact of the bubble on the wider economy looking particularly at Ireland, but also at Scotland, examining how far contemporary perceptions differed from reality.

I

Julian Hoppit has queried whether the bubble had an impact on the English provinces, let alone Ireland or Scotland. Drawing upon an impressive array of English evidence he has shown how contemporaries exaggerated the effect on property prices, on the availability of credit and on local financial structures.[22] Questions remain, however, over whether this analysis can be fully translated to other parts of Britain and Ireland. Anecdotal and banking evidence from Scotland suggests the picture north of the border may have been more complicated, while Irish economic historians have long noted an external impact on the domestic economy following the London crash, which they have attributed to the bursting of the bubble.[23] Multiple sources of evidence can be brought forward to demonstrate the repercussions, including some indication of increased strain on the Irish banking system, trade and taxation figures, as well as extensive complaints about the difficulties in collecting rental income across the kingdom.

The impact of the bursting of the bubble on the Irish banking world remains somewhat contested. Swift's poem *The Run upon the Bankers* published in October 1720 condemned the greed and avarice of the Dublin bankers, traits he suggested had contributed to a run on their balances earlier in the same month. The evidence for this 'run', however, remains quite slight and its seriousness is difficult to gauge. Swift's clerical colleague, Bishop Nicolson, in a letter to the Archbishop of Canterbury described how in order to 'answer the demands of our adventures in your Exchange Alley' there had been a run on the Dublin bankers, which was only ended by the intervention – 'wisely and stoutly (as is his manner)' – of Speaker Conolly.[24] Ireland's most powerful politician had it seemed saved the local financial

---

21   Paul, p. 103.
22   Hoppit, 'Myths of the South Sea Bubble', p. 158.
23   For Scotland see Walsh, 'Bubble on the Periphery', pp. 120–4. For Ireland see L. M. Cullen, 'Economic Development, 1691–1750', in *New History of Ireland*, ed. T. W. Moody, F. X. Martin and F. J. Byrne, 9 vols (Oxford, 1986), vol. 4, pp. 123–58 (pp. 144–5); and David Dickson, *Old World Colony: Cork and South Munster 1630–1830* (Cork, 2005), p. 124.
24   Nicolson to Wake, 21 Oct. 1720 (BL, Add MS 6116, fol. 114). The copy of this letter

sector, demonstrating both Conolly's great wealth and prestige as well as the small scale of the Dublin banking scene. There is surprisingly little other contemporary evidence for the run, with Conolly himself playing down his own role. In a letter to the lord lieutenant he explained that 'the bad effect of the South Sea has reached this kingdom to a great degree, insomuch that numbers are ruined by it. There has been a run upon all the banks here, who have all hitherto stood it.'[25] Despite Conolly's assertions to the contrary, at least one banker, James Swift, did temporarily go to the wall. Swift absconded to the Continent taking his balances with him, though within a year he was back in business in Dublin.[26] Legislation passed in the Irish parliament in the 1721 session for 'better securing the payment of banker's notes', which allowed creditors to proceed against an absconding or deceased banker's estate was, however, probably influenced by his temporary insolvency.[27]

The exposure of the Dublin bankers to the ripple effects of the bubble can be identified in other ways. The investing experiences of David La Touche and Sir Alexander Cairnes have been described previously, and it is possible that other members of their banking brethren also invested in London. Some bankers were certainly active in transferring funds to London for their clients' use during the months of greatest speculation: in early August it was reported that 'there was such a demand for money that the bankers themselves wanted it prodigiously, and got vast exchange for money in England'.[28] This anecdotal evidence is confirmed by information from surviving bank ledgers as well as from exchange rate data. La Touche & Kane's ledgers from 1720, although incomplete, show how the bank issued a much greater volume of notes in that year than in the succeeding one, while they also enjoyed higher profits in 1720.[29] Such statistical evidence is indicative of the bank's experience during the bubble, and of that of the Irish banking sector more generally.

The extant exchange rate data is also highly suggestive. Contemporaries noted how the Anglo-Irish exchange rate rose to new heights in autumn 1720, attributing its negative effects to the consequences of the bubble.[30] Table 5.1 shows how their observations are borne out by the published rates. The figures for 1720 are quite revealing: there were very high rates in April,

in the British Library is dated 1721 in error, but the internal evidence shows that it is clearly 1720.

25 Conolly to Grafton, 18 Oct. 1720 (IAA, MS 97/84 A3/17).
26 John Busteed, 'Irish Private Banks', *Journal of the Cork Historical and Archaeological Society*, 53 (1948), 31–7 (p. 32).
27 8 Geo I, c. 14 [Irish], *An Act For the Better Securing the Payment of Banker's Notes*.
28 Henry Ingoldsby to William Smyth, 9 Aug. 1720 (NLI, MS 41,581/2).
29 Information extracted from table 27 in L. M. Cullen, *Anglo-Irish Trade, 1660–1800* (Manchester, 1968), p. 198.
30 Nicolson to Wake, 21 Oct. 1720 (BL, Add MS 6116, fol. 114).

Table 5.1. Exchange rates: London on Dublin, 1719–21.

	Jan.	Feb.	Mar.	Apr.	May	June	July	Aug.	Sep.	Oct.	Nov.	Dec.
1719	12.50	12.50	11.75	14.50	13.00	12.75	10.75	10.00	9.75	10.75	10.00	12.00
1720	12.75	12.25	12.50	15.00	12.50	11.75	12.75	14.25	14.00	14.75	15.50	11.00
1721	12.00	12.00	13.50	12.75	11.00	9.50	9.00	10.25	11.75	9.50	9.50	9.00

Par rate = 9.33 (i.e. £109.33 Irish = £100 sterling). Rates quoted are those for the first of each month. See John McCusker, *Money and Exchange in Europe and America, 1660–1775: A Handbook* (London, 1978), p. 39.

with a persistent rise from June onward, while the rates for the August–November period have no parallel in either the preceding or succeeding years. It is clear that something different was going on – investment in the South Sea scheme. The higher than normal exchange rates during the summer months add credence to the contemporary belief that Irish investors came late to the London markets, although the April rates might point to a significant outflow of Irish funds just as the South Sea share price began to climb. The unprecedented rates for the August–November period in 1720 probably indicate heavy purchases of bills in London that would be used to purchase stock there, or to pay off English merchants and bankers either for bills purchased earlier in the summer, or to settle residual liabilities accruing to Irish customers from the collapse of the South Sea share price. This is the most likely explanation of this data, and here it is worth noting that the Dublin–London rate followed a similar pattern to the Dutch rate on London in 1720.[31] An alternative reading would be that the high rate at the end of the year could be partly explained by London merchants becoming increasingly distrustful of their merchant brethren in the metropolitan capital and having more confidence in bills from their credit-worthy Irish correspondents.[32]

The extant exchange rate data adds much to the anecdotal information discussed earlier, and helps to illustrate the economic impact of the crash on Ireland. The chronology of the outflow of Irish money to London stands out much more clearly, confirming contemporary descriptions regarding both the late arrival of the 'gentlemen of Ireland' and the drain of Irish money to England towards the end of 1720. Irish observers regularly bemoaned this latter phenomenon, which extended into early 1721. Writing to a leading English government official in December 1720, William Conolly described

[31] T. S. Ashton, *Economic Fluctuations in England, 1700–1800* (Oxford, 1959), pp. 120–1; and Larry Neal, *The Rise of Financial Capitalism: International Capital Markets in the Age of Reason* (Cambridge, 1990), p. 66.
[32] Cullen, *Anglo-Irish Trade*, p. 176.

Table 5.2. Abstract of Irish imports and exports, 1715–25.

Year	Exports (£)	Imports (£)	Balance (£)
1715	1,529,766	972,688	557,078
1716	1,255,084	875,566	379,518
1717	1,180,013	907,161	272,852
1718	1,115,304	887,759	227,545
1719	1,038,382	891,678	146,704
1720	859,581	683,364	176,217
1721	986,347	730,559	255,788
1722	1,074,270	829,368	244,902
1723	1,090,676	920,803	169,873
1724	1,053,783	819,762	234,021
1725	1,026,537	889,833	136,704

Source: Arthur Dobbs, *An Essay on the Trade and Improvement of Ireland* (Dublin, 1729), p. 8.

how there was 'no money, no trade, no faith nor confidence' before going on to explain that there was barely enough revenue to pay the 'subsistence of the army'.[33] The weekly receipt of customs revenue had fallen to £53 from a normal average of £1,300 to £1,400 in the week before Christmas. Two weeks later Conolly, in his capacity as Chief Commissioner of the Irish Revenue, was claiming there was barely £5,000 worth of specie left in all Ireland.[34] This rather perilous situation at the Irish Treasury was blamed on the ripple effects of the London crash. Frequent mention was made of the 'decline of trade' in contemporary letters and publications. The volume of such reports and their consistency gives them some credibility, again enhanced by the available statistical evidence.

Table 5.2 shows the official figures for Irish trade for the period 1715–25. Once more 1720 stands out, with both exports and imports recorded at their lowest levels. The significance of this was not lost on Arthur Dobbs, the Irish political economist, who attributed the low figures for the years up to 1722 to the 'disturbances by the rebellion in Great Britain [1715], the confusions in France caused by their calling in and new coining their money, and raising their coin, the Mississippi bubble in France and the South Sea in England'.[35]

---

[33] Conolly to Charles Delafaye, 27 Dec. 1720 (TNA, SP 63/379, fol. 714).
[34] Robert Molesworth to John Molesworth, 9 Jan. 1720 (HMC, *Various Collections*, vol. 8, p. 294).
[35] Dobbs, p. 10.

Figure 5.1. Irish gross revenue (£ Irish), 1715–25.

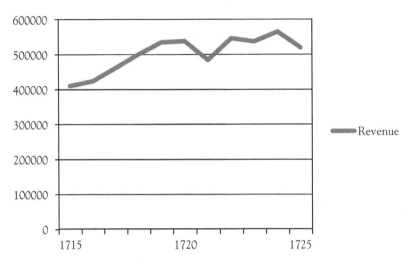

Gross revenue figures have been calculated from the figures for annual revenue receipts presented each session to the Irish parliament. The figures have been adjusted so that all years reflect the state of the accounts at 25 March, the end of the accounting year. Source: *CJI*, vol. 3, Appendix, pp. v, civ, cliv, cxcii, ccxxxiv, cclxxxix and cccxxviii.

In this analysis the bubble was highly significant, although there were other factors neglected by Dobbs. Notably these included the appearance of the plague at Marseille in 1719, which had a significant impact on British and Irish trade following the imposition of quarantine regulations. Some commentators even linked the outbreak, which continued to pose a threat to Britain and Ireland in 1720, to the supposed moral decline that had caused the South Sea bubble.[36] That judgement notwithstanding, it is clear that there were other factors affecting Irish trade at that point, but it is also hard to ignore the contemporary reports, which gave prominence to a post-bubble credit squeeze. Bishop Nicolson, for instance, noted that the demand for exports of linen from Derry to Manchester had collapsed in late 1720, while a dip can also be witnessed in the Cork trade figures for the same period.[37]

This decline in Irish trade can also be clearly seen in the taxation figures for this period. Most Irish taxes, as outlined in chapter 1, were levied on consumption with the customs branch producing the bulk of Irish revenue in

[36] Henry Downes, *A Sermon Preached at Christ's-Church Dublin, before Their Excellencies the Lords Justices on Friday 23rd December 1720* (Dublin, 1721). See also Nicolson to Wake, 24 Jan. 1721 (BL, Add MS 6116, fol. 106).

[37] Nicolson to Wake, 2 June 1721 (BL, Add MS 6116, fol. 109); and David Dickson, *Old World Colony: Cork and South Munster, 1630–1830* (Cork, 2005), p. 124.

this period.[38] Therefore, as foreign trade fell, so too did government income, which is exactly what happened in 1720–21 as demonstrated in figure 5.1. A clear dip is visible for the point indicating the year ending 25 March 1721. While the same caveats apply to these figures as to those recording imports and exports, nevertheless they are indicative of an external shock to the domestic economy. Taking all this evidence together, it is not difficult to appreciate the worries expressed by William Conolly regarding the Irish state's continued ability to pay for its own upkeep.

II

The statistical evidence provided by the exchange rate data and government accounts provides one way of measuring the impact of the bubble on the Irish economy. Other sources tell us even more about the impact on the local economy and of significance here are the glimpses we get of the differing regional effects of the crash. It has been shown elsewhere that the majority of recorded Irish shareholders in the South Sea Company were resident in Dublin, but it was not just the capital city that suffered in the aftermath of the crash, with the northern County Londonderry emerging as one of the worst affected areas. This is not to ignore the repercussions felt by the inhabitants of Dublin, which included not just the contractions in credit described above, but also increased rates of unemployment and poverty across the lower ranks of Irish society.

Among those particularly affected in Dublin were the city's linen weavers, the largest proto-industrial group in the city. Writing in late March 1721, Archbishop King described the situation, explaining that 'at least one half of the city's inhabitants was in a lamentable state and needed charity'. The gentry could not gather their rents, while the merchants had no trade and the 'general cry of the whole people was bread'. He had paid especial attention to the linen and silk workers who largely lived on his doorstep in the Liberties area of the city. Enquiring into their conditions he discovered that 1,300 of these workers, not including their wives and children, were unemployed, and were 'miserable to the highest degree'.[39] Newspaper reports in 1720 also referred to the poverty of the city, with one report describing how the scarcity of money had led to an increase in robberies, making it unsafe to venture out in the streets after ten o'clock at night.[40] Some attempts, led by Archbishop King, were made to alleviate the worst of the

---

[38] Patrick Walsh, 'The Irish Fiscal State, 1690–1769', *Historical Journal*, 56 (2013), 629–56 (pp. 639–40).

[39] Archbishop William King to William Wake, 23 Mar. 1721 (BL, Add MS 6117, fol. 70).

[40] *Daily Post* (London), 28 Apr. 1721.

suffering. Notably these included a production of *Hamlet* performed with a specially written epilogue by Swift in which, repeating the message of his pamphlet published a year previously, he called for the wearing of Irish-made clothes.[41] These charitable efforts yielded £1,500 in total, suggesting there was still some money in Dublin.

Dublin was not the only region to suffer from the effects of the lack of circulating money in the aftermath of the bubble. Bishop Nicolson's letters from his northern diocese of Derry similarly describe scenes of abject poverty, while also commenting on the reduction of the northern port's trade. Such factors contributed to the increasing numbers from this region migrating to the American colonies. There was, however, another feature particular to County Londonderry which worsened local conditions: the county's greatest ground landlords were the livery companies of London and not members of the local gentry or aristocracy as was the case elsewhere in Ireland. Much of the property in the county had been granted to the City of London as part of the Ulster plantation in the early seventeenth century, in other words to the Grocers, Drapers, Vintners and Haberdashers, etc. They then leased their property holdings to local landed interests, but remained the owners of huge Irish estates, which yielded substantial annual rentals. These concerns were managed by an umbrella group called the Irish Society of London, who in early 1721 began to call in their rentals and tried to renegotiate their leases, as the various constituent companies sought to make good their losses suffered during the bubble. In 1721, for instance, attempts were made to improve the yield on the extensive salmon fisheries owned by the Irish Society, although without success.[42]

Specific evidence for the repercussions of the bubble on other Irish regions is much more patchy, although reports emanated from across the kingdom detailing the effect on local markets. Writing from Caledon, County Tyrone, Sligo town and Tuam, County Galway, William Hamilton, Kean O'Hara and Edward Synge all ascribed chronic shortages of specie and trade to the impact of the bubble.[43] Similar testimonies can be found for other parts of the country, indicating the scale of the perceived crisis. In this manner the Irish situation echoed that of Scotland as well as England, where petitions flooded into parliament detailing the effect of the crash on the local economy. Historians have dismissed some of these English reports, and it is important to regard various Irish reports with similar scepticism, especially since some

---

[41] Irvin Ehrenpreis, *Swift: The Man, His Works and The Age, Volume III* (London, 1983), pp. 157–8.

[42] J. S. Curl, *The Londonderry Plantation, 1609–1914: The History, Architecture, and Planning of the Estates of the City of London and its Livery Companies in Ulster* (Chichester, 1986), pp. 108, 130–1, 313 and 381.

[43] William Hamilton to Jane Bonnell, 15. Oct. 1720 (NLI, MS 41,580/9); and Synge to Wake, 22 Mar. 1722, cited in Legg, p. 76.

of the monetary problems reported predated the bubble, and continued long after, notably those concerning the shortage of specie. Reports about wholesale property transfers and heavily fluctuating land prices in England have likewise been treated with caution, and the same should be done for Ireland.[44]

In any case there were few clear-cut cases of Irish property transactions being caused by either the rise or the fall of the stocks. Philip, 1st Duke of Wharton, owner of huge tranches of land in counties Cavan and Dublin, was forced to sell his Irish estates to clear the extensive debts he incurred during the bubble; his losses amounted to £120,000. He attempted to sell his property at Rathfarnham Castle near Dublin for £85,000 or 37 years' purchase in 1720 to a successful English speculator, but this sale fell through, suggesting that the hugely inflated prices seen in parts of England during 1720 did not spread to Ireland.[45] Instead, Wharton's creditors sold the ten-thousand-acre estate to William Conolly in 1723 for £63,000 following the Duke's departure into a financially as well as politically motivated exile at the Jacobite court in Rome.[46] Elsewhere John Maxwell, later 1st Baron Farnham, was obliged to sell his house on Dublin's fashionable Capel Street to cover his London losses.[47] Wharton and Farnham are nonetheless rather isolated examples and it is difficult to see any significant bubble-related impact on the Irish property market in 1720 or 1721. Among the successful speculators, Sir Gilbert Dolben was able to retire to an English estate, while Viscount Doneraile was able to purchase back an English estate he had previously sold, although he paid a premium of £5,000.[48] They were not, however, part of an influx of Irish South Sea nabobs into the English countryside, but again exceptional cases. Others like John Molesworth had their English building ambitions playfully mocked when their paper fortunes stood highest.[49] In this case, a projected Alessandro Galilei-designed palazzo at Edlington in Yorkshire remained but a 'castle in the air'. In the same vein William Conolly's great house at Castletown, County Kildare – partly designed by Galilei – may have had its construction delayed by the economic

[44] Hoppit, 'Myths of the South Sea Bubble', p. 151. For Scotland see Walsh, 'The Bubble on the Periphery', p. 121, where some evidence of rising land prices is presented.
[45] A. P. W. Malcomson, 'A House Divided: The Loftus Family, Earls and Marquesses of Ely, c.1600–c.1900', in *Refiguring Ireland: Essays in Honour of L. M. Cullen*, ed. David Dickson and Cormac O'Gráda (Dublin, 2003), pp. 184–224 (p. 186). For English examples see John Habakkuk, *Marriage, Debt and the Estate System: English Landownership 1650–1950* (Oxford, 1994), p. 511.
[46] Patrick Walsh, *The Making of the Irish Protestant Ascendancy: The Life of William Conolly, 1662–1729* (Woodbridge, 2010), pp. 75–6.
[47] See the entry for John Maxwell in *HIP*, vol. 5, p. 244.
[48] Arthur St Leger to Thomas Pitt, Lord Londonderry, 7 Oct. 1720 (PRONI, T3425/2/25).
[49] Daniel Pulteney to John Molesworth, 12 June 1720 (HMC, *Various Collections*, vol. 8, p. 287).

impact of the bubble. Although first rumoured in 1719–20, building only began in 1722.[50]

More common perhaps were the short-term cash flow problems experienced by Irish landlords who struggled to raise their country rents as a result of the monetary and credit problems witnessed across the kingdom in 1720–21.[51] Such issues were not unique to these years but their incidence in late 1720 and early 1721 seems higher than normal. The slow collection and remittance of rents presumably exacerbated reverses in the stock market for some investors, while also reducing the rate of recovery. It was in the context of such reverses that many of those who had promised funds to a national bank in May 1720 found themselves unable to support revived bank proposals in the summer of 1721. Leaving aside the bank projects to be discussed in the following chapters, it is clear that the bursting of the South Sea bubble had a significant short-term economic impact on Ireland. Much of this resulted from what one observer described as the Irish funds 'they so precipitately and madly returned over to be employed in this chimerical project'.[52] This outflow of specie and bankers' bills had real repercussions on the Irish economy, as demonstrated by the statistical evidence drawn from exchange rate, trade and taxation data. Contemporary perceptions of the London crash, while sometimes influenced by misunderstandings of the financial processes at play in the stock market, therefore reflected reality more readily than some historians have previously allowed.

---

[50] Walsh, *Making of the Irish Protestant Ascendancy*, pp. 183–5.
[51] Conolly to Bonnell, 17 June 1721 (IAA, MS 97/84 A/8); and James Smyth to William Smyth, [n.d.] Sep. 1720 (NLI, MS 41,582/3).
[52] Thomas Brodrick to Alan Brodrick, 1st Viscount Midleton, 13 Sep. 1720 (SHC, MS 1248/4, fols 318–19).

6

'A Thing They Call a Bank':
Irish Projects in the South Sea Year

During the first week of May 1720 a proposal was published in Dublin addressed to 'the Nobility, Gentry and Commonalty of this Kingdom of Ireland', calling for the establishment of a national bank. The proposed bank would address several contemporary economic grievances including the drain of Irish money to the South Sea Company. Public subscriptions were called for to raise the £500,000 capital believed to be necessary for its operation and subscribers' names were to be collected daily in the Merchant's Coffee House in the city from 19 May until the subscription was filled.[1] This was the beginning of a scheme that would dominate Irish political and economic debate over the next eighteen months. The author of the prospectus was John Irwin, a somewhat obscure Dublin projector, and his was one of three projects for a national bank floated in early summer 1720. These bank proposals, together with two plans put forward for an Irish fire insurance company in June 1720, were part of a wider proliferation of 'projects' and bubbles which emerged across Britain and Ireland at this time, as attempts were made to cash in on the investment boom being driven by the South Sea Company. Some of these projects, like the North Sea Fishery in Scotland, the York Buildings Company and arguably the Bank of Ireland, were based on sound fundamentals.[2] Others such as Richard Steele's fish importing business or the scheme for a perpetual motion company floated in London belonged more to the realm of fancy.[3] This chapter examines the rise of the different Irish bank proposals within the context of the speculative

---

1 John Irwin, *To the Nobility, Gentry and Commonalty of this Kingdom of Ireland* (Dublin, 1720). For previous histories of the bank project, which don't fully take into account the wider context of the bubble, see F. G. Hall, *The Bank of Ireland, 1783–1946* (Dublin, 1949), pp. 14–29; Michael Ryder, 'The Bank of Ireland, 1721: Land, Credit and Dependency', *Historical Journal*, 25 (1982), 557–82; and Gordon Hutton, 'Archbishop King, The Bank Scheme (1720–21), and Wood's Halfpence (1722–25)', *Éire-Ireland*, 35 (2000), 81–101.
2 On the North Sea Fishery, see Bob Harris, 'Scotland's Herring Fisheries and the Prosperity of the Nation, c.1660–1760', *Scottish Historical Review*, 79 (2000), 39–60 (pp. 49–50). For the York Buildings Company see A. J. G. Cummings, 'Industry and investment in the Eighteenth-Century Highlands: The York Buildings Company of London', in *Industry, Business and Society*, ed. A. J. G. Cummings and T. M. Devine (Edinburgh, 1994), pp. 24–42.
3 John Carswell, *The South Sea Bubble* (London, 1960), pp. 142–3.

boom of early summer 1720. It shows how the bank schemes were not only developed in response to financial innovations in London, but also how they, as groundbreaking projects in their own right, can be read as echoes of the more dramatic metropolitan financial schemes.

I

The timing of the appearance of the bank schemes is highly significant. There is some dispute as to precisely when the project for a national bank first arose, but it was certainly being discussed by April 1720.[4] The first public statement came with the publication of Irwin's pamphlet in early May and the call for subscriptions in the Dublin newspapers. The first advertisement was published in the *Dublin Courant* of 30 April, with a slightly amended version appearing nine days later.[5] The proposals were sufficiently well known for Jonathan Swift to include an attack on 'a thing they call a bank' in his *Proposal for the Universal Use of Irish Manufacture*, published in early May.[6] Later that month, Lady Molesworth linked the rise of the bank project with the flow of Irish funds to the London stock market.[7] The published proposal had explicitly made this connection, describing the effects on the local economy of Irish investment in the South Sea and Mississippi schemes:

> The expectation of extravagant gain has prevailed on many persons to send over all the money they had credit for to purchase Mississippi and South Sea Stocks, though at most extravagant prices, and when this humour will have an end, nobody knows, but in the meantime the kingdom is exhausted of the greatest part of its current cash.[8]

It is difficult not to view the bank project as a response both to this investment of Irish capital abroad, as well as to the increased willingness of Irish investors to experiment with the latest financial innovations. This could be seen in the remarkable response to Irwin's proposal, whereby promises for £500,000 capital were fully subscribed within four days. This, as is shown below, suggested an Irish appetite both for a bank and for speculative investment.

---

4   Michael Ryder, 'The Bank of Ireland 1721: Land, Credit and Dependency', *Historical Journal*, 25 (1982), 557–82 (p. 559).
5   *Dublin Courant*, 30 Apr. and 9 May 1720; and *Whalley's Newsletter*, 7 May 1720.
6   Jonathan Swift, *Prose Works*, ed. Herbert Davis, 14 vols (Oxford, 1939–68), vol. 9, pp. 21–2. See also Irvin Ehrenpreis, *Swift: The Man, His Works and The Age, Volume III* (London, 1983), p. 124.
7   Letitia, Lady Molesworth to Hon. John Molesworth, 17 May 1720, in HMC, *Report on Manuscripts in Various Collections, vol. 8 The Hon. Frederick Lindley Wood; M. L. S. Clements, Esq.; S. Philip Unwin, Esq.* (London, 1913), p. 287.
8   Irwin, *To the Nobility, Gentry and Commonalty*.

But before moving on to discuss the subscriptions, it is necessary to examine what these subscribers were investing in.

As already stated, the first proposal for a national bank was put forward by John Irwin. Like many projectors during the financial revolution, little is known about him though he may have been an army officer – Archbishop King described him as Colonel Irwin, 'a man of small fortune and little interest' – and he disappeared back into the obscurity from which he had briefly emerged soon after the demise of his scheme.[9] Published in May 1720, the proposal itself was printed in the form of a three-page pamphlet and outlined the manifesto of the proposed Bank of Ireland. Although published under Irwin's name it was probably the product of a consortium. Certainly the project already had a number of influential backers including James Hamilton, 6th Earl of Abercorn, Sir Oliver St George, a prominent Connaught landowner and Michael Ward, a County Down landowner and politician. Both Ward and St George were also investors in the South Sea Company.[10] They may have used Irwin's name partly for cover, to avoid embarrassment should their proposal be ignored.

The pamphlet began by outlining the problems facing the Irish economy, which it hoped a bank would address. These included an increasing negative balance of trade caused by rising imports, remittances of Irish money to London to pay absentee landowners and pensioners on the Irish estab-lishment, as well as military and civil salaries. This outflow was, according to Irwin, contributing to a worsening exchange rate, further draining Ireland of her gold and silver coin, which in turn was causing local trade and commerce to stagnate, leading to unemployment and emigration. The solution he proposed to these problems was the erection of a national bank. His analysis of the difficulties facing the Irish economy would have been familiar to many readers and echoed worries expressed in print and in private by other contemporary commentators. Frequent allusions were made to the lack of specie, and the ruinous effect this was having on Irish trade. Irwin and his fellow promoters were not, however, proposing a new coinage or indeed a separate Irish mint. Instead they were suggesting the establishment of a system of public credit, based on paper money.[11]

The advantages of such a system were, he claimed, self evident for 'whoever considers that almost all the trading nations of Europe, and even the meanest republics have their several banks and that the trade of Great Britain could not be carried on without many millions of paper money, will

9 Archbishop William King to Edward Southwell, 17 Oct. 1721 (TCD, King Papers, MS 750/7, fol. 41).
10 For Ward's investments in London see Michael Ward to James Trail, 9 Jan. 1721 (PRONI, T3041/1/C/3), while for St George see his correspondence with the London banker Nathaniel Gould, 1720–24 (TNA, C 110/46/248–300).
11 Irwin, *To the Nobility, Gentry and Commonalty.*

think it needless to spend more time enquiring into the advantages of it'.[12] The final section of the pamphlet outlined the details of the proposed bank. The total intended capital was £500,000, with individual subscriptions from £500 up to a maximum of £10,000. Stock would be transferable, and was to be paid into the bank when called in by the directors. Subscribers could either pay for their investments in cash, or else transfer mortgages to the bank at 5% interest. The shareholders would control the operation of the bank, with the size of one's holding determining the number of votes each subscriber was entitled to use at a general court. The bank was to be managed by a governor and twelve directors. Finally, Irwin declared that subscriptions were open to all and that the bank was intended for the advantage of 'the landed man, the moneyed man, the widow and the orphan'. Interestingly, no mention was made of religion and Catholics were not formally proscribed from subscribing to the bank. In practice, however, the concentration of landed and commercial wealth within Protestant hands made full participation in economic life more difficult for Irish Catholics under the Penal Laws.[13]

Irwin's pamphlet and newspaper advertisements called for subscribers to come to the Merchant's Coffee House on Essex Street between ten and two o'clock from Thursday 19 May. The choice of newspaper and subscription venue was significant. The *Dublin Courant* was aimed at the local merchant community, and was the only Dublin newspaper to carry London stock prices on a regular basis. The Merchant's Coffee House, meanwhile, was a focal point for Dublin's trading community, a place where they could exchange goods, ideas and gossip. It therefore seemed an appropriate location to collect subscriptions for a bank, which hoped to attract commercial as well as landed support. Coffee-houses were linked with such business proposals throughout northern Europe. Much of the trading in the Amsterdam capital markets took place in the coffee-houses surrounding the exchange, while in Exchange Alley in London, coffee-houses such as Lloyd's, Jonathan's and Garraway's were at the epicentre of the city's financial world.[14] In Dublin, most of the city's coffee-houses were clustered around a small area between Dublin Castle and Custom House Quay.[15] The leading banks were located

---

12 Irwin, *To the Nobility, Gentry and Commonalty*.
13 See David Dickson, 'Catholics and Trade in Eighteenth-Century Ireland: An Old Debate Reconsidered', in *Endurance and Emergence: Catholics in Ireland in the Eighteenth Century*, ed. T. P. Power and Kevin Whelan (Dublin, 1990), pp. 85–100.
14 Natasha Glaisyer, *The Culture of Commerce in England, 1660–1720* (Woodbridge, 2006), pp. 31–3; Brian Cowan, *The Social Life of Coffee: The Emergence of the British Coffeehouse* (London, 2005), pp. 165–7 and 172; and Richard Dale, *The First Great Crash: Lessons From the South Sea Bubble* (Princeton, 2004), pp. 7–21.
15 Colm Lennon, 'Dublin 1610–1756', in *Irish Historic Town Atlas: Dublin, Part II, 1610–1756* (Dublin, 2009), p. 35; Michael Brown, 'The Location of Learning in Mid-Eighteenth-Century Ireland', in *Marsh's Library: A Mirror on the World: Law,*

in the same area. Burton & Harrison and La Touche & Kane occupied addresses on Castle Street, while Hugh Henry and Sir Alexander Cairnes both operated from the opposite bank of the River Liffey, where they were part of a cluster of Ulstermen resident in the Capel Street area.[16] The close geographical proximity of much of Dublin's financial and trading community can only have encouraged collaboration, investment and the spread of information, just as it did in London.[17]

News of the bank project spread quickly. Swift, as we have seen, included a reference to it in his *Proposal for the Universal Use of Irish Manufacture*, which was printed in early May. Swift's scepticism about the project reflected a longstanding hostility to the Irish moneyed interest, and a growing antipathy towards the private bankers in Dublin.[18] His doubts were shared by others including Archbishop King, although clearly other contemporary observers were more welcoming.[19] This enthusiasm for the bank could be seen in the rapidity with which the subscription was filled up. Four days after the subscription books opened, 132 individuals had entered their names promising more than the anticipated £500,000 capital.[20] The speed and volume of the subscriptions was remarkable. Four years earlier, when the Irish parliament sought to raise a £50,000 loan to establish the national debt, it had taken over a month to fill the subscription.[21] In that case several subscribers were also forced to re-enter the lists in order to make up the shortfall, a not uncommon occurrence where such subscriptions were called for.[22] The speed with which the bank received promises for capital that

Learning and Libraries 1650–1750, ed. Muriel McCarthy and Ann Simmons (Dublin, 2009), pp. 104–27 (p. 110); and Patrick Walsh, 'Club Life in Late Seventeenth and Early Eighteenth-Century Ireland: In Search of an Associational World c.1680–c.1730', in *Clubs and Societies in Eighteenth-Century Ireland*, ed. James Kelly and Martyn J. Powell (Dublin, 2010), pp. 36–52 (p. 43).

16 C. M. Tenison, 'The Old Dublin Bankers', *Journal of the Cork Historical and Archaeological Society*, 1 (1893), 17–18, 36–8, 54–6, 102–6, 120–3, 143–6, 168–71, 193–7, 221–2, 241–3 and 256–60 (pp. 36, 143); and Jean Agnew, *Belfast Merchant Families in the Seventeenth Century* (Dublin, 1996), pp. 184–5.

17 For London, see Larry Neal, *The Rise of Financial Capitalism: International Capital Markets in the Age of Reason* (Cambridge, 1990), pp. 20–6.

18 Sean D. Moore, 'Satiric Norms, Swift's Financial Satires and the Bank of Ireland Controversy of 1720–1', *Eighteenth-Century Ireland*, 17 (2002), 26–56 (pp. 30–1).

19 Philip O'Regan, *Archbishop William King of Dublin (1650–1729) and the Constitution of Church and State* (Dublin, 2000), p. 290.

20 Subscription list for the Bank of Ireland, 19–23 May 1720 (NLI, MS 2256, fols 63–5).

21 *CJI*, vol. 3, Appendix, pp. cxiii–cxiv; and C. I. McGrath, 'The Irish Experience of "Financial Revolution" 1660–1760', in *Money, Power and Print: Interdisciplinary Studies on the Financial Revolution in the British Isles*, ed. C. I. McGrath and Chris Fauske (Newark, 2008), pp. 157–88 (p. 168).

22 Douglas Watt, *The Price of Scotland: Darien, Union and the Wealth of Nations* (Edinburgh, 2007), p. 54.

was ten times more than the national loan does, however, demonstrate the success of Irwin's proposal in attracting investors. The national loan had also been raised during a parliamentary session, when there would have been a greater concentration of potential. It should also be remembered that the prospective bank at this point had no royal charter or any other official government backing in Dublin or London.

The project did, however, have a number of influential supporters. Just as the Company of Scotland had enticed politically and socially prominent individuals to back its project in 1696, the bank promoters similarly sought support from the Irish Protestant elite in the hope that this endorsement would trickle down through the social hierarchy.[23] The most notable supporter of the bank was James Hamilton, 6th Earl of Abercorn, an Irish peer with extensive connections in all three British kingdoms. Described as 'an eccentric figure, both personally, and politically', he nevertheless enjoyed considerable political influence, both in Dublin and London.[24] He was an astute, if occasionally pessimistic, observer of the Irish economy: in January 1720 he was expressing his fears that the country was already bankrupt. A month later be bemoaned the possible effects of the French Mississippi Company on British and Irish trade, if Law's scheme was to prove too successful.[25] He was also an early critic of the South Sea Company's debt conversion scheme, and in early June he advised his friend Lord Perceval to 'prudently consider what are the probabilities of further gains, and balance the quantum with the risks of losses in case of any disappointment through the run of humour taking quite unexpectedly a counterturn'.[26] His promotion of the national bank project seems therefore to have been motivated not by the potential for personal enrichment, but instead by the concerns for economic improvement, backed up by extensive knowledge of contemporary practices in Paris and London.

Abercorn was also a major Ulster landowner (his Irish title was Viscount Strabane), as were several others of the leading supporters of the bank. These included his distant relation, Gustavus Hamilton, Viscount Boyne, and his County Donegal neighbour Sir Ralph Gore, the chancellor of the Irish exchequer. Other prominent backers included Arthur Hill and also his fellow County Down landowner, Michael Ward, who had been Gore's chief rival for the chancellorship three years previously and was one of the principle undertakers for the bank project. A would-be subscriber, Hamilton

23 Watt, pp. 49–51. See also W. Douglas Jones, '"The Bold Adventurers": A Quantitative Analysis of the Darien Subscription List (1696)', *Scottish Economic & Social History*, 21 (2001), 22–42.
24 See the entry for James Abercorn in *HIP*, vol. 4, pp. 340–2.
25 Abercorn to John, Lord Perceval, 7 Jan. and 18 Feb. 1720 (BL, Add MS 47029, fols 3–4 and 31–2).
26 Abercorn to Perceval, 2 June 1720 (BL, Add MS 47029, fol. 65).

Maxwell, would later describe the whole enterprise as 'Mr Ward's bank'.[27] Significantly, as the presence of Gore and Ward, together with St John Brodrick (the son of Viscount Midleton, the then lord chancellor) attests, the bank promoters included individuals from across the Irish political spectrum. If Ward and St John Brodrick were closely connected to the lord chancellor, Gore and Boyne were both allies of William Conolly, the speaker of the Irish House of Commons and Midleton's great adversary at the apex of Irish politics.[28] Midleton and Conolly's rivalry dominated virtually every aspect of domestic Irish politics in this period but, at least initially, it was absent from the bank proposals. Similarly, and unlike the South Sea Company, adherents to one party did not dominate the bank.[29] Unsurprisingly, reflecting their controlling interest in Irish politics, the Whigs dominated, but the subscribers and directors included prominent Irish Tories such as the former solicitor general, Francis Bernard, and Colonel Thomas Coote, a suspected Jacobite. The presence of so many politically influential figures among the bank's known supporters gave the scheme credibility within the domestic capital market.

This was reflected within the composition of the subscription list, discussed in more detail in the next chapter. It included several members of the nobility as well as forty-eight Irish MPs, emphasizing the bank's popularity with the domestic political elite. It is significant that their very visible expressions of support for the bank project coincided with the period when many of their British counterparts were entering the South Sea Company's money subscriptions.[30] This was also a time when the level of speculation in the South Sea Company was particularly intense, including investment originating from Ireland.[31] Under such circumstances, Abercorn, Irwin and their fellow promoters must have welcomed the rapid generation of promised capital for the bank. On the day following the close of the subscription book, elections were held for a governor and twelve directors. As specified by Irwin's pamphlet, individuals were allocated up to four votes based on the amount subscribed, although it is unclear how the election process actually worked in practice. Lord Abercorn was elected governor of the bank, while

---

[27] Hamilton Maxwell to Agmondisham Vesey, 15 July 1721 (PRONI, T2524/5). Maxwell's name does not, however, appear on any of the surviving 1720 bank subscription lists.

[28] For this rivalry see D. W. Hayton, *Ruling Ireland, 1685–1742: Politics, Politicians and Parties* (Woodbridge, 2004), esp. pp. 106–30.

[29] For party divisions and their effects on stock trading in London see Bruce C. Carruthers, *City of Capital: Politics and Markets in the English Financial Revolution* (Princeton, 1996), pp. 187–92.

[30] Julian Hoppit, 'The Myths of the South Sea Bubble', *Transactions of the Royal Historical Society*, 6th ser., 12 (2002), 141–65 (p. 150).

[31] See Archbishop William King to Abercorn, 27 May 1720 (TCD, MSS 1995–2008, fol. 1954).

the directors included Gore, Ward, St John Brodrick and John Irwin.[32] The next stage was to secure a royal charter for the bank, which would require extensive political lobbying in both Dublin and London. As we shall see, this campaign was complicated by both the emergence of two rival schemes for a bank, as well as the impact of the South Sea bubble on Irish investor confidence.

II

The bank promoters quickly realized that in order to put their enterprise on a sound legal footing they would need a royal charter, and almost immediately after the appointment of the governor and directors of the scheme began the process of securing one.[33] The first step was to present a petition to the lord lieutenant of Ireland, Charles Paulet, 2nd Duke of Bolton. A memorial was prepared laying out the reasons for a national bank and, as with Irwin's original printed proposal, it was put forward as a solution to a number of the major problems facing the Irish economy. These included the scarcity of coin, the diminution of the King's revenues, the decay of trade, and the new phenomenon of peacetime out-migration. The previous three years had seen the first significant wave of transatlantic migration from Ireland.[34] Those departing were mostly Ulster Presbyterians, often farmers with substantial land holdings, and concerns had begun to be raised about the effect this would have on the northern economy, especially if debts were not paid before departure.[35] The paucity of credit then available meant that it took very little to further disturb the existing equilibrium. Advertising a national bank as a solution to this very real problem was therefore an obvious way in which to curry favour with the Dublin Castle administration. The memorial, which was signed by Abercorn, Boyne, Gore, Ward and St George, was submitted to Speaker Conolly and Viscount Midleton in their capacity as Irish lords justices, the locally based politicians who governed Ireland during the regular absences from Dublin of the lord lieutenant.[36]

Meanwhile the promoters began to gather signatures for a petition in

---

[32] Election results for governor and directors, 23 May 1720 (NLI, MS 2256, fol. 35); and Ryder, p. 560.

[33] For the importance of securing a charter see Mark Freeman, Robin Pearson and James Taylor, *Shareholder Democracies? Corporate Governance in Britain and Ireland before 1850* (Chicago, 2012), pp. 39–46.

[34] Up to 7,500 emigrants departed for the American colonies during these years. For the causes of emigration see R. J. Dickson, *Ulster Emigration to Colonial America, 1718–1776* (Belfast, 1966), pp. 19–32.

[35] See Robert McCausland to William Conolly, 18 Nov. 1718 (IAA, MS 97/84 C27/1–92); and Patrick Brett to Kean O'Hara, 14 Nov. 1718 (PRONI, T2812/6/55).

[36] The memorial of James, Earl of Abercorn, 28 May 1720 (NLI, MS 2256, fol. 8). I

favour of a national bank, which they hoped the lord lieutenant would submit to the King. The resulting petition, containing 159 names, was completed by 2 June 1720, again suggesting that knowledge of the bank project was widespread, and that the campaign for a royal charter was carefully managed. The petitioners represented a significant grouping within Irish elite society. The name of the Duchess of Bolton, the viceroy's wife, headed the petition indicating a level of tacit or unofficial support from the Dublin Castle administration. Although it is interesting to note that neither Lord Justice Conolly nor Midleton gave their formal backing at this juncture, sixty-six members of the Lords, Commons or Privy Council were numbered among the petitioners.[37] They included several of the bank promoters, such as Sir Ralph Gore, Michael Ward and Sir Oliver St George, as well as Revenue Commissioner Thomas Medlycott and former Chief Secretary Edward Southwell. The lords included one bishop, Ralph Lambert of Dromore, as well as seven lay peers.

Lambert was one of many subscribers to the bank who also signed the petition. Unsurprisingly there was a strong correlation between the two lists with only twenty of the bank's subscribers not appearing on the petition. There were also forty-seven petitioners who had not subscribed to the bank proposal including the peers Lord Limerick and Lord Conway, as well as the Dublin bankers, Joseph Nuttall and Daniel Falkiner. Other prominent petitioners absent from the bank list were Bolton's chief secretary, Edward Webster, Edward Southwell and, interestingly, Henry Maxwell, who later emerged as the bank's most vociferous supporter in the paper war that erupted in autumn 1721. Other members of Maxwell's family had, however, subscribed to the bank, including his cousin John, who also invested in the South Sea Company. Notably absent from the petition are the names of the promoters of the two rival bank schemes, George, Lord Forbes and James Swift. The level of support for the petition did, however, suggest an appetite in Ireland for a national bank at this time.

Abercorn's memorial and the accompanying petition were dispatched by the lords justices to Lord Lieutenant Bolton, then in London, for his consideration. Pressure then needed to be put on Bolton and the administration in the capital. Here, the undertakers called on several prominent figures resident in London with influential connections at court and in parliament to lobby on their behalf. On 2 June, Abercorn and his fellow directors wrote formally to John, Lord Perceval to ask him to 'undertake and solicit' in support of the bank. Lord Perceval was asked to liaise with his fellow London-based countrymen, Edward Southwell, Sir John Stanley, Sir

have followed the dates established by Ryder in 'The Bank of Ireland 1721', in which he corrected errors made by earlier scholars.

[37] A list of the petitioners to His Majesty for a charter to erect a bank in Ireland, 28 May 1720 (NLI, MS 2256, fol. 27).

Gustavus Hume, Thomas Brodrick, Joshua Allen and William Maynard, all of whom received letters by the same post.[38] In a private letter of the same date, Abercorn wrote to Perceval requesting that he 'exert his well known abilities on behalf of this his country' and advising him that he had been the unanimous choice of the directors to act on their behalf in London. A letter was also sent to the chief secretary, Edward Webster, asking him to 'contribute his endeavours to render the said petition effectual'.[39]

These endeavours became more complex, when Charles FitzRoy, 2nd Duke of Grafton, replaced Bolton as lord lieutenant on 11 June. His appointment was a product of English political machinations and was an early marker of the rising influence of Sir Robert Walpole at Whitehall, as emphasized by the appointment of Walpole's younger brother, Horatio, as Grafton's chief secretary. The bank's supporters in London immediately began to lobby the new lord lieutenant, telling Abercorn that they hoped that he would 'give some life and motion to this affair'.[40] Ominously they also warned that obtaining a charter was not going to be easy, owing to 'the many chimerical projects that have infested this town of late'.[41] This was a clear reference to the multiplicity of schemes, viable and non-viable, then emerging as a consequence of the apparent success of the South Sea Company. In Edinburgh, for example, a group of politicians and merchants were seeking to establish a competitor to the Bank of Scotland, and had even attempted a run on the bank.[42] They were operating under the guise of an insurance company, but their interests were banking rather than fire insurance. Similarly, the recent success of the York Buildings Company in transferring their business aims from providing waterworks for London to land speculation, had begun to raise concerns for the government about the need for greater scrutiny of chartered companies. The political influence of the South Sea Company, and its desire to restrict competition, was also contributing to the increasing difficulty in obtaining charters for legitimate as well as illegitimate business ideas.[43]

---

38 Abercorn, Boyne, Ralph Gore, Oliver St George, Michael Ward, St John Brodrick, Francis Barnard, Thomas Coote, Henry Sandford, James Macartney and John Irwin to Lord Perceval, 2 June 1720 (NLI, MS 2256, fols 8–9); and Thomas Brodrick to Alan Brodrick, 1st Viscount Midleton, 15 June 1720 (SHC, MS 1248/4, fols 275–6).

39 Abercorn et al. to Edward Webster, 2 June 1720 (NLI, MS 2256, fol. 9).

40 Perceval, John Stanley, Gustavus Hume, Edward Southwell, Joshua Allen and William Maynard to Abercorn, 18 June 1720 [from London] (NLI, MS 2256, fols 18–19).

41 Perceval et al. to Abercorn, 18 June 1720.

42 W. R. Scott, The Constitution and Finance of English, Scottish, and Irish Joint Stock Companies to 1720, 3 vols (Cambridge, 1912), vol. 3, pp. 271–2; and Patrick Walsh, 'The Bubble on the Periphery: Scotland and the South Sea Bubble', Scottish Historical Review, 91 (2012), 106–24 (p. 123).

43 Lord Perceval to Philip Perceval, 14 Apr. 1720 (BL, Add MS 47029, fols 58–9); and P. G. M. Dickson, The Financial Revolution in England: A Study in the Development of Public Credit, 1688–1756 (London, 1967), pp. 147–9.

The struggle to secure a charter for the bank, without which it could not operate, was compounded by the appearance of two rival schemes for an Irish national bank, as well as two proposals for a Dublin fire insurance company. The chronology of their development is slightly confused, but certainly all of them were 'on foot' by mid-June/early July. Both fire insurance schemes were seeking subscribers in Dublin and London in June 1720, and with some success. Philip Perceval thanked his brother for a subscription of £5,000 in one fire insurance company, hoping that at least one of it and the bank might succeed 'so I shall have my chance ... of getting something if they hit'.[44] His hopes seem to have been based on potential opportunities for speculation, and were perhaps influenced by the apparent success of several members of the extended Perceval family from their ventures into the South Sea market. One of the fire insurance schemes, proposed by a Joseph Durden, hoped to lend money on the security of goods and merchants, something that Thomas Brodrick warned against as potentially contravening any charter it received as an insurance company. He also queried the need for such a company in Dublin, where there were not sufficient houses of the requisite value to make it profitable. In doing so, he pointed to the danger of transferring ideas wholesale from 'this great opulent city'.[45] Perhaps revealingly, the insurance companies were concentrating their capital raising efforts in London, suggesting they were more concerned with profiting from the investment mania than with contributing to the Irish public good. Speaker Conolly and Viscount Midleton made this very point writing to the Duke of Grafton about Durden's fire insurance proposal: 'we are apprehensive that in the event this project may prove as prejudicial to the kingdom as some of a like nature have lately been to the neighbouring kingdoms'.[46]

One of the two rival bank schemes was also seeking subscribers and supporters in London at about the same time.[47] This was the proposal fronted by George, Lord Forbes, and Brabazon Ponsonby. Forbes, the eldest son of the 2nd Earl of Granard, was a military officer and diplomat, with extensive connections in London. He had also recently taken over the management of the family estates from his heavily indebted father, and seems to have enjoyed a substantial personal fortune to which he had recently added by serving as a naval adviser to the Austrian Emperor.[48] Ponsonby, MP for County Kildare,

---

44 Philip Perceval to Lord Perceval, 30 June 1720 (BL, Add MS 47029, fol. 70).
45 Thomas Brodrick to Midleton, 13 Aug. 1720 (SHC, MS 1248/4, fols 263a–b). On the fire insurance schemes see R. E. Burns, *Irish Parliamentary Politics in the Eighteenth Century*, 2 vols (Washington, 1989–90), vol. 1, pp. 121–3.
46 Undated (but almost certainly Sep. 1720) notes on the fire insurance companies (SHC, MS 1248/8, fols 126 and 132).
47 Lord Perceval to Abercorn, 16 June 1720 (BL, Add MS 47029, fol. 68).
48 George, Lord Forbes to Josiah Burchett, 22 June 1720, noting his arrival back in London (TNA, ADM 1/1778). See also Polly Molesworth to John Molesworth, 13 Oct. 1719, describing the diamond ring Forbes received from the emperor (HMC, *Various*

was together with his father, William, a leader of a rising Irish political interest.[49] Like Forbes, he benefited from a considerable private fortune. It was later erroneously claimed that their project was unknown in Ireland until September, suggesting their emphasis was on securing support among the Irish community in London, rather than in Dublin. Meanwhile, back in Ireland, Dublin banker James Swift was attempting to raise capital for his own bank project. On 16 June an advertisement appeared in the *Dublin Gazette* calling for subscriptions totalling £600,000.[50] Potential investors were required to contribute ten shillings for every £100 promised in order to cover the cost of procuring a charter, the money to be paid to Swift at his premises on Eustace Street, Dublin. Little attention seems to have been paid to his project at this juncture although he did reappear with a modified version of the scheme later in the summer, proposing a solution to unite the other two contending parties.

Swift's name, however, appears on the surviving subscription list for the Forbes/Ponsonby bank, which was probably drawn up in late summer 1720, suggesting his own project had failed to attract sufficient backing. In all, 207 individuals promised to contribute £521,000 in total.[51] Like the Abercorn/Irwin proposal, Forbes and Ponsonby had garnered an impressive range of signatures taking in forty-four MPs, nine lay peers, three bishops and six women.[52] The maximum subscription was £5,000, with fifty-six people investing this sum including government officials such as surveyor-general Thomas Burgh, military officer General Owen Wynne, and bankers David La Touche, Richard and William Maguire, as well as James Swift. Among the peers who supported the scheme were lords Aylmer, Inchiquin, Limerick, Netterville and Westmeath.[53] The range of subscribers willing to support the proposal suggests there was a large pool of potential creditors for a national bank, despite the well-advertised financial problems facing the Irish economy. From a total of 339 investors in the two potential bank schemes, only three individuals subscribed to both, one of whom was the Bishop of Dromore.

Having secured sufficient interest and support for their scheme, Forbes and Ponsonby presented a petition to the lord lieutenant seeking a charter

---

Collections, vol. 8, p. 281). Lord Forbes' biographical details can be found in Patrick M. Geoghegan, 'Forbes, George (1685–1765)', in *DIB*.

49   *HIP*, vol. 6, pp. 78–81 and 98–9.
50   *Dublin Gazette*, 16 June 1720.
51   Subscription list for Forbes/Ponsonby bank, n.d. (NLI, MS 2256, fols 39–41).
52   C. I. McGrath, '"The Public Wealth is the Sinew, the Life, of Every Public Measure": The Creation and Maintenance of a National Debt in Ireland, 1716–45', in *The Empire of Credit: The Financial Revolution in Britain, Ireland and America, 1688–1815*, ed. Daniel Carey and Christopher Finlay (Dublin, 2011), pp. 171–208 (p. 186).
53   Subscription list for Forbes/Ponsonby bank, n.d. (NLI, MS 2256, fols 39–41).

for their bank in late July.[54] Their proposals differed substantially from those of their rivals: they hoped to raise £1 million in capital, twice that proposed by Irwin. They also took a slightly different approach in terms of justifying the necessity of a bank. Instead of bemoaning the dismal state of the Irish economy they stressed the success of banks in 'his majesty's other dominions and all the other parts of Europe the usefulness of which is so generally understood that it will not be necessary to offer any reasons for it'. Their company structure was to be similar to that proposed by the Abercorn group, with a governor and twelve directors. They did, however, emphasize that their charter would be used solely for banking purposes, addressing the contemporary concern about the diversification of joint-stock companies into activities outside the provisions of their charters. This issue was coming into sharp focus at this time as attempts were made to regulate the booming stock trade in Exchange Alley through the aegis of the Bubble Act, which had become law on 21 June. Passed partly at the behest of the South Sea Company, it was intended to restrict the operation of rival companies.[55] Its passage also ensured that closer attention was going to be paid to the applications for bank charters from the Irish projectors.[56]

III

The appearance of a second proposal for a national bank naturally had implications for the Abercorn/Irwin scheme. Only one charter was likely to be granted and therefore the two bank projects were now in direct competition. On 6 August, Grafton informed Lord Abercorn of the existence of the second proposal, which in his words was supported by 'other gentlemen of quality, consideration and interest in that kingdom'.[57] He suggested to the promoters of both banks that it would be desirable if they could demonstrate the utility of their projects to the nation, reminding them that since its foundation the Bank of England had always provided a service to the crown as well as to its proprietors. The Forbes/Ponsonby group offered to pay off the national loan of £50,000 raised in 1716, which they perceived was in the public interest. Promises to pay off a portion of the public debt or to offer payment of a large

---

[54] The humble petition of George Lord Forbes, Brabazon Ponsonby Esq. on behalf of themselves and several other persons in Ireland who have engaged to subscribe a sum not exceeding a million in order to erect a bank in that kingdom, n.d. (NLI, MS 2256, fol. 11).

[55] Ron Harris, 'The Bubble Act: Its Passage and Its Effects on Business Organization', *The Journal of Economic History*, 54 (1994), 610–27; and Freeman, Pearson and Taylor, pp. 2–10.

[56] Thomas Brodrick to Midleton, 13 Aug. 1720 (SHC, MS 1248/4, fols 263a–b).

[57] Charles FitzRoy, 2nd Duke of Grafton to Abercorn, 6 Aug. 1720 (NLI, MS 2256, fol. 21).

sum to government had become part of the *modus operandi* of projectors seeking charters for joint-stock companies, as demonstrated most famously by the South Sea Company's debt conversion scheme. Lord Perceval had suspected as early as June 1720 that such a payment would be necessary to secure a charter for the bank, while one of the fire insurance companies had offered to pay £100,000 for the privilege of obtaining a charter.[58] The latter's failure to secure a charter suggests that such offers were no guarantee of government approval.

The Abercorn consortium responded to Grafton on 23 August, and a fortnight later the lord lieutenant passed on both proposals together with the various amendments to the Irish lords justices, Viscount Midleton and William Conolly, for their opinion. They too sought further clarification on how the two schemes were 'not only for the good of the kingdom in general, but for the particular advantage of the crown'.[59] Sometime later Lord Abercorn and his colleagues presented a memorial to the lords justices outlining their scheme in greater detail than previously.[60] It highlighted their promise to lend at 5%, a rate of interest that was considerably lower than the existing legal rate of 8%, advocating that this would bring considerable benefits to the trade and commerce of the kingdom. They also stated that they did not dare to offer any sum for His Majesty's use, 'it being the proper business of parliament to supply His Majesty's occasions, and which your memorialists humbly conceive can never be performed by those who have made such an offer, if they act consistent with the interest of the nation'.[61] This was a clear reference to the proposal made by the Forbes/Ponsonby consortium to pay off the national debt.[62] Interestingly, eleven of the investors in Abercorn's proposed bank were public creditors, while only five holders of the national debt had offered their support to the bank scheme of Forbes and Ponsonby. The influence of these public creditors, comprising just over 20% of the total holders of the debt, was therefore probably negligible in determining the different stances taken on paying it off.[63]

The fate of the two bank projects remained in the balance. Sometime after the appearance of the two rival projects, probably in September 1720, the banker James Swift circulated a compromise proposal for a national bank,

---

[58] Lord Perceval to Philip Perceval, 16 June 1720 (BL, Add MS 47029, fol. 68).

[59] Conolly and Midleton to Grafton, 7 Sep. 1720 (*CJI*, vol. 3, Appendix, p. cci).

[60] Memorial of Abercorn etc to lords justices of Ireland, n.d. [but post 7 Sep. 1720] (*CJI*, vol. 3, Appendix, p. cc).

[61] Memorial of Abercorn etc to lords justices of Ireland, p. cc.

[62] Petition of Richard Stewart, Agmondisham Vesey and Thomas Bellew to the Lords Justices, 20 Sep. 1720 (SHC, MS 1248/8, fol. 117).

[63] For a rather different interpretation which puts the Irish public creditors, whom he calls Ireland's Monti, at the forefront of the bank debates, see Sean D. Moore, *Swift, The Book, and the Irish Financial Revolution: Satire and Sovereignty in Colonial Ireland* (Baltimore, 2010), *passim*.

hoping to unite 'the two contending parties … on equal and honourable terms'. The scheme suggested a capital of £1 million and, like the Forbes proposal, promised to pay off the national debt. His detailed prospectus also included regulations designed to prevent 'that pernicious practice of stock-jobbing to the ruin of the public', a clear reference to the South Sea bubble. Unfortunately the proposal was met with a deafening silence and it made no impact on the debate between the other two schemes. However, its existence reveals the extent to which the idea of a bank had permeated the Irish elite if not the public consciousness, and also perhaps, the widespread desire to ensure that any project that succeeded would not be subject to predatory investors. The appearance of the three bank schemes and the two fire insurance schemes over the course of the summer of 1720 did suggest the extension of a variant of the London investment mania to Ireland during these months. A well-established system of paper credit, so long treated with fear and trepidation, had, however briefly, come to be recognized as a viable panacea to Ireland's economic ills.[64]

IV

This seemingly extensive public appetite for a national bank was implicitly recognized by the Duke of Grafton when he passed on the Forbes and Abercorn proposals to the Irish lords justices, Conolly and Midleton, to make a decision on the more suitable of the two projects for the kingdom. These instructions came in September 1720 just as the tide was turning against joint-stock companies. The effects of the Bubble Act, passed in June but only stringently applied in late August, together with reports from France of the collapse of John Law's Mississippi scheme, and the withdrawal of the directors of the South Sea Company from active participation in the stock market, had led to the decline in value of that company's stock. An extraordinary general court held on 8 September failed to halt the slide of the share price.[65] The final bursting of the bubble was imminent, and with it came a breakdown in public trust of schemes for paper credit. The crash when it came in early October had an immediate impact on the Dublin financial markets, leading to a short-lived run on the banks, and the failure of James Swift's bank in particular.[66] This was the local context in which Conolly and Midleton sought to make a choice between the two bank schemes. The situation had changed completely since the beginning of the

---

64 'Mr Swift about a bank' (NLI, MS 10,708), printed in John Busteed, 'Irish Private Banks', *Journal of the Cork Historical and Archaeological Society*, 53 (1948), 31–7 (pp. 36–7).
65 Carswell, pp. 180–1.
66 Midleton to Thomas Brodrick, 8 Oct. 1720 (SHC, MS 1248/4, fols 326–7).

summer when optimism had reigned about the possibilities of paper credit; it had since been replaced by an acute sense of pessimism.

The lords justices did not make their decision until January 1721. This delay in arriving at a conclusion on the superior of the two contending parties owed as much to the multiplicity of their other business as to the careful consideration they gave the subject. Both Conolly and Midleton had held ambivalent attitudes to the bank project since the first appearance of Abercorn's scheme in May. Neither had subscribed to the bank, nor had they been party to the petition to the crown seeking a charter.[67] Both, however, had a number of close connections among the bank's supporters. Conolly noted that both banks were 'full of parliament men', and therefore it would be a difficult decision.[68] Brabazon Ponsonby and Sir Ralph Gore, rival directors of the two schemes, were both close confidants of Conolly's, while Midleton's son, St John, was one of the directors of the Abercorn bank. Midleton's third wife, Anne, was also a subscriber to the same bank as was her son, Arthur Hill. Despite such connections, Midleton was suspicious of the project and his opinion of it was not improved by his dalliance in South Sea stock. Conolly too was wary of the scheme for a national bank, telling his sister-in-law Jane Bonnell in September 1720 that he feared that if any charter was granted it would be for 'stock-jobbing'.[69] He would later become more enthusiastic about the bank project, while Midleton's opposition to it hardened.

Their instructions from Grafton in September 1720 were to examine the merits of the two competing proposals, and particularly to take into account the 'present state of the kingdom'.[70] After much deliberation and some disagreement between themselves, for a number of reasons they came to a decision favouring Lord Abercorn's scheme. First, the lords justices agreed with Lord Abercorn about the role of parliament in raising money for the crown, and were unhappy to transfer this power to a private corporation. This must be seen within the context of the hard-won rights of the Irish parliament to initiate supply legislation over the previous three decades.[71] It also reflected the more recent political anxieties caused by the passage of the Declaratory Act in April 1720, which again threatened the legislative powers of the Irish parliament. If the bank could provide funds for the government to cover any shortfall in the hereditary revenues there would be no need to call parliament. This was a very real eventuality in 1720, and one

---

67 There is some confusion about this in the secondary literature. See Burns, vol. 1, p. 123. See, however, Lord Perceval to Philip Perceval, 16 June 1720 (BL, Add MS 47029, fol. 68), where he bemoans their failure to explicitly endorse the project.

68 Conolly to Grafton, 9 Jan. 1721 (IAA, MS 97/84 A3/21).

69 Conolly to Jane Bonnell, 30 Sep. 1720 (NLI, MS 41,578/2).

70 Report by the Duke of Grafton to His Majesty in council, 21 Apr. 1721 (CJI, vol. 3, Appendix, p. ccii).

71 See C. I. McGrath, *The Making of the Eighteenth-Century Irish Constitution* (Dublin, 2000), *passim*.

which greatly alarmed many members of the Irish political nation. Mounting concerns about the prerogative of parliament to manage the national debt therefore contributed to the rejection of the Forbes proposal.[72]

The second factor that influenced the lords justices was their belief that the Aborcorn scheme was best suited to the economic circumstances prevailing in Ireland following the South Sea crash. The proposed capital of £500,000 for the Abercorn bank, rather than the £1 million desired by their rivals, was thought to be sufficient to meet the needs of the kingdom. Conolly, however, doubted if even this subscription could be filled in the altered economic circumstances of autumn 1720. His correspondence, like so many of his contemporaries, is full of references to the scarcity of money, while his role as de facto chief revenue commissioner gave him further insight into the true state of the money supply. In January 1721 it was reported that he was claiming there was only £5,000 cash in the hands of the revenue board.[73] The scarcity of specie and credit was one of the chief selling points of the bank, but it also presented difficulties in raising subscriptions.[74] The strategy proposed by Abercorn and his associates in their most recent memorial, to lend at a low interest rate to encourage the circulation of their credit throughout the kingdom, was therefore particularly appealing to Conolly and Midleton and led to their endorsement of this scheme.

They relayed their joint decision to Grafton in January 1721. Soon after news of their recommendation filtered out, Lord Forbes withdrew his proposal rather than jeopardizing the prospect of a national bank and some of his potential subscribers switched their support to the Abercorn scheme. A charter was still needed for this bank to proceed, and in April Grafton reported to the British Privy Council on the progress made, outlining the structure of the proposed bank. Reflecting the backlash against speculation and anything that might be seen as stockjobbing that had accompanied the fallout from the investigations into the South Sea Company, special mention was made of the measures intended to prevent this 'pernicious' practice.[75] The South Sea crash had also opened up the potentially baleful influence of foreign investors, and here Grafton's report made reference to the small size of the bank's capital, which would act as a deterrent to foreign speculators trading in its stock. His detailed report, prepared in consultation with three of the bank's directors, Michael Ward, Sir Ralph Gore and Sir Oliver St George, was accepted by the Privy Council and then passed on to the Lords of the Treasury for their opinion. They reported in May 1721, a year

---

72   McGrath, 'Public Wealth is the Sinew', p. 190.

73   Robert Molesworth to John Molesworth, 9 Jan. 1721 (HMC, Various Collections, vol. 8, p. 294).

74   Conolly to Grafton, 8 July 1721 (IAA, MS 97/84 A3/30).

75   Report by the Duke of Grafton to His Majesty in council, 21 Apr. 1721 (CJI, vol. 3, Appendix, p. ccii).

after the project had first emerged, and informed the Privy Council that the bank would need not just a charter, but also official approval from the Irish parliament.[76] In the meantime, the venerable secretary of the Treasury, William Lowndes, began to prepare a draft charter.[77] It duly received royal approval in July, subject to parliamentary approval in the next session of the Irish parliament, scheduled for September 1721.

V

The Bank's promoters, despite the various setbacks suffered during the long gestation of their project, remained hopeful. While the charter was being prepared in May 1721, Michael Ward was busy organizing copper plates for printing their banknotes, at the same time seeking advice from the Bank of England about best banking practice.[78] These measures reflected the promoters' belief that their hard work would bear fruit, but they were to be sadly disappointed when the issue came before the Irish parliament in the autumn. Apart from the brief period when their subscription books were being filled in May 1720, their lobbying attempts had been largely conducted not in the public arena of the press and parliament, but in the corridors of power in Dublin and Whitehall. The necessity for official approval of the charter brought the issue back before the court of parliamentary opinion in Dublin. The ensuing debates would also reveal the change in attitudes to the bank project, and to financial innovation, that had appeared in the intervening period and that owed much to the rise and fall of the South Sea Company. Despite the best efforts of the bank's promoters, the South Sea bubble and their bank proposal would remain inextricably linked, contributing to the downfall of a project that had briefly attracted so much enthusiasm. The fate of the bank both inside and outside parliament is the focus of chapter 8, which shows the level to which the South Sea bubble impacted on the nascent Irish public sphere. Before that it is necessary to examine in more detail the individual subscribers who supported the bank schemes, and to see what they tell can us about the Irish investing public in 1720.

---

[76] Report of the Lords of the Treasury presented to the King re: Bank 27 May 1721 and draft charter (TNA, T 14/10/346 and 357–65).

[77] For Lowndes, secretary of the Treasury since 1695, see A. A. Hanham, 'William Lowndes, 1652–1724', in ODNB.

[78] Michael Ward to John Irwin, 11 and 23 May 1721 (printed in Hall, pp. 372–3).

7

The Proposals for a National Bank and the Irish Investment Community in 1720

The various proposals for an Irish national bank in 1720–21 were ultimately unsuccessful. Nevertheless, the history of the project reveals much about both the impact of the financial revolution on Ireland and the effect of the South Sea bubble on that kingdom. Chapter 6 has shown how the various bank projects' initial fortunes rose and fell in tandem with the South Sea Company's share price. Meanwhile, chapter 8 shows how the debates about the bank, both within and without the Irish parliament in autumn 1721, were influenced and informed by alternative readings of the London and Paris bubbles. These discussions, like contemporaneous arguments in Scotland about 'Scots projects', demonstrated that the transnational impact of the financial revolution was as much about concepts as about the integration of money markets.[1] The public debates about the national bank and the successive calls for subscriptions for the three competing bank schemes also, however, highlighted the presence in Ireland of a community who were prepared to invest in domestic paper credit schemes. This evidence strongly indicates that, given the opportunity to do so, these individuals would have invested in Dublin as readily as in London in 1720. This chapter examines this prospective investment community, relating their potential investments to the actual Irish holdings in the South Sea Company in London in 1720. Influenced by Ivar McGrath's analysis of Irish public creditors, and by research on the ledgers of the Company of Scotland by Douglas Watt and W. Douglas Jones, it shows how the socio-economic composition of prospective and actual public creditors on the British periphery differed from those at the metropolitan centre.[2] In doing so it will also demonstrate how even dogs that didn't bark, like the Irish bank proposals, can be useful in elucidating historical problems.

[1] Patrick Walsh, 'The Bubble on the Periphery: Scotland and the South Sea Bubble', *Scottish Historical Review*, 91 (2012), 106–24; and Stefan Altdorfer, 'State Investment in Eighteenth-Century Berne', *History of European Ideas*, 33 (2007), pp. 440–62.
[2] C. I. McGrath, '"The Public Wealth is the Sinew, the Life, of Every Public Measure": The Creation and Maintenance of a National Debt in Ireland, 1716–45', in *The Empire of Credit: The Financial Revolution in Britain, Ireland and America, 1688–1815*, ed. Daniel Carey and Christopher Finlay (Dublin, 2011), pp. 171–208; Douglas Watt, *The Price of Scotland: Darien, Union and the Wealth of Nations* (Edinburgh, 2007), pp. 49–51; and W. Douglas Jones, '"The Bold Adventurers": A Quantitative Analysis of the Darien Subscription List (1696)', *Scottish Economic & Social History*, 21 (2001), pp. 22–42.

I

The succession of subscription lists for the different proposals for a national bank in 1720–21 reveal much about the Irish moneyed public at this time. Subscription lists are valuable historical sources. They can tell us not just who invested and how much, but also about the levels of confidence in the scheme, the availability of capital and indeed the regional dispersal of this capital. Obviously the Bank of Ireland was not the only investment option available to Irish investors in early summer 1720. Some subscribed to rival banks, or pledged their surplus capital to one of the fire insurance companies seeking supporters at this time.[3] Many others, as we have seen in previous chapters, were investing in the London capital markets, while some travelled even further afield to invest in the Mississippi Company in Paris. Choices were made for political and personal reasons, as well as for financial objectives. While examining these lists it should also be borne in mind that the raising of joint-stock capital was still very much a new idea in Ireland, as compared with the situation in both England and Scotland. As demonstrated in chapter 2, the instability of the Irish political and economic situation in the second half of the seventeenth century had discouraged domestic investment even among those groups most likely to invest elsewhere in the early modern world.[4] Members of many such groups, however, including clergy, widows and army officers, did appear as subscribers both to the national loan in 1716 and to the bank schemes in 1720, suggesting a delayed convergence with investment patterns elsewhere in the British world.

The subscription lists for the various bank schemes allow us both to understand better who the holders of domestic liquid capital were, and also to ask questions about them. Were they primarily based in Dublin or were they representatives of the landed aristocracy and country gentry? How important were immigrant groups, like the Huguenots? Did independent women constitute a significant element within the potential investment community, as they did elsewhere? And finally, what can we discern about the religious make-up of these potential bank subscribers? Did Protestant Dissenters, as in London, play a significant role? Were Catholics entirely excluded from investment by the Penal Laws, which restricted their political, civil and property rights? These are questions of particular concern within an Irish context, but they are also of importance to historians of emergent capital markets more generally, and to those interested in uncovering the investment patterns and the broader impact of the financial revolution on British and Irish society.

---

[3] List of willing subscribers for a Dublin fire insurance company [referred to the Duke of Grafton on 12 July 1720] (SHC, MS 1248/8, fols 135–7).
[4] R. G. Gillespie, *The Transformation of the Irish Economy, 1550–1700* (Dundalk, 1998), p. 54.

The focus of this chapter is on unpicking the information contained in the various bank subscription lists. Before proceeding to this analysis it is necessary to examine the sources of this data, briefly explaining their contexts and highlighting some of the more problematic interpretative issues. As outlined in the previous chapter, the first proposals for a national bank appeared in May 1720, when a call for promises of capital of £500,000 was published in the Dublin press. This generated a very enthusiastic response (although it is important to stress no money was paid down at this point), with 132 individuals entering their names in the subscription books in Dublin's Merchant's Coffee House over the course of just four days.[5] The surviving list provides the names of putative subscribers as well as some indication of the amount promised, even though the exact value of individual subscriptions is not recorded. Instead, in line with contemporary corporate practice, each name is accompanied by a number of asterisks indicating the number of votes each person was entitled to in the elections for the bank's directors. These electoral allocations were based on the value of subscriptions, with the maximum allowed being £10,000, a sum that granted the investor four votes.[6] Incidental details about social rank and profession are also included in the list but in a non-systematic way. Its contents are summarized in table 7.1, which indicates the social breakdown of the subscribers.

The second surviving subscription list is that for the proposed national bank project associated with Lord Forbes and Brabazon Ponsonby. Dating from July 1720, it is especially useful as it gives us a valuable insight into this otherwise very poorly documented project. What is clear from their proposal is that they hoped to secure £1 million in capital.[7] It also appears that their initial efforts to raise funds took place not just in Dublin, but also in London.[8] Although they were unsuccessful in reaching their somewhat optimistic target, they did attract 207 named subscribers, who promised a total of £521,000 in capital.[9] Despite this overall failure these figures are still exceptional, especially when we consider the minimum subscription promised was £1,000, which was greater than the price of a South Sea share at the top of the market. Crucially of course these subscriptions were, like those for the South Sea Company, to be paid for in instalments thereby reducing the necessary initial capital outlay. Their success in raising these

---

[5] Abercorn/Irwin subscription list, May 1720 (NLI, MS 2256, fols 63–5).

[6] John Irwin, *To the Nobility, Gentry and Commonalty of this Kingdom of Ireland* (Dublin, 1720).

[7] The humble petition of George Lord Forbes and Brabazon Ponsonby Esq. on behalf of themselves and several other persons in Ireland who have engaged to subscribe a sum not exceeding a million in order to erect a bank in that kingdom, n.d. (NLI, MS 2256, fol. 11).

[8] John, Lord Perceval to James Hamilton, 6th Earl of Abercorn, 16 June 1720 (BL Add MS 47029, fol. 68).

[9] Forbes/Ponsonby subscription list (NLI, MS 2256, fols 39–42).

Table 7.1. Subscribers to the Abercorn/Irwin bank, May 1720.

Classification	Number of subscribers	%
Peers	5	3.8
Bishops	1	0.8
Judges	2	1.5
MPs	48	36.4
Past or future MPs	8	6.1
Women	3	2.3
Clergy	6	4.5
Merchants	7	5.3
Bankers	1	0.8
Goldsmiths	0	0.0
Military officers	8	6.1
Aldermen	1	0.8
Doctors	0	0.0
Others	42	31.8
Total	132	100.0

Source: Abercorn/Irwin subscription list, May 1720 (NLI, MS 2256, fols 63–65).

promises of capital is especially impressive as they were partly competing for subscribers in a crowded London market, albeit mostly among the growing London-Irish community. It is important to note here that the Irish bank proposals, like the Irish national debt previously, did not attract foreign investors, despite the high rates of interest on offer.

As with the subscribers to the Abercorn/Irwin proposal, the 207 individuals who subscribed to the Forbes/Ponsonby bank represented a diverse cross-section of Irish landed and commercial society, as shown by table 7.2. There is certainly a higher number of those that might only be gathered into the group titled 'others' but not all of those classified as such are necessarily obscure. They included individuals such as the prominent Irish portrait painter Charles Jervas, as well as Thomas Prior, the noted improver and author of pamphlets on economic subjects.[10] Such figures escape easy categorization in tabular

[10] Rebecca Minch, 'Jervas, Charles (1675–1735)', in *DIB*. For Prior, author of the famous *A list of the absentees of Ireland, and the yearly value of their estates and incomes spent abroad. With observations on the present state and condition of that kingdom* (Dublin, 1729), see D. W. Hayton, *The Anglo-Irish Experience, 1680–1730: Religion, Identity and Patriotism* (Woodbridge, 2012), pp. 174–99.

Table 7.2. Subscribers to the Forbes/Ponsonby bank, July 1720.

Classification	Number of subscribers	%
Peers	9	4.3
Bishops	3	1.4
Judges	0	0.0
MPs	44	21.3
Past or future MPs	15	7.2
Women	6	2.9
Clergy	1	0.5
Merchants	19	9.2
Bankers	3	1.4
Goldsmiths	1	0.5
Military officers	3	1.4
Aldermen	3	1.4
Doctors	0	0.0
Others	100	48.3
Total	207	100.0

Source: Forbes/Ponsonby subscription list (NLI, MS 2256, fols 39–42).

manner. They do, however, together with presence of two doctors, Henry Cope and Haniball Hall, highlight the success of this bank's promoters in obtaining subscriptions from the ranks of the Irish 'middling sort', as well as from the traditional holders of Irish wealth, the landed gentry.[11]

The next section examines these two subscription lists in greater detail. Comparisons are also drawn with a further bank list drawn up in autumn 1721, when the bank proposals came before the Irish parliament. By this juncture some of the original subscribers had withdrawn their financial and political support for the project (as discussed in chapter 6), but other new subscribers were prepared to take their place and so this adds a further 117 names to the list of potential investors. It also allows careful consideration of the impact of the bursting of the South Sea bubble in the intervening period, on both the project and the Irish investment community. This is further explored through comparative analysis of the bank lists with records of the known Irish investors in the South Sea Company.[12]

[11] For Hall and the social position of eighteenth-century Irish doctors, see Toby Barnard, *A New Anatomy of Ireland: The Irish Protestants, 1649–1770* (London, 2003), p. 137.

[12] Unlike McGrath, I have not included in my analysis the names entered on the

II

It is perhaps not entirely surprising that the profile of the subscribers to the two bank schemes is strikingly similar. As suggested in the previous chapter, while both lists were 'full of parliament men' they were not divided by ideological or factional differences. Divisions between Whig and Tory, court and country, city financier and landlord, were not reflected in the two lists. Instead they cumulatively represented the interest in, and support for, a national bank within the moneyed ranks of the Irish elite. As such, rather than attempting to engage in a futile hair-splitting exercise designed to demonstrate real differences between the two bank subscriptions, the following analysis examines them together, allowing a fuller picture of potential Irish bank investors to emerge. However, occasional differences are emphasized, especially in relation to religion.

The importance of attracting eighteenth-century British and Irish society's 'natural leaders', namely members of the peerage, has been highlighted by historians of English and Scottish subscription lists, while royal and political support for the South Sea Company is well known.[13] In Ireland too, peers were prominent in their support of both bank projects, reflecting the traditional ordered nature of an *ancien régime* society. Lords Abercorn and Boyne were chief promoters of one scheme, while Lord Forbes, the dominant force behind the other putative bank, was the eldest son of the 2nd Earl of Granard. Numbered among the other peers who subscribed to either of the two bank projects were some of the recent creations in the Irish peerage, including lords Aylmer, Carbery, Ferrard, Gowran, Limerick and Molesworth. They had all received their titles since the Hanoverian succession in 1714, and may have seen the bank schemes as a way of exerting their recently acquired social role.[14] Some of these lords, including Aylmer, Limerick and Molesworth, were usually resident not in Dublin but in London, where they were prominent figures within political and administrative circles. For instance, Lord Aylmer of Balrath, a former distinguished naval commander, was governor of Greenwich Hospital, while Robert, 1st Viscount Molesworth, was a prominent Westminster MP.[15]

Considering the other London-based Irish peers whose titles appear on the Forbes/Ponsonby list, two names stand out: Lord Netterville and Lord

petition forwarded to the lord lieutenant, the Duke of Bolton, in support of a national bank in June 1720. Expressing support for a bank did not equate to pledging financial backing for one of the bank projects.

[13] Watt, pp. 49–51; and Jones, 'The Bold Adventurers', pp. 29–30. For the South Sea Company see Anon., *Index Rerum & Vocabulorum For the Use of Freeholders of Counties and Freemen of Corporations* (London, 1722).

[14] For the Irish peerage in this period see F. G. James, *Lords of the Ascendancy: The Irish House of Lords and its Members, 1600–1800* (Dublin, 1995).

[15] Helen Andrews, 'Mathew, Lord Aylmer (1650–1720)', in *DIB*.

Westmeath. John, 4th Viscount Netterville and Thomas Nugent, 4th Earl of Westmeath, who subscribed £1,000 and £2,000 respectively, were both Catholics, and also among the very small number of their co-religionists within the Irish peerage who had retained their estates and wealth following the Williamite land settlement in the 1690s.[16] Their presence among the proposal's subscribers, along with the evidence for investment by the Irish Catholic elite in the South Sea Company, suggests that Irish Catholics were not entirely excluded from participation in the financial revolution. The presence of Netterville and Westmeath, together with a small but significant number of Catholic mercantile interests among the subscribers to the Forbes/Ponsonby bank, also complicates further perceptions about Catholic investment in the post-revolutionary Irish Protestant state. Their bank subscriptions can perhaps be best compared with the willingness of Scottish Jacobite peers, such as Lord and Lady Panmure, to invest in the South Sea Company.[17] Financial self-interest in such cases might have trumped political ideology. It is probably significant in this regard, and indeed a further warning against historical reductionism, that Westmeath would emerge later in the 1720s as one of the prime movers of a proposed address of political loyalty to the Hanoverian monarchy from the Irish Catholic community.[18]

Past, present and future members of the Irish House of Commons made up the largest identifiable grouping, which reflects the continued concentration of Irish wealth among the political and landed elite.[19] The names of ninety-two Irish MPs, or almost one third of those who sat in the Irish House of Commons, appear across the two summer 1720 lists with a further twenty-three past or future MPs also appearing as subscribers.[20] Speaker Conolly's comments about their almost equal division between the two schemes have already been noted, as has the inclusion of a number of the leading members of both major factions in the Irish Commons. Indeed the election of representatives of both the Conolly and Midleton factions as directors of the Abercorn bank, notably the Conolly supporters Sir Ralph Gore and Lord Boyne on one side, and on the other St John Brodrick and Michael Ward, whom Gore had defeated for the chancellorship in 1717, suggests that this was an avowedly bi-partisan project.[21]

Similarly members of both 'parties' can be found among the subscribers to the other bank. Lord Forbes' own political inclinations remain largely

---

16 James, Lords of the Ascendancy, pp. 90–2.
17 Walsh, 'Bubble on the Periphery', pp. 119–20.
18 Ian McBride, 'Catholic Politics in the Penal Era: Father Sylvester Lloyd and the Delvin Address of 1727', in New Perspectives on the Penal Laws, ed. John Bergin, Eoin Magennis, Lesa Ni Mhunghaile and Patrick Walsh (Dublin, 2011), pp. 115–47.
19 Barnard, New Anatomy, p. 61.
20 Biographical information on Irish MPs has been taken from HIP.
21 Patrick Walsh, The Making of the Irish Protestant Ascendancy: The Life of William Conolly, 1662–1729 (Woodbridge, 2010), pp. 122–3.

obscure, partly because he had spent much of the years previous to the bank scheme absent from parliament, either on naval duty, or in the service of the Austrian Emperor.[22] His business partner, Brabazon Ponsonby, was regarded as being close to Speaker Conolly.[23] Other members of Conolly's circle, including Agmondisham Vesey and General Owen Wynne, were also putative subscribers to this bank, while Thomas Carter and Lord Hillsborough were among Midleton's allies who pledged their financial support.[24] In summary, as suggested above, it is difficult to ascribe a particular political character to either bank. Instead it is worth noting the presence of most of those MPs generally regarded as politically active among the supporters of the two banks.

The large number of MPs pledging their financial support to these banks suggests two things: first, that a national bank was seen as an attractive idea by a significant portion of the parliamentary elite, something that was also plainly demonstrated in the petition forwarded to the lord lieutenant in June; and secondly, that MPs were, perhaps unsurprisingly, still holders of much of the kingdom's liquid capital. This was clearly seen in 1716 when subscriptions were called for the national loan, and would be shown again when a new loan was raised in 1729. On the former occasion eighteen MPs, as well as seven peers, were numbered among the sixty-three public creditors, while thirteen years later fifty MPs would be included in the 163 holders of newly issued government debt.[25] In both cases, government office holders, whether parliamentary officials or other administrative figures such as senior revenue officials, were prominent investors. The true test of parliamentary support for a national bank would not come, however, until autumn 1721 when a modified version of the Abercorn/Irwin proposal was laid before the House of Commons for their approval.

Beyond the two houses of parliament other members of the Irish lay and clerical elites were enthusiastic subscribers to the two bank proposals. Three Church of Ireland bishops, Thomas Vesey of Ossory, Timothy Goodwin of Kilmore and Ralph Lambert of Dromore, all subscribed to the Forbes/Ponsonby bank. Lambert, interestingly, also subscribed to the Abercorn bank, which made him the only person to definitively subscribe to both schemes.[26] Below the ranks of the episcopal bench, other Irish Anglican clergy were keen to subscribe to both banks. In total seven clergymen, outside the bishops, appear on the two 1720 bank subscription lists, including two

---

[22] John Forbes, *Memoirs of the Earls of Granard* (London, 1868), pp. 140–51.

[23] For Ponsonby see his entry in *HIP*, vol. 6, pp. 78–81.

[24] Hayton, *Anglo-Irish Experience*, pp. 124–48.

[25] McGrath, 'The Public Wealth is the Sinew, the Life, of Every Public Measure', p. 187.

[26] It is possible that the otherwise obscure Andrew Wilson and Lewis Jones also subscribed to both banks, but without further evidence it is impossible to assume these were not merely namesakes.

deans, Josiah Hort and Benjamin Pratt, both of whom enjoyed substantial livings in the church. Pratt, like fellow subscriber William Brownlow, was also Lord Abercorn's son-in-law and such family relationships were undoubtedly important for persuading potential investors.[27] The presence of members of the clergy among the subscribers to the banks is not surprising: clergymen across the early modern world often had access to liquid capital and were not adverse to investment, or even to engage in private moneylending. Indeed Sean Moore has suggested that significant numbers of the clergy opposed the funding of a national bank because its lower rates of interest would undercut their private lending activities, although much further research is needed to prove this point.[28] His conclusions, based on close reading of the contemporary pamphlet literature, are further tempered somewhat by the acknowledgement that some Irish clergymen did subscribe to both bank schemes as well as investing in the Irish and British national debts in this period.

It is also possible to identify a number of members of the increasingly important Dublin mercantile and civic elite among the bank subscribers. Several of this group, including James Galbally and Henry Irwin, have the appellation 'merchant' beside their names on the subscription list. The civic offices they currently held, or had held in the past, defined other merchant subscribers such as Sir William Fownes and John Porter. Fownes was a former Tory lord mayor and a prominent figure within the corporation, while Porter, who was later elected a putative director of the bank, was an alderman in the city.[29] Another growing interest in the city were the private bankers, and those identified supporting the Abercorn scheme included business partners Benjamin Burton and Francis Harrison, as well as Sir Alexander Cairnes and Hugh Henry.

Conspicuous by his absence from the Abercorn list was the already significant banking figure of David La Touche, who instead subscribed to Lord Forbes' proposal. Some of La Touche's Huguenot co-religionists, an important subset among Dublin's mercantile and military interests, did subscribe to Abercorn's bank demonstrating they were not only active in the London capital markets, as shown in chapter 2, but also within their Dublin equivalents. Alderman John Porter was the most prominent Huguenot subscriber. A wine merchant and a ship owner, he also enjoyed extensive connections on the Continent.[30] Among Porter's fellow Huguenot subscribers was

---

[27] For Pratt, a former provost of Trinity College Dublin, see John Bergin, 'Pratt, Benjamin (1669–1721)', in *DIB*.

[28] Sean D. Moore, '"Vested" Interests and Debt Bondage: Credit as Confessional Coercion in Colonial Ireland', in Carey and Finlay (eds), *The Empire of Credit*, pp. 209–28.

[29] Jacqueline Hill, *From Patriots to Unionists: Dublin Civic Politics and Irish Protestant Patriotism, 1660–1840* (Oxford, 1997), p. 75.

[30] Vivien Costelloe, '"Pensioners, Barbers, Valets or Markees"?: Jonathan Swift and Huguenot Bank Investors in Ireland, 1721', *Proceedings of the Huguenot Society of Great Britain and Ireland*, 29 (2008), 62–92 (p. 77).

Nicholas Grueber, another successful merchant, who was active in the civic life of the city, and three military men: Captain Theophilus Debrisay, his son (also Theophilus) and Captain William Duponet. Debrisay senior acted as an agent to several Irish regiments, allowing him access to extensive funds.[31] Each of these five subscribers was also a signatory to the petition presented to George I in June 1720. Meanwhile, at least five different members of the local Huguenot community, including La Touche and his cousin Daniel Delamotte, who was active in the Amsterdam, London and Dublin financial markets in 1720, subscribed to Lord Forbes' bank project.[32] A total of twenty-six new Huguenot subscribers also appeared among the supporters of the bank scheme in its final iteration in November 1721.[33] The willingness of the Dublin Huguenot community to invest in the bank schemes reflected their growing economic influence as well as their integration into the commercial life of the city.

The visible support for the bank by the Huguenots, most of whom gradually conformed to the established Church of Ireland, does raise again the issue of religion and investment, previously touched upon briefly in relation to the South Sea Company. Religious minorities were often dispro-portionately represented among financial and commercial interests in early modern Europe, and Ireland was no different. Aside from the Huguenots, Quakers such as Edward Hoare and Joseph Fade, and Presbyterians such as Sir Alexander Cairnes, Benjamin Burton and Hugh Henry, were prominent in Irish private banking circles. This was not surprising as their businesses often grew out of existing kinship and religious networks. This was certainly the case for the Cairnes' banking empire, which stretched from Dublin to Cork, Limerick and London by 1720. Cairnes was one of a select band of identifiable Presbyterians, including the Dublin merchant James Steevenson, Colonel John Upton and the banker Benjamin Burton, who subscribed to Abercorn's bank. These numbers are quite low relative to their position within Irish economic life, suggesting that most of the bank subscribers were resident in Dublin, rather than in smaller cities and towns like Belfast and Derry where Protestant Dissenters dominated mercantile and business life.[34]

Irish Catholics were similarly largely absent from the two subscription lists. This reflected their exclusion from Irish political, social and economic life under the Penal Laws. Unlike other oppressed religious groups across

---

[31] John Bayly, deputy clerk of the pells, was another army agent and subscriber to the bank. See A. P. W. Malcomson, *Nathaniel Clements: Government and the Governing Elite in Ireland, 1725–75* (Dublin, 2005), pp. 145–6.

[32] For Delamotte's investments see the La Touche & Kane Accounts, 1719–25 (NLI, MS 2785).

[33] Jonathan Swift, *Subscribers to the Bank Plac'd according to Their Order and Quality. With Notes and Queries* (Dublin, 1721), printed in *Prose Works*, ed. Herbert Davis, 14 vols (Oxford, 1939–68), vol. 9, pp. 288–90; and Costelloe, p. 67.

[34] Jean Agnew, *Belfast Merchant Families in the Seventeenth Century* (Dublin, 1996).

Europe, however, they were largely unable to surmount these difficulties through commercial prowess.[35] It is therefore significant that some Catholics did subscribe to at least one of the bank proposals in 1720. These subscribers to the Forbes/Ponsonby proposal included, as we have seen, two leading Catholic peers and members of the surviving Catholic gentry, as well as a select number of Catholic merchants and at least one prominent Catholic solicitor, Joseph Nagle.[36] Among the Catholic landowners who subscribed to the Forbes bank were Sir Walter Blake, a leading member of the Galway gentry, and John and Valentine Quin, members of a prominent Limerick family, who each subscribed the not insignificant sum of £5,000.[37] Dublin-based merchants supporting Forbes' bank included Augustus Clarke, Patrick Creagh and Michael Bodkin. They were among the small number of Catholic merchants active in the city, with Creagh one of only seven Catholics identifiable out of 372 Dublin traders who signed a petition against the introduction of the hotly contested 'Wood's Halfpence' in 1724.[38]

These subscriptions suggest that there remained a small Catholic financial interest in Ireland, which had not been obliterated by the effects of the Williamite wars and the penal legislation passed by the Irish parliament. This was something that Protestant contemporaries feared, leading at least one pamphleteer, the MP Hercules Rowley, to argue against a national bank on the grounds that it would encourage the Catholic interest.[39] His objections led to restrictions being included in the bank's eventual charter, barring Catholics from being directors though not investors. Similar fears were expressed about the potential of Jacobite/Catholic investors to destabilize Scottish projects and indeed the South Sea Company, although on occasion the converse argument was also expressed that investment could bind Catholics to the state.[40] It is unlikely, however, that this small number

[35] David Dickson, 'Catholics and Trade in Eighteenth-Century Ireland: An Old Debate Reconsidered', in *Endurance and Emergence: Catholics in the Eighteenth Century*, ed. T. P. Power and Kevin Whelan (Dublin, 1990), pp. 85–100.

[36] David Dickson, *Old World Colony: Cork and South Munster, 1630–1830* (Cork, 2005), p. 267, where Nagle is described as the 'leading Catholic lawyer of his generation in the region'.

[37] David Fleming, *Politics and Provincial People: Sligo and Limerick, 1691–1761* (Manchester, 2010), p. 88.

[38] Patrick Fagan, *Catholics in a Protestant Country: The Papist Constituency in Eighteenth-Century Dublin* (Dublin, 1998), pp. 65 and 165. For Bodkin, see L. M. Cullen, 'Galway Merchants in the Outside World, c.1650–1800', in *Economy, Trade and Irish Merchants at Home and Abroad, 1600–1998* (Dublin 2012), pp. 165–92 (pp. 179–80).

[39] Hercules Rowley, *An Answer to a Book Intitled Reasons Offered for Erecting a Bank in Ireland in a Letter to Henry Maxwell Esquire* (Dublin, 1721), p. 40; and *An Answer to Mr Maxwell's Second Letter Concerning the Bank* (Dublin, 1721), p. 16.

[40] Lord Perceval to Charles Dering, 23 June 1720 (BL, Add MS 47029, fol. 67); and Henry Maxwell, *Mr Maxwell's Second Letter to Mr Rowley: Wherein the Objections Against the Bank Are Answered* (Dublin, 1721), pp. 11–12.

of bank subscribers posed a serious threat to the Anglican establishment. They were not all inherently disloyal, or part of a covert Jacobite interest: Sir William Blake, for instance, had been the first Catholic of distinction to declare his support for William of Orange.[41]

If early financial markets and institutions have been identified as significant in breaking down religious boundaries, they have also been recognized as important in subverting gender barriers, with an impressive literature now extant chronicling female investment during the financial revolution. The sums invested were not always substantial, although a few exceptional case studies warn us against unduly dismissing these investments as 'mere pin money'.[42] In Ireland, four women had contributed a total of £3,400 or 6.8% to the national loan raised in 1716.[43] As shown elsewhere, Irish women invested in the South Sea Company, and they were likewise attracted to the national bank proposals. The Abercorn group's subscription list included three women, Ann Dowling, Lady Midleton and Lady Mahon. Nothing is known of the first of these women, while Lady Midleton was not only the lord chancellor's wife, but also the mother of Arthur Hill, one of the bank's promoters and greatest individual financial backers.[44] Lucy, Lady Mahon, was the wife of prominent British politician, James Stanhope, and daughter of Thomas 'Diamond' Pitt, an exceedingly wealthy London merchant and speculator. Her brother Thomas, Lord Londonderry, was one of the greatest speculators in South Sea stock. However, despite her brother's title, there is little evidence of any Irish connection and her presence among the subscribers remains a mystery. The Forbes/Ponsonby bank meanwhile attracted six female subscribers of whom details are only known of two, namely the widow and daughter of Sir Thomas Bligh, a wealthy County Meath landowner. These ladies subscribed £8,000 between them, something that attracted unfavourable comment in one anti-bank pamphlet.[45] Their subscriptions, together with those of the other four women, amounted to £14,000 out of the £521,000 raised by the bank promoters, or just 2.7% of the total. This compares unfavourably with the 6.8% of the first Irish national loan held by women, and suggests that domestic Irish female investment continued to lag behind investment patterns elsewhere in the British world.

---

[41] Eoin Kinsella, 'Dividing the Bear's Skin Before She is Taken: Irish Catholics and Land in the Late Stuart Monarchy, 1683–1691', in *Restoration Ireland: Always Settling Never Settled*, ed. Coleman Dennehy (Aldershot, 2008), pp. 161–78 (p. 175); and McBride, pp. 130–1.

[42] For an overview see Anne Laurence, Josephine Maltby and Janette Rutterford (eds), *Women and Their Money 1700–1950: Essays on Women and Finance* (London, 2009).

[43] *CJI*, vol. 3, Appendix, pp. cxiii–cxiv.

[44] Hill was Lady Midleton's son by her first marriage: *HIP*, vol. 4, pp. 117–18.

[45] Swift, *Prose Works*, vol. 9, p. 289.

III

Examining the two bank subscription lists more broadly allows us to further develop a portrait of the potential Irish investment community at the time of the South Sea bubble, and to see how they fitted into wider trans-national investment patterns. The dominance of the Irish political class has already been noted and quantifying the investments of Irish parliamentarians adds further ballast to this conclusion. Although peers and MPs, including past, current and future members, comprised just under 33% of the Forbes/Ponsonby list (as opposed to 46% of the subscribers to the Abercorn/Irwin bank) they subscribed £211,000 or 40% of its promised capital. This compares with the £71,000 or 14% of the total capital subscribed to the same bank by the twenty-nine identifiable members of the Dublin civic and financial elite, a category defined as including the city aldermen, merchants, bankers and goldsmiths. This figure could probably be revised upwards if more information was available on the occupational activity of the rather nebulous category of 'others' in table 7.2 above.

Such methodological difficulties make it more difficult to compare the Irish data across time and space. Nevertheless, some tentative conclusions can be broached. Comparing the profile of Irish bank subscribers with those who subscribed to the national banks actually realized in England and Scotland in the 1690s, it is immediately evident that the Irish case is more similar to the Scottish than the English situation. In Ireland, like Scotland, the landed gentry continued to be the pre-eminent holders of potential banking capital.[46] This also had implications for the geographical spread of investors, with Irish bank subscribers, like their Scottish counterparts, resident across the kingdom on their estates, even if some also maintained residences in their respective capital cities. As in Scotland, some Irish subscriptions also came from the expatriate community in London.[47] In England, meanwhile, London mercantile interests dominated the initial subscription for the Bank of England in 1694, a trend that continued on an upward trajectory into the eighteenth century.[48] Irish women, as we have seen, were underrepresented in the bank lists, at least as compared with English investment patterns, although their proportional investment in the South Sea scheme, relative to the Irish total, was closer to the figure for England. Here too they conform to the pattern witnessed in Scotland, where few women subscribed to the Bank of Scotland as compared with those investing in the more speculative Company of Scotland in the 1690s.[49]

---

[46] Jones, 'The Bold Adventurers', p. 37.
[47] Jones, 'The Bold Adventurers', p. 38.
[48] P. G. M. Dickson, *The Financial Revolution in England: A Study in the Development of Public Credit 1688–1756* (London, 1967), p. 297.
[49] Jones, 'The Bold Adventurers', p. 31.

The speed with which both sets of bank promoters were able to fill their subscriptions was reminiscent not just of the Company of Scotland's successful drive for funds in the 1690s, but more generally of the manner in which investors flocked to invest in joint-stock enterprises elsewhere in 1720.[50] In this respect perhaps, the bank proposals can be compared with the multiplicity of 'projects' appearing contemporaneously in London, a point of comparison regularly made at the time.[51] Diverting the perceived flow of Irish capital from these London schemes was after all one of the stated aims of the bank promoters, as outlined in their respective manifestos. Their success in doing so might be gauged by examining the bank subscription lists in comparison with the available data on actual Irish investors in the South Sea Company in 1720, which is the focus of the next section of this chapter.

The two schemes for a national bank were not the only investment opportunities open to Irish investors in 1720, nor indeed were they necessarily the most lucrative. The bank schemes, like their earlier counterparts in London and Edinburgh, promised a safe return on investment.[52] In contrast, the South Sea Company, and its London and European rivals, offered greater rewards albeit with greater risks attached, although it is important not to overstate these risks with the benefit of hindsight. It is therefore not surprising that there was some crossover between those individuals who invested in the South Sea Company and those whose names appeared on the subscription lists for the bank projects. More unexpected is the fact that their numbers were very small. Only sixteen out of the 132 people who subscribed to the Abercorn/Irwin bank in May 1720 and only eight of the 207 putative subscribers to the Forbes/Ponsonby bank are known to have also invested in the South Sea Company. These figures might be explained by the incompleteness of the available data on holders of South Sea shares, especially during the period of greatest movement in the market for company stock in midsummer 1720.[53] They might also suggest that contemporary reports about extensive Irish investment in London were unnecessarily alarmist. The activities of prominent individuals like Viscount Molesworth

---

[50] Jones, 'The Bold Adventurers', p. 39. See also Watt, pp. 79–89, where he sees the speed with which the Company of Scotland recruited investors as evidence of a speculative mania.

[51] William Conolly to Jane Bonnell, 30 Sep. 1720 (NLI, MS 41,578/2). Anon., *Remarks on Mr Maxwell's and Mr Rowley's Letters: Setting Forth the Advantages of a Bank and Lumbards in Ireland, in a Letter to a Friend* (Dublin, 1721), p. 4.

[52] The same could be said of the competing claims of the Company of Scotland and the Bank of Scotland in the 1690s: Jones, 'The Bold Adventurers', p. 38.

[53] Irish investors in the South Sea Company have been identified from the Bank of England records described in chapter 3, and from a range of personal papers and correspondence from the period. Therefore the nature of these records means there might be some further correlation between as yet unidentified South Sea investors and the bank subscription lists.

and David La Touche, who publicly supported one or other of the schemes for a national bank while also investing in London, may therefore have distorted contemporary perceptions. An alternative possibility is, of course, that the bank promoters' arguments against foreign investment, as expressed in the manifestos for both projects and in Lord Abercorn's private conversations and correspondence, had a significant and immediate impact.

Looking more closely at the twenty-four named individuals who invested in the South Sea Company and also supported the bank projects, some interesting details emerge. Only three of the named promoters of either bank scheme are known to have held South Sea stock, namely Brabazon Ponsonby, Michael Ward and Sir Oliver St George. Significantly perhaps, most of the dual investors were resident in London rather than Dublin at this time. Among those who came into this category were Charles Dering, Lord Gowran and Edward Southwell, who all subscribed to Lord Forbes' bank, while Sir Alexander Cairnes, Sir Gustavus Hume, Sir Oliver St George, Viscount Molesworth and Sir John St Leger were some of the Abercorn/Irwin subscribers known to be in London at this time. Otherwise these twenty-four individuals have more in common with their fellow bank subscribers than with their fellow Irish investors in the South Sea Company. There were, for instance, only four Huguenots in this group, including the ubiquitous David La Touche and his financier cousin Daniel Delamotte, as compared with the sizeable Huguenot majority among the Irish investors in London more generally. Also interestingly, none of the women who subscribed to the bank proposals appear to have invested in the South Sea Company.

If these figures are considered in isolation, it would appear that the bursting of the South Sea bubble could have had little impact on the fate of the bank projects. Such a view would be mistaken, however, and ignores other factors such as the impact on Irish credit networks, as well as the important shift in broader market sentiment during the course of summer and autumn 1720 when the bank subscriptions were being raised. If the early enthusiasm for the bank projects in May 1720 can be linked to wider transnational market forces then logically so too can the changed perceptions of the remaining consolidated bank proposal in late 1720 and early 1721. Contemporaries doubted whether some of the original subscribers would be able to make good their pledged subscriptions.[54] This applied not just to those who were known to have suffered significant losses in the London stock market, such as James Barry and John Maxwell, but also to those who were affected by the ripple effect on Irish credit networks.

---

[54] Conolly to Charles FitzRoy, 2nd Duke of Grafton, 18 Oct. 1720 (IAA, MS 97/84 A3/17).

IV

Broader concerns about the wisdom of a national bank in the aftermath of the London crash were also notable in the public and private discourses when the issue came before the Dublin parliament in autumn 1721. These are addressed more fully in the next chapter, but they were clearly evident in the composition of the final subscription list for the bank, which was published in October 1721.[55] This final list contains the names of those who were still prepared to subscribe to the bank despite the difficulties experienced in obtaining its draft charter, and the impact of the bubble. Unlike the earlier more prospective, or speculative, lists, investors were required to make a down payment of 10% of their total subscription. Even though it is unclear if this actually happened, greater commitment was obviously expected. It was also received: the bank's promoters, still led by Abercorn, Irwin and Ward, were able nevertheless to fill their subscription with remarkable ease.

The final list, published in Dublin in October 1721, contains 209 names.[56] Of these, fifty-six had subscribed to the original Abercorn/Irwin proposal almost eighteen months earlier, while only thirty-one of the 207 subscribers to the Forbes/Ponsonby proposal continued to pledge their support. This means that 122 new individuals appeared in the final subscription list, indicating that this was much more than the 'composite' list that some historians have previously assumed.[57] As such it deserves careful examination, as well as comparison with the earlier lists. Just who were the prospective national bank investors in October 1721? This question similarly exercised contemporaries with Jonathan Swift famously dismissing the subscribers in a pamphlet entitled *The Eyes of Ireland Open, in A Letter from a Lady at Dublin to Her Friend in the Country*. The dean suggested that while 'there were some persons of honour, estates and good distinction among the subscribers, they were in some alliance with the directors and chief promoters of the bank: and generally speaking, the rest consisted of pressed men and *French* volunteers'.[58] This commentary has attracted some attention, both because of its author, and also because of its particular targeting of the Huguenot financial interest. As always with Swift's writings, it needs to be carefully analysed: his characterization of the bank subscribers was rather unfair and reductive, as table 7.3 indicates. Even if a proportion of the names had changed, the overall profile of these 209 subscribers was quite similar to those who had

---

[55] William Nicolson to William Wake, 28 Oct. 1721 (Christ Church Library, Oxford, MSS 231, vol. 13, fol. 292).
[56] Anon., *A List of the Subscribers to the Bank of Ireland* (Dublin, 1721).
[57] McGrath, 'The Public Wealth is the Sinew, the Life, of Every Public Measure', p. 186.
[58] Jonathan Swift, *The Eyes of Ireland Open, in A Letter from a Lady at Dublin to Her Friend in the Country* (Dublin, 1721), printed in *Prose Works*, p. 301, and quoted in Costelloe, p. 63.

Table 7.3. Subscribers to the Bank of Ireland, October 1721.

Classification	Number of subscribers	%
Peers	4	1.9
Bishops	2	1.0
Judges	1	0.5
MPs	45	21.5
Past or future MPs	13	6.2
Women	9	4.3
Clergy	8	3.8
Merchants	26	12.4
Bankers	5	2.4
Goldsmiths	0	0.0
Military officers	19	9.1
Aldermen	2	1.0
Doctors	5	2.4
Others	70	33.5
Total	209	100.0

Source: Anon., A List of the Subscribers to the Bank of Ireland (Dublin, 1721).

previously enlisted for either of the two previous iterations of the bank project. This becomes even clearer when we compare the three subscriptions in tabular format and consider the percentage contribution of the different categories enumerated in tables 7.1–7.3, as is shown in table 7.4.

Members of the political and clerical elites, comprising almost 30% of the total subscribers, continued to be heavily represented although their numbers relative to the total had fallen. Significantly, there were also many different names. This partly reflected natural wastage, some subscribers to the previous lists like Samuel Dopping and Lord Aylmer, for instance, having died during 1720. Others had clearly changed their minds, both positively and negatively, about the prospects of the project. Among the newly visible converts to the utility of a national bank was Henry Maxwell, MP for Donegal town, who in late 1721 was already the most vociferous defender of the scheme in the printed sphere, writing two lengthy pamphlets arguing for its erection. Maxwell, sometimes referred to as 'the speaker's shadow', was politically and personally close to William Conolly, and supporters of the speaker are readily identifiable among the bank's parliamentary subscribers, suggesting the entry of the factional disputes into the debates on the bank. This hypothesis is given further credence by the absence of St John Brodrick,

Table 7.4. Subscribers to the three Irish banks compared (%).

Classification	Abercorn/Irwin	Forbes/Ponsonby	Bank of Ireland
Peers	3.8	4.3	1.9
Bishops	0.8	1.4	1.0
Judges	1.5	0.0	0.5
MPs	36.4	21.3	21.5
Past or future MPs	6.1	7.2	6.2
Women	2.3	2.9	4.3
Clergy	4.5	0.5	3.8
Merchants	5.3	9.2	12.4
Bankers	0.8	1.4	2.4
Goldsmiths	0.0	0.5	0.0
Military officers	6.1	1.4	9.1
Aldermen	0.8	1.4	1.0
Doctors	0.0	0.0	2.4
Others	31.8	48.3	33.5
Total	100.0	100.0	100.0

Source: Abercorn/Irwin subscription list, May 1720 (NLI, MS 2256, fols 63–65); Forbes/Ponsonby subscription list (NLI, MS 2256, fols 39–42); and Anon., *A List of the Subscribers to the Bank of Ireland* (Dublin, 1721).

Viscount Midleton's son and spokesman in the Commons, from the October list, while the inclusion of Conolly's land agent Robert McCausland might also be construed as similarly significant.[59] McCausland's presence meanwhile points to the continuing diverse profile of the bank subscribers, showing that they were not all drawn from the higher political and mercantile ranks of Irish society.

This diversity was recognized in the pamphlet literature, where the Huguenot presence among the military and mercantile subscribers was highlighted. The number of 'Frenchmen' had certainly risen, with thirty-one Huguenots identified among the 209 subscribers, amounting to 14.8% of the total investors as compared with 3.8% and 2.4% of the original Abercorn and Forbes subscription lists respectively. If the Huguenot element had increased, the Catholic element had evaporated, with none of the Catholics listed as subscribers to the Forbes bank reappearing on the October list. This must

---

[59] For McCausland see Walsh, *Making of the Irish Protestant Ascendancy*, pp. 113–15.

have done much to assuage contemporary fears about a potentially threatening Catholic moneyed interest, although the actual paltry number of Catholic investors as described earlier suggests these fears were exaggerated for rhetorical purposes.[60]

The final element of this subscription list worth considering in some detail is the correlation between its entries and the names of known Irish holders of South Sea stock. Only ten subscribers on the October bank list are known to have invested in the South Sea Company. They included Francis Hutchinson, Bishop of Down, a prominent public supporter of the bank, as well as two of the bank's promoters, Michael Ward and Sir Oliver St George. Ward and St George incurred personal financial losses as a result of their South Sea investments, while Hutchinson made a profit during the bubble period.[61] A further three subscribers were members of the Dublin Huguenot community, namely the military officers William Duponet and Theophilus Debrisay, and the clergyman Peter Maturin. The four remaining investors were the MPs William Maynard and General Owen Wynne, the future MP and economic thinker Arthur Dobbs, and a Dublin merchant, John Shaw, who was the only one not to have participated previously in either bank scheme.[62] These ten subscribers comprised less than 5% of the total subscription, and their numbers compared unfavourably with the twenty-four South Sea investors who had appeared on the previous bank lists. This may reflect the impact of the bubble. Certainly some South Sea Company investors who had previously supported one or other of the earlier bank schemes, like Viscount Molesworth, would have been unable to meet the cost of a bank subscription in October 1721, although it is impossible to know how many would have fitted into this category.

V

The resilience of the Irish investing public in 1720, both of those who invested in London, and of those who chose to speculate elsewhere, is, however, demonstrated by the 209 individuals who were prepared to subscribe to the national bank in October 1721. Their subscriptions suggest a continued interest in financial innovation, and indicate that the impact of the South Sea bubble whether on individual pockets, financial sentiment, or on the

---

[60] Hercules Rowley, *An Answer to a Book Intitled Reasons Offered for Erecting a Bank in Ireland in a Letter to Henry Maxwell Esquire* (Dublin, 1721).

[61] Michael Ward to James Trail, 9 Jan. 1720 (PRONI, T3041/1/C/3).

[62] For Dobbs see Eoin Magennis, 'Dobbs, Arthur (1689–1765)', in *DIB*. Dobbs describes the impact of the South Sea bubble on Ireland in *An Essay on the Trade and Improvement of Ireland* (Dublin, 1729), p. 10. For Wynne and Maynard, who was also revenue collector at Cork, see *HIP*, vol. 5, p. 233 and vol. 6, pp. 562–3.

local economic and financial structures, was not quite as all-encompassing as some contemporaries suggested. Nevertheless the bank project failed to materialize: the proposal was defeated following an intensive parliamentary and extra-parliamentary debate over its merits. This debate and its contexts reveal another dimension to the impact of the London stock-market crash on Ireland, and they are the focus of the final chapter.

8

'A Strong Presumption That This Bank May be a Bubble': Misreading the Bubble and the Bank of Ireland Debates, 1721

In September 1721 the Irish parliament sat for the first time in almost two years. Much had changed since its last meeting. The passage of the Declaratory Act at Westminster in April 1720 had seen the British parliament reassert its legislative and constitutional superiority over its Irish counterpart. The South Sea bubble had also burst with consequences for British and Irish politics. In London, the political fallout that followed the stock-market crash had led to a changing of the guard at the apex of British politics with Sir Robert Walpole successfully manipulating the crisis to establish himself as *de facto* prime minister;[1] his rise to power would have important consequences for the government of Ireland. However, the immediate political impact of the crash in Dublin was its effect on the proposal for a national bank.[2] Parliamentary approval was needed for the bank charter which had been drawn up in London in July 1721 and the debates over this charter would dominate the parliamentary session that opened in September. These debates were partly informed by political rivalries and the influence of vested interests, but crucially they were also dictated by reactions to, and misreading of, the South Sea crash. This was clear from the views expressed in the House of Commons, and importantly also in the voluminous pamphlet material concerning the arguments over the bank that were produced in the extra-parliamentary public sphere. The language and vocabulary used in both London and Paris could be just as contagious as the financial effects of the stock-market crash. Considering these Irish debates, this chapter offers a new perspective on the political, cultural and literary responses to the bubble, showing how quickly what Hoppit has termed the 'myths of the South Sea bubble' were established.

The debates over the bank have been much studied by historians and literary scholars, eager to disentangle what is a well-documented, if complicated and knotty problem. For historians of high politics, the bank episode

---

[1] John Carswell, *The South Sea Bubble* (London, 1960), pp. 226–64; and Julian Hoppit, *A Land of Liberty? England 1689–1727* (Oxford, 2000), pp. 403–7.
[2] D. W. Hayton, *Ruling Ireland, 1685–1742: Politics, Politicians and Parties* (Woodbridge, 2004), pp. 237–75.

offers a window into the increasingly fractious disputes between the leading
figures on the Irish scene – Speaker Conolly and Lord Chancellor Midleton
– while the surviving division lists (rare in an Irish context) have been much
mined for evidence of political and ideological allegiances in the House
of Commons.[3] Meanwhile, the magnetic presence of Jonathan Swift has
drawn other scholars towards the extra-parliamentary debates on the bank.[4]
Michael Ryder, in the best account of the episode, has nonetheless demonstrated how the influence of the dean has been overstated and has shown
that many of the pamphlets have been mistakenly attributed to Swift.[5]

Instead Ryder has argued that the bank was defeated because of widespread
fears that a national bank would be 'corrosive of the political society and
values of the country gentry' in its own right.[6] This 'court' versus 'country'
argument, while useful does not fully explain the apparent volte-face in
attitudes to the bank over the last four months of 1721. More recently, in
an innovative and thought-provoking study, Sean Moore has returned to
Swift, reassessing his printed contributions and seeing his objections to the
bank not as an anti-modern crusade against paper credit but rather as a
critique of the bank project as the best way to remedy Ireland's economic
woes in the wake of the South Sea bubble.[7] Moore's work has situated the
bank debates more firmly in the context of the aftermath of the London
crash, but the particular focus of his study has meant that the impact of the
'fall of the stocks' on the attitudes of a wider section of Irish public opinion
remains to be fully elucidated. This chapter argues that the influence of the
bubble was central to the framing of the debates around the bank and that
these debates in turn allow us to appreciate how the bubble was understood
or indeed misunderstood in Dublin. Before looking at the pamphlet debates

[3]   R. E. Burns, *Irish Parliamentary Politics in the Eighteenth Century*, 2 vols (Washington,
1989–90), vol. 1, pp. 113–33; also D. W. Hayton, *The Anglo-Irish Experience, 1680–1730:
Religion, Identity and Patriotism* (Woodbridge, 2012), pp. 114–16; C. I. McGrath, '"The
Public Wealth is the Sinew, the Life, of Every Public Measure": The Creation and
Maintenance of a National Debt in Ireland, 1716–45', in *The Empire of Credit: The
Financial Revolution in Britain, Ireland and America, 1688–1815*, ed. Daniel Carey and
Christopher Finlay (Dublin, 2011), pp. 171–208; and Patrick Walsh, *The Making of the
Irish Protestant Ascendancy: The Life of William Conolly, 1662–1729* (Woodbridge, 2010),
pp. 170–2.
[4]   See for example, J. M. Hone, 'Berkeley and Swift as National Economists', *Studies*,
23 (1934), 421–32; and Oliver Ferguson, *Jonathan Swift and Ireland* (Urbana, IL, 1962),
pp. 60–75.
[5]   Michael Ryder, 'The Bank of Ireland, 1721: Land, Credit and Dependency', *Historical
Journal*, 25 (1982), 557–82.
[6]   Ryder, pp. 563–4.
[7]   Sean D. Moore, 'Satiric Norms, Swift's Financial Satires and the Bank of Ireland
Controversy of 1720–1', *Eighteenth-Century Ireland*, 17 (2002), 26–56. See also Moore's
Swift, The Book, and the Irish Financial Revolution: Satire and Sovereignty in Colonial Ireland
(Baltimore, 2010), esp. pp. 59–89.

over the bank it is first necessary to examine the trajectory of the bank question through parliament.

In late July 1721 the British Privy Council granted Lord Abercorn and his fellow bank promoters a royal charter for twelve years, subject to the approval of the Irish parliament. This act of parliament was seen as necessary by the Lords of the Treasury so as to:

> prevent the bank borrowing beyond its capital, and to make members personally liable if capital fell below debts and to exempt them from becoming bankrupts; to protect members' private property against corporation forfeitures as in the Bank of England; to make sealed bills assignable by endorsement and to make the counterfeiting of these and of cash notes a felony; and to avoid transfers of stock not registered in the bank's books within a certain time to prevent stockjobbing.[8]

This last reason proffered by the Treasury Lords hints perhaps at the impact of the bubble, although much of their advice followed contemporary practice in terms of incorporating a major new company.[9] The necessity for a charter and the prospect of further delays caused some impatient grumbles among the bank promoters, but there was little they could do about it.[10] It had taken approximately fifteen months to get this far, and the story was not yet finished.

The lord lieutenant, the Duke of Grafton, in his speech opening the new parliamentary session in 1721, informed the assembled legislators that 'His Majesty leaves it to the wisdom of the parliament to consider what advantages the public may receive by the erecting a bank and in what means it may be settled upon a safe foundation so as to be beneficial to the kingdom'.[11] The bank charter was now firmly on the Dublin political agenda. It remained to be seen, however, how well disposed Irish parliamentarians were to the idea of a national bank. Many of them had subscribed to the two bank proposals floated in early summer 1720, but the political and, also crucially, the economic circumstances of the kingdom had changed dramatically in the intervening period. It was therefore inevitable that some members of both the Commons and the Lords were going to be sceptical of the merits of an innovatory project like a bank. Bishop William Nicolson, in a letter anticipating the opening of the new session, explicitly linked the bank's prospects to the recent experience of the South Sea crash:

> One of the first matters that is likely to fall under consideration in both houses is the ratification of letters patent which are said to have been lately granted for the

---

8   Ryder, p. 563.
9   Mark Freeman, Robin Pearson and James Taylor, *Shareholder Democracies? Corporate Governance in Britain and Ireland before 1850* (Chicago, 2012), pp. 39–46.
10   Michael Ward to John Irwin, 11 and 23 May 1721, printed in F. G. Hall, *The Bank of Ireland, 1783–1946* (Dublin, 1949), pp. 372–3.
11   *CJI*, vol. 3, p. 249.

erecting of a new bank in this kingdom where so many have lately perished in the South Sea, that few are left among us that have any great stomach of launching any more into such dangerous gulfs.[12]

Nicolson had of course incurred some personal losses during the bubble, and he was also particularly attuned to the economic impact of the London crash on his diocese in Derry. However, he was not alone in doubting the appetite for the bank among the assembled MPs and peers. Both George Berkeley and Philip Perceval in their letters to Lord Perceval forecast that the bank charter would be lucky to pass through the Commons and that it would fail either in the House of Lords or at the Irish Privy Council. They saw little unity among MPs on the issue, and therefore little incentive for the lord lieutenant to push the issue too hard.[13] Circumstances would show that their political antennae in this instance were correctly tuned.

The proposed legislation for establishing the bank by an act of parliament was introduced into the House of Commons on 25 September 1721. Proposed by the chief secretary, Edward Hopkins, it immediately met with some opposition. In speeches railing against the proposed bank, the MPs Clotworthy Upton and Henry Maxwell declared it would 'ruin the kingdom' and compared it to the Mississippi and South Sea schemes. They went on to suggest that the list of subscribers should be published to show that the bank's only supporters in parliament were those with a financial interest in the project. Their contributions were countered by a 'violent' speech from St John Brodrick, who had previously been nominated as one of the putative directors of the proposed Abercorn bank in 1720, defending the integrity of the bank's supporters.[14] On this occasion the bank's supporters carried the day, winning out seventy-three votes to forty-seven on a division to consider the matter further in a committee of the whole house.[15] This committee reported back three days later and recommended that a bank established 'upon a solid and good foundation' would 'greatly contribute to the restoring of credit and support the trade and commerce of the kingdom'.[16]

The next stage in the process was to prepare the heads of a bill laying

---

[12] William Nicolson to William Wake, 15 Aug. 1721 (BL, Add MS 6116, fol. 110).
[13] Philip Perceval to John, Lord Perceval, 5 Oct. 1721; and George Berkeley to Lord Perceval, 21 Oct. 1721 (BL, Add MS 47029, fols 140 and 142–3).
[14] Sir Richard Levinge to Edward Southwell, 25 Sep. 1721, in Sir Richard G. A. Levinge, *Jottings of the Levinge Family* (Dublin, 1857), p. 64. See also Hayton, *Anglo-Irish Experience*, p. 114. Maxwell would emerge as the leading supporter of the bank, writing two influential pamphlets in its favour. The inconsistencies between his spoken and written statements on the bank have been attributed by David Hayton to the exigencies of party politics, although doubts must also remain about the accuracy of Levinge's report, his being the only source for this seemingly contradictory speech of September 1721.
[15] Ryder, p. 564.
[16] *CJI*, vol. 3, p. 258.

out the draft legislation for parliamentary scrutiny. This was duly done, and the 'heads' were introduced into the Commons on 7 October and scheduled for debate a week later, on 14 October, to determine the future prospects of the project.[17] The debate focused on the first paragraph of the proposed legislation, which declared that 'a bank on a solid foundation would be beneficial to the Kingdom', and contemporary reports describe rather heated exchanges in front of a crowded house and public gallery.[18] According to Bishop Nicolson, the bank's supporters, led by St John Brodrick, were very confident of success and described the 'great advantages' that 'Venice, Genoa and Amsterdam had gained by such expedients', noting that it was hoped that Ireland would likewise reap the same benefits.[19] Not everyone was convinced of these arguments. Drawing on rather different international precedents, the bank's opponents compared it both to the South Sea Company, and to the ill-fated Company of Scotland.

They described how it was no coincidence that the three proposals for a national bank appeared when the 'South Sea was in its most flourishing state', arguing that 'every director here promised himself as fair a fortune as any man of his denomination had met in Exchange Alley'.[20] Such statements linking the directors of the proposed bank to the now disgraced directors of the South Sea Company were designed to inflame opinion against the bank, regardless of the veracity of such connections. Moving on to counter the favourable comparisons drawn between the proposed Irish bank and those in Italy and the Netherlands, the bank's opponents pointed to the constitutional differences between Ireland and those 'free and independent commonwealths'. Here the example of the Scottish misfortunes in the 1690s was employed. The bank projectors were advised to consider the fate of the 'adventurers of Darien', who though possessing an 'irrecoverable' charter, found it dissolved by royal proclamation when their interests in the West Indies threatened those of the great merchants of London.[21] A similar fate, it was warned, would befall the directors of the Irish bank if they met with any real success in their venture.

These pessimistic and somewhat distorted claims about the bank's purpose and potential fate met with support in parliament when a vote was called on this clause: MPs voted by a majority of eight votes, 102 to ninety-four, to throw out the bill.[22] This caused some surprise among those watching the

---

17 Ryder, p. 565.
18 Alan Brodrick, 1st Viscount Midleton to Thomas Brodrick, 14 Oct. 1721 (SHC, MS 1248/5, fols 97–8). For the heated debate see Philip Perceval to Lord Perceval, 16 Oct. 1721 (BL, Add MS 47029, fol. 146), where he describes it from his position in the packed public gallery, where 'everyone needed no bagnio to sweat'.
19 Nicolson to Wake, 21 Oct. 1721 (BL, Add MS 6116, fol. 115).
20 Nicolson to Wake, 21 Oct. 1721.
21 Nicolson to Wake, 21 Oct. 1721.
22 CJI, vol. 3, p. 262.

debate from the public gallery while attempts were also made by the bank's advocates to rescue the situation. A second vote was called suggesting that the proposals be revisited the following week, but the bill's opponents countered this by proposing that the discussion be delayed for two months. This latter measure was carried by ninety-eight votes to ninety-one and was recognized as effectively killing off the bill, with one bank supporter describing how the bank 'though zealously sought for' had been 'hissed out'.[23] It was assumed that the two-month delay would mean it would not be raised again in that parliamentary session, a well-known political tactic.[24] For opponents of the scheme, the possible 'enslavement' of Ireland had been avoided.[25]

The reasons for the bank's parliamentary defeat have been much debated. Some contemporaries blamed the 'violence' of language used by the bank's proponents for its miscarriage, while others pointed to the covert influence of Dublin's private bankers who stood to lose out if the current legal interest rate of 8% was lowered to the bank's proposed 5%.[26] Some modern historians have also highlighted the influence of factional rivalries between different groups of MPs, although disentangling the voting patterns of the different blocs of MPs on this issue is extremely complicated, with the usual Conolly versus Midleton lines somewhat blurred.[27] St John Brodrick, for instance, was a prime advocate for the bank, possibly the leading voice on that side and certainly the loudest, if Sir Richard Levinge's written reports of the debates are to be believed.[28] However, Brodrick's father, Viscount Midleton, was actively canvassing for its defeat, although many of his allies, including, of course, his own son, appeared among the bank's supporters when the vote was called.[29] The influence of the comparisons made between the bank and the South Sea Company should not be discounted either.[30] It is clear that they were an important feature of the speeches made for and against the bank, and it would be strange if they had no impact on the assembled listeners.

While many contemporaries were convinced that the vote on 14 October spelled the end of the scheme, the bank's promoters and supporters had other ideas. They were not prepared to give up so easily after all the effort they had expended soliciting first for subscribers, and then for a charter. Aware that many of the original subscribers had withdrawn their support for the project,

---

23 Thomas Medlycott to Edward Southwell, 19 Oct. 1721, quoted in Ryder, p. 565.
24 Levinge to Southwell, 14 Oct. 1721, in Levinge, p. 69.
25 Midleton to Thomas Brodrick, 11 Oct. 1721 (SHC, MS 1248/5, fols 95–6).
26 Levinge to Southwell, 14 Oct. 1721, in Levinge, p. 69.
27 Burns, vol. 1, pp. 120–3; and Hayton, *The Anglo-Irish Experience*, p. 114–15.
28 Levinge to Southwell, 25 Sept and 14 Oct. 1721, in Levinge, p. 69. In the first of these letters he suggested such was the violence of Brodrick's language, he was surprised that his opponents did not challenge him to a duel.
29 Midleton to Thomas Brodrick, 11 and 14 Oct. 1721 (SHC, MS 1248/5, fols 95–8).
30 McGrath, 'Public Wealth is the Sinew', pp. 188–9.

they reopened their subscription list. Within this context it is worth noting that twenty-three of the forty-eight MPs who had subscribed to the original Abercorn list, and twenty-nine of the forty-four MPs who had subscribed to the Forbes list in early summer 1720, had voted against the bank.[31] This new call for subscribers was published by 28 October, and was met with some enthusiasm.[32] A total of 209 subscribers entered their names, many of them appearing on a bank list for the first time (see table 7.3). In an attempt to boost their political support, efforts were made to convince the hugely influential Speaker Conolly to add his name to the subscription list, but these failed, much to the disappointment of the bank's promoters, who were still led by Lord Abercorn.[33]

The success of this renewed subscription, even as Swift and others mocked it in the press, meant that the bank question was still very much on the political agenda.[34] The project's advocates continued to muster support in both houses of parliament.[35] In the Commons, a motion was passed expressing thanks to Conolly and Midleton for their original favourable report on the bank proposal, made in the previous January. This motion's successful passage was helped by the absence of many of the bank's opponents who had not expected such a measure to be presented that day, and had therefore retired to the country. Such clever political strategizing was not going to be of much use in the House of Lords, where the opponents of the bank had a much larger majority. Led by Lord Chancellor Midleton, who made a speech stressing the dangers of stockjobbing in a clear reference to the perceived ills of the South Sea Company, the lords condemned the bank as a threat to the nation.[36] The only dissenters were six peers who had previously subscribed to the bank: lords Abercorn, Boyne, Limerick and Ferrard, and the bishops of Dromore and Down.[37] The two houses of parliament now seemed to be on a collision course over the bank question, with the pro-bank lobby in the Commons becoming more emboldened. Rumours were rife that two of Speaker Conolly's close associates, Henry Maxwell and the Revd William Gore, the speaker's chaplain, were dispatched to meet MPs in a tavern to

---

[31] Calculated from their individual entries in *HIP*, vol. 4, pp. 76–7 and vol. 6, p. 321. One MP on the Abercorn list, Samuel Dopping, and one on the Forbes list, James Stannus, had died in the period between their subscriptions and the vote.

[32] Levinge to Southwell, 28 Oct. 1721, in Levinge, p. 73; and Ryder, p. 566.

[33] Levinge to Southwell, 11 Nov. 1721, in Levinge, p. 77.

[34] Jonathan Swift, *Subscribers to the Bank Plac'd according to Their Order and Quality. With Notes and Queries* (Dublin, 1721), printed in *Prose Works*, ed. Herbert Davis, 14 vols (Oxford, 1939–68), vol. 9, pp. 288–90. See also extracts appended to Lord Perceval to Philip Perceval, 11 Nov. 1721 (BL, Add MS 47029, fols 176–7).

[35] Nicolson to Wake, 9 Nov. 1721 (BL, Add MS 6116, fol. 117); and Midleton to Thomas Brodrick, 5 Nov. 1721 (SHC, MS 1248/5, fols 107–8).

[36] Ryder, p. 566.

[37] Lords division list in Midleton to Brodrick, 9 Nov. 1721 (SHC, MS 1248/5, fol. 129).

'proselytise' on behalf of the bank among its former opponents.[38] It was time for the lord lieutenant to intervene, and on 11 November Grafton called for parliament to be adjourned until the beginning of December.[39]

This adjournment, intended to lower the temperature in parliament, did not mean an end to the debate. Instead it changed location. Ryder has pointed out how much of the pamphlet literature on the subject (discussed below) was published during this period taking the debate out-of-doors, where the bank's promoters continued to stoke the flames of public and parliamentary opinion.[40] This could be clearly seen when on 20 November, having completed their latest subscription, they again elected their directors with Lord Abercorn once more being nominated as governor.[41] A week later the bank's directors, perhaps hoping to bypass the Commons, petitioned the lord lieutenant for their charter but were told to wait until parliament met again. This it did on 9 December, and there it dealt the final 'deathstroke' to the bank with the Commons voting 150 to eighty to reject the project.[42] Two days later they passed a motion declaring that 'erecting a bank would be of the most dangerous and fatal consequence to His Majesty's service, and the trade and liberties of this nation'. Furthermore they declared that any person soliciting for a bank in the future would be regarded as 'an enemy of the country'.[43] The lords expressed similar sentiments when it convened later in the month. The bank proposals had been roundly defeated and the promoters began to return the subscriptions that had been paid in, keeping sixpence in the pound to cover expenses incurred.[44] The reasons why the bank was finally defeated are complex. Political machinations undoubtedly played a part with both Conolly and Midleton using the debates for their own ends in their never-ending battle for political supremacy in Ireland.[45] There was, however, more involved than that alone, with the paper war that raged in parallel with the parliamentary session revealing the persistent use of language and arguments borrowed and bowdlerized from the debates over the demise of the South Sea Company. These arguments are the focus of the next section.

---

[38] Midleton to Brodrick, 11 Nov. 1721 (SHC, MS 1248/5, fol. 130).
[39] The motivations of the principal political players at this point – Conolly, Midleton and Grafton – are somewhat disputed in the historiography: see Hayton, *Anglo-Irish Experience*, pp. 114–15; Ryder, pp. 567–9; and Walsh, *Making of the Irish Protestant Ascendancy*, pp. 171–2.
[40] Ryder, p. 567.
[41] Nicolson to Wake, 21 Nov. 1721 (BL, Add MS 6116, fol. 118).
[42] Nicolson to Wake, 9 Dec. 1721 (BL, Add MS 6116, fol. 119).
[43] Quoted in Ryder, p. 569.
[44] Levinge to Southwell, 23 Dec. 1721, in Levinge, p. 80.
[45] Hayton, *Ruling Ireland*, pp. 232–3; and Walsh, *Making of the Irish Protestant Ascendancy*, p. 172.

I

For many contemporaries the Irish national bank and South Sea schemes were inextricably linked. They had risen together in the late spring and early summer of 1720, cresting on the same wave of financial optimism. The bank's parliamentary denouement in the autumn and winter of 1721, meanwhile, came at the same time as the British state was attempting to 'financially reconstruct itself' in the aftermath of the crisis of the previous year.[46] This context, Sean Moore has persuasively argued, is essential to any understanding of the bank scheme, and its unravelling. The comparisons with the South Sea scheme were there from the very beginning. In their initial promotional flurry in May 1720, as shown in chapter 6, the bank's projectors had stressed what they perceived as the pernicious influence of the Mississippi and South Sea schemes while simultaneously declaring that their project was very different. Despite considerable evidence to support their position, not all of their contemporaries were convinced and such misconceptions would continue to dog the project right through to its final moments. Indeed John Irwin, reflecting on the debates over the bank at the very end of 1721, described how the manipulation of the 'havock made by the Mississippi and the South Sea by which they have infused such fears, jealousies and prejudices against a bank' had rendered 'such a design ineffectual'.[47] He clearly held the perceived links between the bank and the South Sea scheme responsible for the former's demise. We have seen how the example of the London crash was used in parliamentary debates to object to the bank, but how were such arguments employed in the printed debates going on outside the walls of the Dublin parliament?

The final four months of 1721 saw an unprecedented level of political pamphleteering in Dublin, with more than a dozen pamphlets and poems published as both pro and anti-bank writers put pen to paper to explain their position. These printed debates marked a new departure in Irish politics, and have been seen together with the more famous debates on the so-called 'Wood's Halfpence' controversy in 1723–25 as central to the creation of an Irish public sphere.[48] The contributors to these debates included experienced political writers like the MP Henry Maxwell, who was also the author of a

---

46 Moore, 'Satiric Norms', p. 50.
47 John Irwin, *The Phoenix, or a New Scheme for Establishing Credit on the Most Solid and Satisfactory Foundation and Entirely Free From All the Objections Made to the Late Intended Bank* (Dublin, 1721), p. 4.
48 Moore, *Swift, The Book and the Irish Financial Revolution*, pp. 59–89. On the debates around Wood's halfpence see Sabine Baltes, *The Pamphlet Controversy about Wood's Halfpence (1722–25) and the Tradition of Irish Constitutional Nationalism* (Frankfurt, 2003); Albert Goodwin, 'Wood's Halfpence', *English Historical Review*, 51 (1936), 647–74; and Patrick McNally, 'Wood's Halfpence, Carteret and the Government of Ireland, 1723–26', *Irish Historical Studies*, 30 (1997), 354–76.

famous 1703 pamphlet advocating an Anglo-Irish political union, Francis
Hutchinson, Bishop of Down, and of course Jonathan Swift, as well as
novice writers like Maxwell's uncle Hercules Rowley, an Irish MP himself,
together with a number of anonymous authors. Their respective arguments
focused on a small number of key issues, including reflections on the utility
of banks, Ireland's constitutional status, and fears about the potential for the
bank to achieve a position of dominance in Irish political and financial life.[49]
This last theme – fears about the oligarchic nature of the proposed bank –
reflected some of the concerns raised about the South Sea Company during
its emergence as the British government's greatest creditor in early 1720. It
was not the only echo of the debates surrounding the South Sea Company
heard in Dublin at this time.

'The general and popular argument against the bank is that it may become
a bubble.'[50] So wrote one anonymous defender of the bank in a pamphlet
in November 1721 after discussing the individual arguments put up against
the scheme both inside and outside parliament.[51] The general tenor of these
arguments, the unknown author stated, was that although the proponents
of the bank claimed that their scheme was advantageous to the public, the
reality was that they were actually delusional, and that the bank would lead
to the 'same misfortunes we have lately seen England, France, and Holland
drawn into by their South Sea, Mississippi Company and insurance offices'.[52]
However, the bank project and these 'wicked schemes', he argued, were not
parallel cases. Instead the bank was modelled on the successful English and
Dutch banks, which had provided 'effective remedies to their recent evils'.[53]
This particular pamphlet, written towards the end of the political dispute,
demonstrates how misconceptions about the bank's structural similarities to
the South Sea Company were widespread within contemporary debate.

Both sides sought to use the rise and fall of the South Sea Company's
fortunes to bolster their arguments. Henry Maxwell, author of one of the
most cogent and sophisticated pamphlets in the project's favour and a reprise
of John Irwin's arguments fifteen months earlier, used the outflow of Irish
capital to Exchange Alley and the consequent decline in the balance of
trade to illustrate the necessity for founding a bank. Maxwell also drew
attention to the salutary lessons that could be learned from the South Sea

---

[49] For a detailed analysis of these and other themes found in the bank literature see
Ryder, pp. 570–82.
[50] Anon., *Remarks on Mr Maxwell's and Mr Rowley's Letters: Setting Forth the Advantages
of a Bank and Lumbards in Ireland, in a Letter to a Friend* (Dublin, 1721), p. 4.
[51] He was responding to Henry Maxwell, *Reasons Offer'd for Erecting a Bank in Ireland;
in a Letter to Hercules Rowley, Esq* (Dublin, 1721), and Hercules Rowley, *An Answer to
a Book Intitled Reasons Offered for Erecting a Bank in Ireland in a Letter to Henry Maxwell
Esquire* (Dublin, 1721).
[52] Anon., *Remarks on Mr Maxwell's and Mr Rowley's Letters*, p. 4.
[53] Anon., *Remarks on Mr Maxwell's and Mr Rowley's Letters*, p. 5.

Company's fall from grace. He argued that the imposition of limits on transferring bank stock, except in the case of death, would prevent the 'vile trade of stock-jobbing', and he further suggested that if such restrictions had been in place in the South Sea Company that 'they would never have done mischief in England'.[54] Maxwell, according to Richard Levinge, had made similar statements condemning the company in the House of Commons, although as already noted he was also reported to have declared the national bank scheme 'ruinous to the kingdom', a statement that contradicted his later written opinions.[55]

Other contributors to the printed debate played up the coincidence of the timing of the bank projects and the South Sea Company's rise to prominence. One anonymous author asked, 'Is not the first setting up of the bank on foot in May 1720 by a person of no fortune or interest in Ireland, and in the season of bubbles when the South Sea was at high tide a strong presumption that this bank may be a bubble?'[56] Similar statements were also made in parliament leading one pro-bank writer, Bishop Francis Hutchinson of Down, to describe it as a misfortune that the bank had risen at a time 'when men's heads were indeed set upon bubbles'. This caused two problems, the first being the negative connotations associated with the South Sea Company after the crash, and the second that 'many still flattered themselves with over great hopes from it with wrong mistaken arguments'. For some misguided advocates of the bank, in Hutchinson's eyes at least, its attraction was the possibility that it would actually be a 'bubble'. He, however, regarded these beliefs as equal to the objections to the bank raised by its opponents, seeing them as mostly 'chimerical'.[57]

The most substantive contributions to the pamphlet debate were made by Henry Maxwell and by his uncle Hercules Rowley, MP for County Londonderry.[58] Maxwell's initial pamphlet took the form of a printed letter, a standard contemporary stylistic convention, addressed to Rowley and was almost certainly printed at the beginning of the parliamentary session in September. In it, Maxwell described the advantages of the bank in great detail, highlighting particularly the benefits of a low rate of interest, using the printed works of contemporary political economists like William Petty, Josiah Child and Charles Davenant to advance his argument.[59] In response Rowley,

---

54 Maxwell, *Reasons Offer'd for Erecting a Bank in Ireland*, p. 7.

55 Hayton, *Anglo-Irish Experience*, p. 114.

56 Anon., *A Strange Collection of Maybes Fully Answered and Cleared Up By a Subscriber and Well Wisher to the Bank* (Dublin, 1721).

57 Francis Hutchinson, *A Letter to the Gentlemen of the Landed Interest in Ireland Relating to a Bank* (Dublin, 1721), p. 4.

58 For Rowley see his entry in *HIP*, vol. 6, p. 196.

59 Maxwell, *Reasons Offer'd for Erecting a Bank in Ireland*, pp. 18, 20, 41 and 43. The works he cites are William Petty's *Political Anatomy of Ireland* (1718 edition), Sir Josiah Child's *A New Discourse of Trade* (n.d.) and Charles Davenant's *Essay on Ways and Means* (n.d.).

writing as the voice of country gentlemen in parliament, acknowledged that he could find little fault with the superstructure of the bank but that he still had reason to oppose it. Among his reasons were scepticism about the advantages of low interest rates, abhorrence of luxury, worries about the potential political power of the bankers, and fears that Catholics would gain a foothold in the bank.[60] These were all typical 'country' arguments against banks, and echoed the English critiques of the Bank of England of the 1690s.[61] Adding a contemporary flavour to these objections, he expressed a fear that the directors would be corruptible, and that there was a likelihood of an Irish Mr Knight, running off with the bank holdings to Antwerp.[62] These were clear allusions to the South Sea Company, with 'Mr Knight' being the company's cashier who had fled to the Continent, probably with the British government's connivance, following the collapse of the bubble.[63] Another respondent to Maxwell was more direct in his international comparisons, describing in somewhat indecorous language that this 'pernicious bank is a bastard by Law got by one Mississippi on the body of a South Sea whore'.[64]

In his published response, Maxwell rebutted all of Rowley's claims, pointing out that the latter's worries about paper credit could be countered by the (exaggerated) fact that up to £600,000 worth of banker's notes already circulated in Ireland. He took particular care to dismiss the comparisons made with the South Sea Company, reassuring his readers that there could be no Irish Mr Knight because of the strict operating rules as stipulated in the bank's Treasury-approved charter. Furthermore, Maxwell explained, the structure of the South Sea Company's subscriptions was quite different from those of the bank 'for a thousand pound given for a hundred pound capital was a profit so immense that they were able to make princely fortunes all at once; and in this case they had no regard to the future dividends of the company or the prospect of their trade'.[65] This could be seen as further demonstrating his suspicion of stockjobbing or trading in bank shares in a secondary market, while also distancing the bank from such practices. It also, of course, reflected contemporary misunderstandings of the South Sea Company's trading prospects, a myth that has been comprehensively debunked by modern historians.[66] He concluded this section with the statement that 'it

[60] Rowley, *An Answer to a Book Intitled Reasons Offered for Erecting a Bank in Ireland*.

[61] Ryder, p. 571.

[62] Rowley, *An Answer to a Book Intitled Reasons Offered for Erecting a Bank in Ireland*.

[63] Carswell, pp. 224–5.

[64] Anon., *Letter to Henry Maxwell: Plainly Showing the Great Danger that the Kingdom has Escaped and the Great Inconveniences that Must of Necessity Have Happened if the Bank had been Established* (Dublin, 1721), p. 16.

[65] Henry Maxwell, *Mr Maxwell's Second Letter to Mr Rowley: Wherein the Objections Against the Bank are Answered* (Dublin, 1721), p. 14.

[66] H. J. Paul, *The South Sea Bubble: An Economic History of its Origins and Consequences* (London, 2010), pp. 54–65.

was as easy to make the poles meet as it was to draw a parallel between the bank and the South Sea Company'.[67] Maxwell's continued need to reinforce this point emphasizes the association that was being made between the bank and the South Sea Company, showing the extent to which reports of the crash in London had impacted on the opinions of the Dublin elite.

This was clear not just from the references made in pamphlets on the bank, but also in contemporary private correspondence, as well as through the republication in Dublin of material that had originated in London during the bubble. These included an Irish imprint of Swift's poem *The Bubble*, itself first published in London, as well as cautionary tales such as the anonymous *A letter from a Gentleman in the Country to a Member of Parliament in England*, which detailed a by then already stereotypical bubble-induced rise and fall in fortune.[68] Swift himself, of course, intervened in the debates on the bank, publishing a number of works of both prose and poetry on the subject.[69] The most significant of these was his *Subscribers Placed in Their Order and Quality with Notes and Queries*, with its famous breakdown of the bank's subscription list, and its attacks on the Huguenot or 'French' interest among the subscribers. Its xenophobia was not unique and indeed echoed some of the language employed by Rowley as well as the anti-Catholic rhetoric of the anonymous author, possibly Swift, of *The Swearer's Bank, or Parliamentary Security for a New Bank*.[70] Swift's printed interventions in the bank debate made little direct reference to the South Sea scheme. Two of his poems on the subject, *The Wonderful Wonder of Wonders* and *The Wonder of All the Wonders That Ever the World Wondered At*, did critique paper credit or 'air money' and should, therefore, be seen as responses to the broader financial climate that spawned both the South Sea Company and the bank.[71] His final contributions to the subject, *An Account of the Short Life, Sudden Death and Pompous Funeral of Michy Windybank, Only Child to Sir Oliver Windybank*, and *The Bank Thrown Down*, were instead preoccupied with expressing glee at the fate of the bank's directors.[72]

The focus on indigenous factors and circumstances in Swift's writings warn us of the dangers of looking for the bubble within every contemporary commentary on the bank. Nevertheless, it is clear from a survey of the surviving printed works that the fate of the South Sea Company cast a long shadow and dictated the terms of the debate, with the bank being seen either

[67] Maxwell, *Second Letter to Mr Rowley*, p. 14.
[68] Anon., *A Letter from a Gentleman in the Country to a Member of Parliament in England* (Dublin, 1721).
[69] Moore, *Swift, The Book and the Irish Financial Revolution*, pp. 77–8.
[70] Moore, *Swift, The Book and the Irish Financial Revolution*, p. 79, where Moore dismisses some modern scholars' attribution of this pamphlet to Swift.
[71] Moore, *Swift, The Book and the Irish Financial Revolution*, p. 78.
[72] Jonathan Swift, *Poems*, ed. Harold Williams, 3 vols (Oxford, 1958), vol. 1, pp. 286–8.

as a panacea to, or a symptom of, the monetary situation created by events in London. The experiences of Irish investors in London and the press reports emanating from the English capital hardened existing attitudes against 'stock-jobbing', allowing this somewhat peripheral issue to feature heavily in the parliamentary and extra-parliamentary debates and divert attention from the bank's fundamentals.[73] Similarly, the exposure of the corrupt practices of the South Sea Company directors in the comprehensively reported and well-publicized parliamentary investigations of 1721 created suspicions among the bank's opponents about the potential power of that institution's prospective directors.[74] Fears were expressed about their possible control of future parliamentary elections, again something that owed much to English commentaries on the South Sea Company.[75] Such Irish concerns owed their genesis not only to contemporary readings of the London bubble but also, even if to a much lesser extent, the Parisian one too. Some objections were based on fact while others were misjudged and reflected the tendency recognized by one contemporary author to 'call all public projects in South Sea time by the odious name of bubbles'.[76] Whatever the truth of this, it is clear that the bursting of the South Sea bubble had a significant and detrimental impact on the debates surrounding the Irish bank.

II

The failure of the national bank proposals had important consequences. In the short term, the bank's promoters suffered a blow to their reputation, while the individual subscribers had to bear a very small financial loss. Much greater, however, were the repercussions in the medium and long term. The tone and sentiment of the resolutions issued by both houses of parliament decrying any future bank projects cast a long shadow over future attempts at domestic financial innovation. This could be seen in the stillborn proposals for a new scheme of public credit proposed by John Irwin, the original bank

---

[73] See Anon., *A Strange Collection of Maybes*, p. 1.

[74] For the spread of news of the these investigations see the following local reprints: John Aislabie, *The Speech of the Right Honourable John Aislabie, Esq; upon his Defence made in the House of Lords Against the Bill for Raising Money Upon the Estates of the South-Sea Directors, on Wednesday the 19th of July 1721* (Dublin, 1721); and Anon., *The Nation Preserved; Or, the Plot Discover'd Containing an Impartial Account of the Secret Policy of Some of the South-Sea Directors; With Copies of Their Letters to Each Other; and the Substance of their Debates in Several of Their Private Conferences Taken Before a Notary-Publick* (Dublin, 1721).

[75] Anon., *A Letter to a Member of Parliament Concerning the Late Bank* (Dublin, 1721), p. 22; and Patriophilus Misoletes, *Objections Against the General Bank in Ireland* (Dublin, 1721), p. 3. For such English concerns, see Anon., *Index Rerum & Vocabulorum For the Use of Freeholders of Counties and Freemen of Corporations* (London, 1722).

[76] Anon., *A Strange Collection of Maybes*, p. 2.

projector, at the end of 1721. In his optimistically titled pamphlet *The Phoenix, or a New Scheme for Establishing Credit*, he not only acknowledged, as discussed earlier, the negative influence of the South Sea bubble on the bank's failure, but also other contemporary criticisms of the project.[77]

These concerns included those raised about the reduction in the legal rate of interest, and its impact on existing lenders. Irwin's *New Scheme* proposed a rate of 6%, a marginally higher rate than previously promised by any of the bank schemes, in an attempt to placate the local banking lobby, whose hostility to lower rates was alleged to have contributed to the failure of the national bank proposals.[78] In this context it is worth noting that the four Dublin bankers who sat in the Commons – Benjamin Burton, Francis Harrison, Hugh Henry and Sir Alexander Cairnes – had voted against the measure in parliament. It should be noted though that their parliamentary actions did not stop them subscribing to the bank: their names all appear on the subscription lists published in both May 1720 and October 1721, with each subscribing at least £5,000. It seems therefore that the private bankers were afraid of being left out, and thus subscribed to the bank, while also publicly opposing it. Their chief objection was a fear of competition on the lending market if interest rates were cut to 5%. They were on the winning side in the parliamentary battle over the bank, but it is hard not to see the lowering of the legal interest rate from 8% to 7% in 1721 as a form of legislative compromise between the bankers and the erstwhile supporters of the national bank.[79]

Irwin's *New Scheme* also proposed that any new banking proposal should not be run by a private corporation but instead should be managed by parliament.[80] This addressed the concerns raised about the potential power of the bank's directors, a question linked to readings of the South Sea fallout, as well as wider disquiet about the bank's potential to reduce the need to call regular parliaments in Ireland. The latter issue had been, alongside the bubble, the other key theme of the debates inside and outside parliament, and it reflected the anxieties created by the passage of the Declaratory Act in April 1720, as well as reports of a possible plan to tax Ireland from Westminster. This project, as well as even less credible rumours of a potential political union, died with the change of ministry amid the general political and economic upheaval that followed the bursting of the bubble.[81] It was clear that any future bank scheme would have to place the Dublin parliament at its core if it was to

---

77 Irwin, *The Phoenix, or a New Scheme for Establishing Credit*.
78 Philip Perceval to Lord Perceval, 16 Oct. 1721 (BL, Add MS 47029, fol. 146).
79 8 Geo. I, c. 13 [Irish], *An Act for Reducing the Interest of Money to Seven Per Cent*; Moore, 'Satiric Norms', pp. 51–2.
80 Irwin, *The Phoenix, or a New Scheme for Establishing Credit*.
81 Burns, vol. 1, pp. 115–17; and for the union rumours see Nicolson to Wake, 28 Oct. 1721 (BL, Add MS 6116, fol. 116).

have any chance of succeeding. Lord Perceval expressed similar views in a long discourse on European banks contained in a letter to George Berkeley, although he also stressed the need for the bank to remain as an independent entity to prevent its reserves being used to make up government shortfalls.[82]

Perceval's correspondence with Berkeley on the subject of the bank demonstrates both men's deep intellectual engagement with the subject. Berkeley would return to these questions in the 1730s when he came to write his famous *Querist*, which was informed both by his earlier correspondence with Perceval and by his observations of monetary developments in the American colonies.[83] Laid out as a series of questions, this fascinating and complex work proposed solutions to the continuing and manifold problems facing the Irish economy at this time. Many of these problems were the same or similar to those visible in 1720–21, showing that some of these issues, while exacerbated by the particular contexts of the bubble, were also endemic to the Irish situation.[84] The 1720s had seen various efforts to solve these issues, the most notable being the botched introduction of 'Wood's Halfpence' in an attempt to counter the continuing problem of insufficient circulating small coin or specie. The same decade had also seen an increase in the amount of printed material focusing on Irish economic issues, building on arguments that had first emerged during the bank debates in 1721. The quantity of this printed literature and the later reputations of some of its contributors, notably Swift, Berkeley, Arthur Dobbs and Thomas Prior, has led historians to see this as the 'golden age of Irish political economy'.[85] Aside from the always exceptional figure of Swift, Berkeley is perhaps the best known of these authors, and it was he who briefly put the issue of a national bank back on the Irish agenda in 1737.

The concept of a national bank as a solution to Irish economic ills had largely disappeared from view in the later 1720s, suggesting that the 1721 parliamentary resolutions had some influence. Instead the Dublin private bankers, having recovered from their negative experience of the bubble, grew in strength only to suffer a major reverse in 1733 when Burton & Harrison's bank ignominiously collapsed.[86] The ensuing run on the city's

[82] Lord Perceval to Berkeley, 9 Nov. 1721 (BL, Add MS 47029, fols 158–74, esp. fol. 168). This important document, which informs much of the author's argument, is erroneously credited to Berkeley in Moore, *Swift, The Book and The Financial Revolution*, p. 5.
[83] George Berkeley, *The Querist: Containing Several Queries, Proposed to the Consideration of the Public*, 3 vols (Dublin, 1735–37).
[84] See James Kelly, 'Harvests and Hardship: Famine and Scarcity in Ireland in the late 1720s', *Studia Hibernica*, 26 (1992), 65–106, for a valuable overview of the problems facing the Irish economy in this decade.
[85] P. H. Kelly, 'The Politics of Political Economy in Mid-Eighteenth-Century Ireland', in *Political Thought in Eighteenth-Century Ireland*, ed. S. J. Connolly (Dublin, 2000), pp. 105–29.
[86] Eoin Magennis, 'Whither The Irish Financial Revolution? Money, Banks and Politics in Ireland in the 1730s', in *Money, Power and Print: Interdisciplinary Studies on the Financial*

banks sparked comparisons with the London crash thirteen years previously, with one government official, perhaps hyperbolically, describing the situation as being 'like the South Sea'.[87] This incident revealed again the fragility inherent in the Irish banking system and it should be seen as one of the catalysts for Berkeley's renewed focus on money, credit and banking in a large section of the first part of *The Querist*, which was published in Dublin two years later in 1735. In 'Query 223', Berkeley asked 'whether a bank of national credit, supported by public funds and secured by parliament, be a chimera or impossible thing? And if not what would follow from the supposal of such a bank?'[88]

Berkeley clearly thought a national bank *could* be more than 'a chimera', with several of the queries that followed advocating the virtues of a well-managed paper credit system. He was careful to disabuse his readers of any prejudices they might have about monetary innovations, arguing that the problems witnessed in London and Paris in 1720 had more to with speculation and gambling than with money or credit. This was evident in a number of the queries but made explicit in 'Query 229': 'Whether the ruinous effects of the Mississippi, South Sea and such schemes were not owing to an abuse of paper money or credit, in making it a means for idleness and gaming, instead of a motive and help to industry?'[89] This commentary reflected the already well-established, if disputed, narrative of the bubble as an example of a 'gambling mania' as well as demonstrating the continuing impact of the vocabulary of the South Sea crash on Irish monetary debates.[90]

Berkeley didn't leave his ideas about a national bank buried inside the pages of *The Querist*. Instead, a selection of the relevant queries on this subject were published alongside a pamphlet entitled *A Plan or Sketch of Such Bank* in 1737.[91] Here he described his scheme in detail, stressing the need for any bank to be controlled by parliament rather than by private directors and echoing the earlier arguments of Irwin and Perceval. Berkeley's proposed bank would be funded by a tax on imported wines, with parliament both guaranteeing its reserves and acting as auditors of its transactions. This was a very different scheme from the 1720–21 bank proposals and, if anything, more closely echoed Irwin's second set of proposals, which were republished in a Dublin newspaper in late 1737, six months after Berkeley's *Plan*

Revolution in the British Isles, ed. C. I. McGrath and Chris Fauske (Newark, 2008), pp. 189–208 (p. 196).

[87] Walter Cary to Charles Delafaye, 27 Jan. 1734 (TNA, SP 63/397, fol. 34).

[88] George Berkeley, *The Querist: Containing Several Queries, Proposed to the Consideration of the Public*, 3 vols (Dublin, 1735–37), vol. 1, p. 41.

[89] Berkeley, vol. 1, pp. 144–5.

[90] For an important modern refutation of the 'gambling mania' interpretation see Paul, pp. 7–8 and 85–6.

[91] George Berkeley, *Queries Relating to a National Bank, Extracted from the Querist. Also the Letter Containing a Plan or Sketch of Such Bank* (Dublin, 1737).

appeared. Neither Irwin's republished second set of proposals nor Berkeley's scheme, which he intended to introduce into the House of Lords, came to anything and the idea of a national bank was once again abandoned.[92] It is unclear precisely why the bishop gave up his plans, with most scholars attributing his decision either to the pressure of other preoccupations or perhaps more likely the hostility of his parliamentary contemporaries.[93] In any case, 1737 was not a propitious time to launch a new bank scheme as MPs were still focused on resolving the coinage problems that had dogged Ireland for so long. This end was finally achieved after some debate with the value of the gold coins in circulation reduced by proclamation and the introduction of small denomination copper coinage. Eoin Magennis has persuasively argued that the ongoing intellectual and parliamentary concentration on coinage at the expense of paper money reflected the continuing slow adoption of the financial revolution in Ireland.[94]

III

The failure to set up an Irish national bank until 1783, when the Bank of Ireland was finally established almost ninety years after the foundation of its English and Scottish counterparts, was the logical result of this slow engagement with the innovations witnessed elsewhere in the British world.[95] The reasons for this are manifold but it is clear that the best opportunity to establish such an institution was the bank proposal that so nearly passed through the Irish parliament in 1721. Its failure then owed much to the effects of the South Sea bubble, and the fears, both justified and unjustified, that events in London created about schemes for paper credit, investment and stockjobbing. These concerns are visible both in the surviving accounts of parliamentary debates and in the contemporary printed literature. From there they continued to influence economic and political discourses in Ireland about banking, money and credit, until the very different economic and political circumstances created by the granting of legislative independence in 1782 gave the Irish legislature and investing public the confidence to successfully launch a national bank.

[92] Magennis, pp. 198–200.
[93] P. H. Kelly, 'Berkeley and the Idea of a National Bank', *Eighteenth-Century Ireland*, 25 (2010), 98–117; and C. George Caffentzis, 'The Failure of Berkeley's Bank: Money and Libertinism in Eighteenth-Century Ireland', in Carey and Finlay (eds), *The Empire of Credit*, pp. 229–48.
[94] Magennis, p. 204. For the continuing problems faced by Irish banks in succeeding years see Mary-Lou Legg, 'Money and Reputations: The Effects of the Banking Crises of 1755 and 1760', *Eighteenth-Century Ireland*, 11 (1996), 74–87.
[95] Hall, *passim*. L. M. Cullen, *An Economic History of Ireland since 1660* (London, 1972), p. 95.

Conclusion

In March 1733, on reporting the death of Sir Ralph Gore – the long-time chancellor of the Irish exchequer and one-time national bank promoter – a leading Irish politician, Marmaduke Coghill, noted with some surprise that Gore had 'no ready money or any out on securities'.[1] Almost thirteen years after the South Sea bubble, it was clearly expected that members of the Irish elite would have some of their wealth laid out in stocks or securities, whether in London or Dublin. This is evident from other sources too. The diaries for the same period of John Perceval, now 1st Earl of Egmont, are replete with references to his investments, both his own, and on behalf of his Irish and English relations, including regular purchases of South Sea stock. His negative personal experience, of what Egmont still termed in 1737 'that vile scheme', had not led him to retreat entirely from investment in the stock market.[2] Instead, despite his losses during the bubble, income from stocks and shares continued to be important for him and his extended family circle. In this he had much in common with many, if not most, investors during the bubble. The 'plaguy South Sea', while it initially led to increased levels of suspicion and distrust among the British and Irish investing public, did not mark a watershed in terms of wider financial and investing practices.[3] The innovations and developments of the financial revolution had become too embedded in contemporary society for them to be easily undone.

This is important, as it warns us against reading the impact of the bubble in overly negative terms, of seeing it simply in terms of losers, of bemoaning its impact both on the wider economy and contemporary projects. Nevertheless it was the great crisis of the financial revolution in that it forced contemporary observers to rethink and reconceptualize their understanding of the changes that they had witnessed over the previous thirty years. The rise and fall of the South Sea Company in 1720 seemed to offer lessons about investment, speculation and the dangers of human folly, lessons that were quickly promulgated across Britain, Ireland and beyond. These contemporary readings of events had an enormous effect, an impact that was perhaps even

---

[1]   Marmaduke Coghill to Edward Southwell, 8 Mar. 1733, in *Letters of Marmaduke Coghill, 1722–1738*, ed. D. W. Hayton (Dublin, 2005), p. 121.
[2]   Entry for 26 Apr. 1737, in HMC, *Egmont Diary*, 3 vols (London, 1923), vol. 2, p. 397.
[3]   Henry Tichborne, 1st Baron Ferrard to Robert, 1st Viscount Molesworth, 14 June 1721, in HMC, *Report on Manuscripts in Various Collections, vol. 8 The Hon. Frederick Lindley Wood; M. L. S. Clements, Esq.; S. Philip Unwin, Esq.* (London, 1913), p. 316.

greater than the strictly financial consequences of the crash. We have seen how they contributed to the demise of the various schemes for a national bank in Dublin. These projects had, of course, like contemporary 'Scots projects', initially ridden on the crest of the South Sea wave in early summer 1720, only to collapse in the aftermath of the London crash in the autumn.

The central argument of this book has been that participation in, and the consequences of, the South Sea bubble extended beyond its geographic and financial centre in London. This was not just evident in its influence on contemporary schemes and projects in Dublin, Edinburgh and elsewhere, but in the profile of the investors who came to London to invest in the South Sea Company, following its highly successful, and carefully manipulated, launch in spring 1720. These investors, as chapter 2 has shown, came not just from across Britain and Ireland but also from continental Europe, and even in a few cases from further afield. These 'foreign' investors comprised a small but significant element within the wider London investment community during the bubble and added to its transnational dimension. The South Sea scheme drew in a cosmopolitan mix of investors, both novice and experienced. These included the Irish and Scottish landed, military and mercantile elites described in this book alongside the international traders and speculators already very familiar with the London, Paris and Amsterdam markets, as well the transnational and international kinship groups such as the many members of the European Jewish and Huguenot diasporas who ventured a portion of their mobile capital in London.

Together these groups helped to shape a global phenomenon. The impact of their investments also crucially had a transnational effect. This could be seen at the local and personal scale with individual gains and losses often clearly visible to contemporaries, whether in terms of conspicuous or restrained consumption, or in their correspondence and conversation. It could also be seen in the broader effects on society. These included the visible strains on local credit markets, the runs on the Dublin and Edinburgh banks, and the poverty and distress partly caused by declining trade balances. Taken together, all of these elements suggest that any reading of the crash that ignores its impact beyond the metropolitan centre is somewhat deficient. The South Sea bubble was more than just a London event; it was one that reverberated around the known world, impacting on many lives in many different places. These included not just the investors and speculators who came to Exchange Alley, but also those who benefited and suffered from the consequences of their actions. This book has integrated some of their stories into the already dramatic story of the 'year of the bubbles', providing a new perspective on both the London crash and the wider British financial revolution.

Bibliography

MANUSCRIPT PRIMARY SOURCES

Bank of England Archives

AC27/6437–80	Stock Ledger: Old South Sea Annuities, 1723–51.
M1/1	List of Original Subscribers to the Bank of England, 1694.

British Library

Add MS 6116	Letters to Archbishop William Wake from Bishop William Nicolson.
Add MS 6117	Letters to Archbishop William Wake from Archbishops Edward Synge and William King.
Add MS 36161	Hardwicke Papers.
Add MS 38151	Southwell Papers.
Add MS 47029	Egmont Papers.

Christ Church Library, Oxford

MS 231	Papers of William Wake (consulted on microfilm in the NLI).

Irish Architectural Archive

MS 97/84	Castletown Papers (property of the Castletown Foundation).

The National Archives (United Kingdom)

ADM 1/1778	Admiralty Papers In-Letters.
ADM 1/2037	Admiralty Papers In-Letters.
C 110/46	Chancery: Master Horne's Exhibits, St George Correspondence.
CUST 1/15	Minutes of the Irish Revenue Commissioners, 1720–21.
SP 63/371–97	State Papers, Ireland, 1714–34.
T 14/10	Treasury: Books of out-letters concerning Ireland, 1715–23.

National Library of Ireland

MSS 2056	Letters of William King, Archbishop of Dublin, largely on public affairs, 1716–1728.

MS 2256   A collection of miscellaneous papers (manuscript and printed) relating to the abortive project to establish a Bank of Ireland at Dublin, including various petitions for a Royal Charter, lists of subscribers and of persons qualified to hold offices and vote c.1720–1721.

MS 2534   Ormonde Papers.

MS 2785   La Touche Papers: 'Photostat' copies of abstracts of ledger accounts (of Kane and La Touche, bankers?) Dublin, 1719–1726.

MS 10,708   F. S. Bourke Collection: Accounts of profit and loss of Swift's Bank, Dublin, 1722–1724 and a proposal by Swift, the banker for a chartered Bank of Ireland 1720.

MSS 41,563–603   Papers of the Family of Smythe of Barbavilla.

P3752   Molesworth Papers.

National Records of Scotland (Edinburgh)

GD18   Papers of the Clerk family of Penicuik, Midlothian.

GD45/1/217   Papers of the Maule Family, Earls of Dalhousie: Manifesto by the Pretender on the occasion of the South Sea Bubble, 10 Oct 1720.

GD220/5/833/1   Papers of the Graham Family, Dukes of Montrose (Montrose Muniments).

GD248/170/3/79   Papers of the Ogilvy family, Earls of Seafield (Seafield Papers).

Public Record Office, Northern Ireland

D654/B/1/1AA   Londonderry Papers: Robert Cowan letterbook.

D2707   Shannon papers.

D2092   Castleward Papers, 1718–25.

D2977/2/7   Earl of Antrim Estate Papers: Vane v Burton's Bank.

D3000/27/1   Extracts from records for the most part relating to the Falkiner family.

D4151   Kenmare Papers.

T2524/5   Kirk papers: Hamilton Maxwell, Drumbeg, to Agmondisham Vesey, Dublin, 15 July 1721.

T2812   O'Hara Papers.

T3041/1/C/3   Bruce family papers: Michael Ward, Dublin, to James Traill, Killyleagh, 9 January 1720.

T3425/2   Chancery papers: Ridgeway Pitt estate.

Staffordshire Record Office

D641/2/K   Stafford Family Collection: Persons connected with Stafford Howard family.

Surrey History Centre

MS 1248   Brodrick Family of Peper Harow and Midleton (Cork),
Viscounts Midleton: Family Correspondence and Papers.

Trinity College Dublin

MSS 750/2–13   Letterbooks of Archbishop William King.
MSS 1995–2008 Lyons (King) Collection.

PRINTED PRIMARY SOURCES

Pamphlets and Other Contemporary Printed Sources

Aislabie, John, *The Speech of the Right Honourable John Aislabie, Esq; upon his Defence made in the House of Lords Against the Bill for Raising Money Upon the Estates of the South-Sea Directors, on Wednesday the 19th of July 1721* (Dublin, 1721).

Anderson, Adam, *An Historical and Chronological Deduction of the Origins of Commerce from the Earliest Accounts to the Present Time*, 2 vols (London, 1764).

Anon., *The Case of the Governor and Company for making Hollow Sword Blades* (London, 1709).

——, *Index Rerum & Vocabulorum For the Use of Freeholders of Counties and Freemen of Corporations* (London, 1722).

——, *A Letter from a Gentleman in the Country to a Member of Parliament in England* (Dublin, 1721).

——, *Letter to Henry Maxwell: Plainly Showing the Great Danger that the Kingdom has Escaped and the Great Inconveniences that Must of Necessity Have Happened if the Bank had been Established* (Dublin, 1721).

——, *A Letter to a Member of Parliament Concerning the Late Bank* (Dublin, 1721).

——, *A List of the Subscribers to the Bank of Ireland* (Dublin, 1721).

——, *The Nation Preserved; Or, the Plot Discover'd Containing an Impartial Account of the Secret Policy of Some of the South-Sea Directors; With Copies of Their Letters to Each Other; and the Substance of their Debates in Several of Their Private Conferences Taken Before a Notary-Publick* (Dublin, 1721).

——, *Proposals for Raising A Million of Money out of the Forfeited Estates in Ireland Together, With the Answer of the Irish to the Same, and a Reply Thereto* (London, 1694).

——, *Remarks on Mr Maxwell's and Mr Rowley's Letters: Setting Forth the Advantages of a Bank and Lumbards in Ireland, in a Letter to a Friend* (Dublin, 1721).

——, *South Sea Playing Cards* (London, 1721).

——, *A Strange Collection of Maybes Fully Answered and Cleared Up By a Subscriber and Well Wisher to the Bank* (Dublin, 1721).

Berkeley, George, *Queries Relating to a National Bank, Extracted from the Querist. Also the Letter Containing a Plan or Sketch of Such Bank* (Dublin, 1737).

——, *The Querist: Containing Several Queries, Proposed to the Consideration of the Public*, 3 vols (Dublin, 1735–37).

Castaing, John, *Course of the Exchange* (London, 1720).

Chamberlain, Hugh, *A Proposal and Considerations relating to an Office of Credit upon Land Security: Proposed to their Excellencies the Lords Justices: and to the Lords of the Privy Council; and the Parliament of Ireland* (London, 1697).

Defoe, Daniel, *The Anatomy of Exchange Alley* (London, 1719).

——, *A Tour thro' the Whole Island of Great Britain*, 3 vols (London, 1724–26).

Dobbs, Arthur, *An Essay on the Trade and Improvement of Ireland* (Dublin, 1729).

Downes, Henry, *A Sermon Preached at Christ's-Church Dublin, before Their Excellencies the Lords Justices on Friday 23rd December 1720* (Dublin, 1721).

Holt, Richard, *Seasonable Proposals for a Perpetual Fund or Bank in Dublin* (Dublin, 1696).

Hutcheson, Archibald, *Four Treatises Related to the South Sea Scheme* (London, 1721).

Hutchinson, Francis, *A Letter to the Gentlemen of the Landed Interest in Ireland Relating to a Bank* (Dublin, 1721).

Irwin, John, *The Phoenix, or a New Scheme for Establishing Credit on the Most Solid and Satisfactory Foundation and Entirely Free From All the Objections Made to the Late Intended Bank* (Dublin, 1721).

——, *To the Nobility, Gentry and Commonalty of this Kingdom of Ireland* (Dublin, 1720).

Maxwell, Henry, *Reasons Offer'd for Erecting a Bank in Ireland; in a Letter to Hercules Rowley, Esq* (Dublin, 1721).

——, *Mr Maxwell's Second Letter to Mr Rowley: Wherein the Objections Against the Bank are Answered* (Dublin, 1721).

Misoletes, Patriophilus, *Objections Against the General Bank in Ireland* (Dublin, 1721).

Prior, Thomas, *A list of the absentees of Ireland, and the yearly value of their estates and incomes spent abroad. With observations on the present state and condition of that kingdom* (Dublin, 1729).

Ramsay, Allan, *Poems by Allan Ramsay* (Edinburgh, 1721).

Rowley, Hercules, *An Answer to a Book Intitled Reasons Offered for Erecting a Bank in Ireland in a Letter to Henry Maxwell Esquire* (Dublin, 1721).

——, *An Answer to Mr Maxwell's Second Letter Concerning the Bank* (Dublin, 1721).

Tattler, Tom [J. Swift], *The Life and Character of Mr Joseph Damer* (Dublin, 1720).

Trenchard, John, *A Letter From A Soldier to The Commons of England Occasioned by an Address Now Carrying On By The Protestants in Ireland, In Order to Take Away the Fund Appropriated For the Payment of the Arrears of the Army* (London, 1702).

Newspapers

Daily Post (London).
Dublin Courant.
Dublin Gazette.
Dublin Intelligence.
The Flying Post.
Harding's Impartial Newsletter.
London Mercury.
New England Courant.
Whalley's Newsletter.

Modern Collections of Printed Primary Sources

Emmett, Ross B. (ed.), *Great Bubbles*, 3 vols (London, 2000).

Forbes, John, *Memoirs of the Earls of Granard* (London, 1868).

Giblin, Cathaldus, 'Catalogue of Material of Irish Interest in the Collection Nunziatura di Fiandra, Vatican Archives: Part 5, vols 123–132', *Collectanea Hibernica*, 9 (1966), 7–70.

Graham, J. M., *Annals and Correspondence of the Viscount and First and Second Earls of Stair*, 2 vols (Edinburgh, 1875).

Hayton, D. W. (ed.), *Letters of Marmaduke Coghill, 1722–1738* (Dublin, 2005).

Historical Manuscripts Commission, *Egmont Diary*, 3 vols (London, 1923).

——, *Report on Manuscripts in Various Collections, vol. 8 The Hon. Frederick Lindley Wood; M. L. S. Clements, Esq.; S. Philip Unwin, Esq.* (London, 1913).

Levinge, Sir Richard G. A, *Jottings of the Levinge Family* (Dublin, 1857).

Luce, A. A. and T. E. Jessop (eds), *The Works of George Berkeley*, 9 vols (Edinburgh, 1948–57).

MacLysaght, Edward (ed.), *The Kenmare Manuscripts* (Dublin, 1942).

Ohlmeyer, Jane and Éamonn Ó Ciardha (eds), *The Irish Statute Staple Books, 1596–1687* (Dublin, 1998).

Redington, Joseph (ed.), *Calendar of Treasury Papers Volume 6: 1720–28* (London, 1889).

Swift, Jonathan, *Poems*, ed. Harold Williams, 3 vols (Oxford, 1958).

——, *Prose Works*, ed. Herbert Davis, 14 vols (Oxford, 1939–68).

Williams, Harold (ed.), *The Correspondence of Jonathan Swift*, 5 vols (Oxford, 1963–65).

Parliamentary Papers

The Journals of the House of Commons of the Kingdom of Ireland, 3rd edn, 20 vols (Dublin, 1796–1800).

SECONDARY WORKS

Books and Articles

Agnew, Jean, *Belfast Merchant Families in the Seventeenth Century* (Dublin, 1996).

Altdorfer, Stefan, 'State Investment in Eighteenth-Century Berne', *History of European Ideas*, 33 (2007), 440–62.

Ashton, T. S., *Economic Fluctuations in England, 1700–1800* (Oxford, 1959).

Bailey, Craig, *Irish London: Middle-Class Migration in the Global Eighteenth Century* (Liverpool, 2013).

——, 'Metropole and Colony: Irish Networks and Patronage in the Eighteenth-Century Empire', *Immigrants and Minorities*, 23 (2005), 161–81.

——, 'The Nesbitts of London and their Networks, 1747–1817', in *Irish and Scottish Mercantile Networks in Europe and Overseas in the Seventeenth and Eighteenth Centuries*, ed. David Dickson, Jan Parmentier and Jane Ohlmeyer (Gent, 2007), pp. 231–50.

Ball, F. E., *The Judges in Ireland, 1221–1921*, 2 vols (London, 1926).

Baltes, Sabine, *The Pamphlet Controversy about Wood's Halfpence (1722–25) and the Tradition of Irish Constitutional Nationalism* (Frankfurt, 2003).

Barnard, Toby, '"Grand Metropolis" or "The Anus of the World"? The Cultural Life of Eighteenth-Century Dublin', in *Two Capitals, London and Dublin, 1500–1840*, ed. Peter Clark and R. G. Gillespie (Oxford, 2001), pp. 185–211.

——, *A New Anatomy of Ireland: The Irish Protestants, 1649–1770* (London, 2003).

——, 'A Tale of Three Sisters: Katherine Conolly of Castletown', in *Irish Protestant Ascents and Descents, 1641–1770*, ed. Toby Barnard (Dublin, 2004), pp. 266–89.

Barrow, G. L., *The Emergence of the Irish Banking System, 1820–1845* (Dublin, 1975).

Bell, Stuart, '"A Masterpiece of Knavery"? The Activities of the Sword Blade Company in London's Early Financial Markets', *Business History*, 54 (2012), 623–38.

Bergin, John, 'The Irish Catholic Interest at the London Inns of Court, 1674–1800', *Eighteenth-Century Ireland*, 24 (2009), 36–61.

Bergin, John, Eoin Magennis, Lesa Ni Mhunghaile and Patrick Walsh (eds), *New Perspectives on the Penal Laws* (Dublin, 2011).

Bialuschewski, Arne, 'Greed, Fraud, and Popular Culture: John Breholt's Madagascar Schemes of the Early Eighteenth Century', in *Money, Power and Print: Interdisciplinary Studies on the Financial Revolution in the British Isles*, ed. C. I. McGrath and Chris Fauske (Newark, 2008), pp. 104–14.

Bowen, H. V., 'From Supranational to National: Changing patterns of investment in the British East India Company, 1750–1820', in *Colonial Empires Compared: Britain and the Netherlands, 1750–1850*, ed. Bob Moore and Henk Van Nierop (Aldershot, 2003), pp. 131–44.

Braddick, M. J., *The Nerves of State: Taxation and the Financing of the English State, 1558–1714* (Manchester, 1996).

Braudel, Fernand, *The Wheels of Commerce* (London, 1982).

Brewer, John, 'Commercialization and Politics', in *The Birth of a Consumer Society: The Commercialization of Eighteenth-Century England*, ed. John Brewer, J. H. Plumb and Neil McKendrick (London, 1982), pp. 203–60.

——, *The Sinews of Power: War, Money and the English State, 1688–1783* (London, 1989).

Brown, Michael, 'The Location of Learning in Mid-Eighteenth-Century Ireland', in *Marsh's Library: A Mirror on the World: Law, Learning and Libraries 1650–1750*, ed. Muriel McCarthy and Ann Simmons (Dublin, 2009), pp. 104–27.

Burns, R. E., *Irish Parliamentary Politics in the Eighteenth Century*, 2 vols (Washington, 1989–90).

Busteed, John, 'Irish Private Banks', *Journal of the Cork Historical and Archaeological Society*, 53 (1948), 31–7.

Caffentzis, C. George, 'The Failure of Berkeley's Bank: Money and Libertinism in Eighteenth-Century Ireland', in *The Empire of Credit: The Financial Revolution in Britain, Ireland and America, 1688–1815*, ed. Daniel Carey and Christopher Finlay (Dublin, 2011), pp. 229–48.

Caldicott, C. E. J., Hugh Gough and J. P. Pittion (eds), *The Huguenots and Ireland: Anatomy of an Emigration* (Dun Laoghaire, 1987).

Carey, Daniel and Christopher Finlay (eds), *The Empire of Credit: The Financial Revolution in Britain, Ireland and America, 1688–1815* (Dublin, 2011).

Carlos, Ann M. and Larry Neal, 'The Micro-Foundations of the Early London Capital Market: Bank of England Shareholders During and After the South Sea Bubble, 1720–25', *Economic History Review*, 59 (2006), 498–538.

——, 'Women Investors in Early Capital Markets, 1720–25', *Financial History Review*, 2 (2004), 197–224.

Carlos, Ann M., Larry Neal and Karen Maguire, '"A Knavish People ...": London Jewry and the Stock Market during the South Sea Bubble', *Business History*, 50 (2008), 728–48.

Carruthers, Bruce C., *City of Capital: Politics and Markets in the English Financial Revolution* (Princeton, 1996).

Carswell, John, *The South Sea Bubble* (London, 1960).

Champion, Justin, '"Mysterious Politicks": Land, Credit and Commonwealth Political Economy, 1656–1722', in *Money and Political Economy in the Age of Enlightenment*, ed. Daniel Carey (Oxford, 2014), pp. 117–62.

——, *Republican Learning: John Toland and the Crisis of Christian Culture, 1696–1722* (Manchester, 2003).

Chancellor, Edward, *Devil Take the Hindmost: A History of Financial Speculation* (London, 1999).

Checkland, S. G., *Scottish Banking: A History, 1695–1973* (Glasgow, 1975).

Coffmann, D'Maris, *Excise Taxation and the Origins of Public Debt* (Basingstoke, 2013).

Coffmann, D'Maris, Adrian Leonard and Larry Neal (eds), *Questioning Credible Commitment: Perspectives on the Rise of Financial Capitalism* (Cambridge, 2013).

Connolly, S. J., *Religion, Law and Power: The Making of Protestant Ireland 1660–1760* (Oxford, 1992).

Conway, Stephen, *Britain, Ireland, & Continental Europe in the Eighteenth Century: Similarities, Connections, Identities* (Oxford, 2011).

Costelloe, Vivien, '"Pensioners, Barbers, Valets or Markees"?: Jonathan Swift and Huguenot Bank Investors in Ireland, 1721', *Proceedings of the Huguenot Society of Great Britain and Ireland*, 29 (2008), 62–92.

Cowan, Brian, *The Social Life of Coffee: The Emergence of the British Coffeehouse* (London, 2005).

Cox, Gary W., 'Was the Glorious Revolution a Constitutional Watershed', *Journal of Economic History*, 72 (2012), 567–600.

Crouzet, Francois, 'The Huguenots and the English Financial Revolution', in *Favorites of Fortune: Technology, Growth and Economic Development since the Industrial Revolution*, ed. Patrice Higonnet, David S. Landes and Henry Rosovsky (Cambridge, MA, 1991), pp. 221–66.

Cullen, L. M., *Anglo-Irish Trade 1660–1800* (Manchester, 1968).

——, 'Economic Development, 1691–1750', in *New History of Ireland*, ed. T. W. Moody, F. X. Martin and F. J. Byrne, 9 vols (Oxford, 1986), vol. 4, pp. 123–58.

——, *An Economic History of Ireland since 1660* (London, 1972).

——, 'The Exchange Business of the Irish banks in the Eighteenth Century', *Economica*, 25 (1958), 326–38.

——, 'Galway Merchants in the Outside World, c.1650–1800', in *Economy, Trade and Irish Merchants at Home and Abroad, 1600–1998* (Dublin 2012), pp. 165–92.

——, 'The Huguenots from the Perspective of the Merchant Networks of W. Europe (1680–1790): The Example of the Brandy Trade', in *The Huguenots and Ireland: Anatomy of an Emigration*, ed. C. E. J. Caldicott, Hugh Gough and J. P. Pittion (Dun Laoghaire, 1987), pp. 129–50.

——, 'Landlords, Bankers and Merchants: The Early Irish Banking World, 1700–1820', in *Economists and the Irish Economy from the Eighteenth Century to the Present Day*, ed. Antoin E. Murphy (Dublin, 1984), pp. 25–44.

——, 'The Scottish Exchange on London, 1663–1778', in *Conflict, Identity and Economic Development in Ireland and Scotland, 1600–1939*, ed. S. J. Connolly, R. A. Houston and R. J. Morris (Preston, 1995), pp. 29–44.

——, 'The Two George Fitzgeralds of London, 1718–59', in *Irish and Scottish Mercantile Networks in Europe and Overseas in the Seventeenth and Eighteenth Centuries*, ed. David Dickson, Jan Parmentier and Jane Ohlmeyer (Gent, 2007), pp. 251–70.

Cummings, A. J. G., 'Industry and Investment in the Eighteenth-Century Highlands: The York Buildings Company of London', in *Industry, Business and Society*, ed. A. J. G. Cummings and T. M. Devine (Edinburgh, 1994), pp. 24–42.

Cunningham, Jessica, 'Dublin's Huguenot Goldsmiths, 1690–1750: Assimilation and Divergence', *Irish Architectural and Decorative Studies*, 12 (2009), 159–85.

Curl, J. S., *The Londonderry Plantation, 1609–1914: The History, Architecture, and Planning of the Estates of the City of London and its Livery Companies in Ulster* (Chichester, 1986).

Dale, Richard, *The First Crash: Lessons from the South Sea Bubble* (Princeton, 2004).

Dawes, Margaret and C. N. Ward-Perkins, *Country Banks of England and Wales: Private Provincial Banks and Bankers, 1688–1953* (Canterbury, 2000).

De Bruyn, F., 'Reading *Het Groote Tafereel der Dwaasheid*: An Emblem Book of the Folly of Speculation in the Bubble Year 1720', *Eighteenth-Century Life*, 24 (2000), 1–42.

De Goede, M., 'Mastering "Lady Credit": Discourses of Financial Crisis in Historical Perspective', *International Feminist Journal of Politics*, 2 (2000), 58–81.

Dehing, Pit and Marjolhein 't Hart, 'Linking the Fortunes: Currency and Banking, 1500–1800', in *A Financial History of the Netherlands*, ed. Marjolhein 't Hart, Joost Jinker and Jan Luiten Van Zanden (Cambridge, 1997), pp. 37–61.

Devine, T. M., 'The Scottish Merchant Community, 1680–1740', in *The Origins and Nature of the Scottish Enlightenment*, ed. R. H. Campbell and Andrew S. Skinner (Edinburgh, 1982), pp. 26–41.

Dickson, David, 'Catholics and Trade in Eighteenth-Century Ireland: An Old Debate Reconsidered', in *Endurance and Emergence: Catholics in Ireland in the Eighteenth Century*, ed. T. P. Power and Kevin Whelan (Dublin, 1990), pp. 85–100.

——, 'Huguenots in the Urban Economy of Eighteenth-Century Dublin and

Cork', in *The Huguenots and Ireland: Anatomy of an Emigration*, ed. C. E. J. Caldicott, Hugh Gough and J. P. Pittion (Dun Laoghaire, 1987), pp. 321–32.

——, *New Foundations: Ireland 1660–1800* (Dublin, 2000).

——, *Old World Colony: Cork and South Munster, 1630–1830* (Cork, 2005).

Dickson, David and Richard English, 'The Latouche Dynasty', in *The Gorgeous Mask: Dublin 1750–1850*, ed. David Dickson (Dublin, 1987), pp. 17–30.

Dickson, David, Jan Parmentier and Jane Ohlmeyer (eds), *Irish and Scottish Mercantile Networks in Europe and Overseas in the Seventeenth and Eighteenth Centuries* (Gent, 2007).

Dickson, P. G. M., *The Financial Revolution in England: A Study in the Development of Public Credit, 1688–1756* (London, 1967).

Dickson, R. J., *Ulster Emigration to Colonial America, 1718–1776* (Belfast, 1966).

Dillon, Malcolm, *The History and Development of Banking in Ireland from the Earliest Times to the Present Day* (Dublin, 1889).

Doherty, Richard, *The Williamite War in Ireland, 1688–91* (Dublin, 1998).

Downie, J. A., 'Gulliver's Travels, The Contemporary Debate on the Financial Revolution and the Bourgeois Public Sphere', in *Money, Power and Print: Interdisciplinary Studies on the Financial Revolution in the British Isles*, ed. C. I. McGrath and Chris Fauske (Newark, 2008), pp. 115–34.

——, *To Settle the Succession of the State: Literature and Politics, 1678–1750* (London, 1994).

Dudley, Rowena, *The Irish Lottery, 1780–1801* (Dublin, 2005).

Ehrenpreis, Irvin, *Swift: The Man, His Works and The Age, Volume III* (London, 1983).

Fagan, Patrick, *Catholics in a Protestant Country: The Papist Constituency in Eighteenth-Century Dublin* (Dublin, 1998).

Fauske, Chris, 'Misunderstanding What Swift Misunderstood, or the Economy of a Province', in *Money, Power and Print: Interdisciplinary Studies on the Financial Revolution in the British Isles*, ed. C. I. McGrath and Chris Fauske (Newark, 2008), pp. 135–56.

Ferguson, Oliver, *Jonathan Swift and Ireland* (Urbana, IL, 1962).

Flavell, Julie, *When London was Capital of America* (London, 2010).

Fleming, David, *Politics and Provincial People: Sligo and Limerick, 1691–1761* (Manchester, 2010).

Freeman, Mark, Robin Pearson and James Taylor, *Shareholder Democracies? Corporate Governance in Britain and Ireland before 1850* (Chicago, 2012).

Garber, Peter, *Famous First Bubbles: The Fundamentals of Early Manias* (Cambridge, MA, 2000).

Genet-Rouffiac, Nathalie, 'The Irish Jacobite exiles in France, 1692–1715', in *The Dukes of Ormonde, 1610–1745*, ed. Toby Barnard and Jane Fenlon (Woodbridge, 2000), pp. 195–210.

Gillespie, R. G., 'Irish Protestants and James II', *Irish Historical Studies*, 28 (1992), 124–33.

——, *The Transformation of the Irish Economy, 1550–1700* (Dundalk, 1998).

Glaisyer, Natasha, *The Culture of Commerce in England, 1660–1720* (Woodbridge, 2006).

Goldgar, Anne, *Tulipmania: Money, Honor and Knowledge in the Dutch Golden Age* (Chicago, 2007).

Goodwin, Albert, 'Wood's Halfpence', *English Historical Review*, 51 (1936), 647–74.

Grell, Ole Peter, *Brethren in Christ: A Calvinist Network in Reformation Europe* (Cambridge, 2011).

Griffin, Patrick, *The People With No Name: Ireland's Ulster Scots, America's Scots Irish and the Creation of the British Atlantic World* (Princeton, 2001).

Gwynn, Julian, 'Financial Revolution in Massachusetts: Public Credit and Taxation, 1692–1774', *Histoire Sociale – Social History*, 27 (1984), 59–77.

Gwynn, Robin, 'The Huguenots in Britain, the "Protestant International" and the defeat of Louis XIV', in *From Strangers to Citizens: The Integration of Immigrant Communities in Britain, Ireland and Colonial America, 1550–1750*, ed. Randolph Vigne and Charles Littleton (Brighton, 2001), pp. 412–26.

Habakkuk, John, *Marriage, Debt and the Estate System: English Landownership 1650–1950* (Oxford, 1994).

Hall, F. G., *The Bank of Ireland, 1783–1946* (Dublin, 1949).

Hancock, David, *Citizens of the World: London Merchants and the Integration of the British Atlantic Community, 1735–1785* (Cambridge, 1995).

Harris, Bob, 'Scotland's Herring Fisheries and the Prosperity of the Nation, c.1660–1760', *Scottish Historical Review*, 79 (2000), 39–60.

Harris, Ron, 'The Bubble Act: Its Passage and Its Effects on Business Organization', *The Journal of Economic History*, 54 (1994), 610–27.

Harris, Tim, *Revolution: The Great Crisis of the British Monarchy, 1685–1720* (London, 2006).

Hartley, James, 'The Chameleon Daniel Defoe: Public Writing in the age before Economic Theory', in *Money, Power and Print: Interdisciplinary Studies on the Financial Revolution in the British Isles*, ed. C. I. McGrath and Chris Fauske (Newark, 2008), pp. 26–50.

Hayton, D. W., *The Anglo-Irish Experience, 1680–1730: Religion, Identity and Patriotism* (Woodbridge, 2012).

——, 'Contested Kingdoms, 1688–1756', in *Short Oxford History of the British Isles: The Eighteenth Century*, ed. Paul Langford (Oxford, 2002), pp. 35–70.

——, *Ruling Ireland, 1685–1742: Politics, Politicians and Parties* (Woodbridge, 2004).

——, 'The Stanhope/Sunderland Ministry and the Repudiation of Irish Parliamentary Independence', *English Historical Review*, 113 (1998), 610–36.

Hill, Jacqueline, *From Patriots to Unionists: Dublin Civic Politics and Irish Protestant Patriotism, 1660–1840* (Oxford, 1997).

Holmes, Geoffrey, *British Politics in the Age of Anne*, rev. edn (London, 1987).

Hone, J. M., 'Berkeley and Swift as National Economists', *Studies*, 23 (1934), 421–32.

Hoppit, Julian, *A Land of Liberty? England 1689–1727* (Oxford, 2000).

——, 'The Myths of the South Sea Bubble', *Transactions of the Royal Historical Society*, 6th ser., 12 (2002), 141–65.

Humphries, Jane and Steve Hindle, 'Editors' Introduction', *Economic History Review*, 62, Special Issue: Finance, Investment and Risk (2009), 1–7.

Hutton, Gordon, 'Archbishop King, The Bank Scheme (1720–21), and Wood's Halfpence (1722–25)', *Éire-Ireland*, 35 (2000), 81–101.

Hylton, Raymond, *Ireland's Huguenots and their Refuge 1662–1745* (Brighton, 2005).

Ingrassia, Catherine, *Authorship, Commerce and Gender in Early Eighteenth-Century England: A Culture of Public Credit* (Cambridge, 2005).

James, F. G., 'The Irish Lobby in the Early Eighteenth Century', *English Historical Review*, 81 (1966), 543–57.

——, *Lords of the Ascendancy: The Irish House of Lords and its Members, 1600–1800* (Dublin, 1995).

Johnston, Joseph, *Bishop Berkeley's Querist in Historical Perspective* (Dundalk, 1970).

Jones, D. W., *War and Economy in the Age of William III and Marlborough* (Oxford, 1988).

Jones, W. Douglas, '"The Bold Adventurers": A Quantitative Analysis of the Darien Subscription List (1696)', *Scottish Economic & Social History*, 21 (2001), 22–42.

Kelly, James, 'Harvests and Hardship: Famine and Scarcity in Ireland in the Late 1720s', *Studia Hibernica*, 26 (1992), 65–106.

——, 'The Historiography of the Penal Laws', in *New Perspectives on the Penal Laws*, ed. John Bergin, Eoin Magennis, Lesa Ni Mhunghaile and Patrick Walsh (Dublin, 2011), pp. 27–54.

Kelly, P. H., 'Berkeley and the Idea of a National Bank', *Eighteenth-Century Ireland*, 25 (2010), 98–117.

——, '"Industry and Virtue Versus Luxury and Corruption": Berkeley, Walpole and the South Sea Bubble Crisis', *Eighteenth-Century Ireland*, 7 (1992), 57–74.

——, 'Ireland and the Glorious Revolution, from Kingdom to Colony', in *The Revolutions of 1688*, ed. Robert Beddard (Oxford, 1991), pp. 162–90.

——, 'The Irish Woollen Export Prohibition Act of 1699: Kearney revisited', *Irish Economic and Social History*, 7 (1980), 22–44.

——, 'The Politics of Political Economy in Mid-Eighteenth-Century Ireland', in *Political Thought in Eighteenth-Century Ireland*, ed. S. J. Connolly (Dublin, 2000), pp. 105–29.

Kinsella, Eoin, 'Dividing the Bear's Skin Before She is Taken: Irish Catholics and Land in the Late Stuart Monarchy, 1683–1691', in *Restoration Ireland: Always Settling Never Settled*, ed. Coleman Dennehy (Aldershot, 2008), pp. 161–78.

Lamoreaux, Naomi, *Insider Lending: Banks, Personal Connections and Economic Development in Industrial New England* (Cambridge, 1994).

Laurence, Anne, 'The Emergence of a Private Clientèle for Banks in the Early Eighteenth Century: Hoare's Bank and Some Women Customers', *Economic History Review*, 61 (2008), 565–86.

——, 'Lady Betty Hastings, Her Half-sisters, and the South Sea Bubble: Family Fortunes and Strategies', *Women's History Review*, 15 (2006), 533–40.

——, 'Women Investors, "That Nasty South Sea Affair" and the Rage to Speculate in Early Eighteenth-Century England', *Accounting, Business & Financial History*, 16 (2006), 245–64.

Laurence, Anne, Josephine Maltby and Jeanette Rutherford (eds), *Women and Their Money, 1750–1950: Essays on Women and Finance* (London, 2009).

Legg, Mary-Lou, 'Money and Reputations: The Effects of the Banking Crises of 1755 and 1760', *Eighteenth-Century Ireland*, 11 (1996), 74–87.

Lenman, Bruce, An Economic History of Modern Scotland (London, 1977).

Lennon, Colm, Irish Historic Town Atlas: Dublin, Part II, 1610–1756 (Dublin, 2009).

Livesey, James, Civil Society and Empire: Ireland and Scotland in the Eighteenth Century Atlantic World (London, 2009).

Lyons, Mary Ann, '"Digne de Compassion": Female Dependents of Irish Jacobite Soldiers in France, c.1692–c.1730', Eighteenth-Century Ireland, 23 (2008), 55–75.

MacCarthy-Morrogh, Michael, 'Credit and Remittance: Monetary Problems in Early Seventeenth-Century Munster', Irish Economic and Social History, 14 (1987), 5–19.

Mackay, Charles, Extraordinary Popular Delusions and the Madness of Crowds (Ware, 1995).

Magennis, Eoin, 'Whither The Irish Financial Revolution? Money, Banks and Politics in Ireland in the 1730s', in Money, Power and Print: Interdisciplinary Studies on the Financial Revolution in the British Isles, ed. C. I. McGrath and Chris Fauske (Newark, 2008), pp. 189–208.

Malcomson, A. P. W., 'Absenteeism in Eighteenth-Century Ireland', Irish Economic and Social History, 1 (1974), 15–35.

——, 'A House Divided: The Loftus Family, Earls and Marquesses of Ely, c.1600–c.1900', in Refiguring Ireland: Essays in Honour of L. M. Cullen, ed. David Dickson and Cormac O'Gráda (Dublin, 2003), pp. 184–224.

——, Nathaniel Clements: Government and the Governing Elite in Ireland, 1725–75 (Dublin, 2005).

McBride, Ian, 'Catholic Politics in the Penal Era: Father Sylvester Lloyd and the Delvin Address of 1727', in New Perspectives on the Penal Laws, ed. John Bergin, Eoin Magennis, Lesa Ni Mhunghaile and Patrick Walsh (Dublin, 2011), pp. 115–47.

McGowan, Padraig, Money and Banking in Ireland: Origins, Development and Future (Dublin, 1990).

McGrath, C. I., Ireland and Empire, 1692–1770 (London, 2012).

——, 'The Irish Experience of "Financial Revolution" 1660–1760', in Money, Power and Print: Interdisciplinary Studies on the Financial Revolution in the British Isles, ed. C. I. McGrath and Chris Fauske (Newark, 2008), pp. 157–88.

——, The Making of the Eighteenth-Century Irish Constitution (Dublin, 2000).

——, 'Money, Politics and Power: The Financial Legislation of the Irish Parliament', in The Eighteenth-Century Composite State: Representative Institutions in Ireland and Europe, 1689–1800, ed. D. W. Hayton, James Kelly and John Bergin (Basingstoke, 2010), pp. 21–43.

——, '"The Public Wealth is the Sinew, the Life, of Every Public Measure": The Creation and Maintenance of a National Debt in Ireland, 1716–45', in The Empire of Credit: The Financial Revolution in Britain, Ireland and America, 1688–1815, ed. Daniel Carey and Christopher Finlay (Dublin, 2011), pp. 171–208.

McGrath, C. I. and Chris Fauske (eds), Money, Power and Print: Interdisciplinary Studies on the Financial Revolution in the British Isles (Newark, 2008).

McGuire, James, 'The Irish Parliament of 1692', in Penal Era and Golden Age:

Essays in Irish History, 1690–1800, ed. Thomas Bartlett and D. W. Hayton (Belfast, 1979), pp. 1–31.

McNally, Patrick, '"Irish and English interests". National Conflict within the Church of Ireland Episcopate in the Reign of George I', *Irish Historical Studies*, 24 (1995), 295–314.

——, 'Wood's Halfpence, Carteret and the Government of Ireland 1723–26', *Irish Historical Studies*, 30 (1997), 354–76.

Melton, Frank T., *Sir Robert Clayton and the Origins of English Deposit Banking, 1658–1685* (Cambridge, 1986).

Moore, Sean D., 'Satiric Norms, Swift's Financial Satires and the Bank of Ireland Controversy of 1720–1', *Eighteenth-Century Ireland*, 17 (2002), 26–56.

——, *Swift, The Book, and the Irish Financial Revolution: Satire and Sovereignty in Colonial Ireland* (Baltimore, 2010).

——, '"Vested" Interests and Debt Bondage: Credit as Confessional Coercion in Colonial Ireland', in *The Empire of Credit: The Financial Revolution in Britain, Ireland and America, 1688–1815*, ed. Daniel Carey and Christopher Finlay (Dublin, 2011), pp. 209–28.

Muldrew, Craig, *The Economy of Obligation: The Culture of Credit and Social Relations in Early Modern England* (New York, 1998).

Murphy, Anne, 'Lotteries in the 1690s: Investment or Gamble?', *Financial History Review*, 12 (2005), 227–46.

——, *The Origins of English Financial Markets: Investment and Speculation before the South Sea Bubble* (Cambridge, 2009).

Murphy, Antoin E., *John Law: Economic Theorist and Policy Maker* (Oxford, 1997).

——, *Richard Cantillon: Entrepreneur and Economist* (Oxford, 1986).

Musielak, Ruth, 'Madame da Cunha Prefers Her Own "Dunghill" to a Palace: City Lodging and Country Visiting in Early Eighteenth-Century London', *Irish Architectural and Decorative Studies*, 14 (2011), 56–77.

Neal, Larry, *'I Am Not Master of Events': The Speculation of John Law and Lord Londonderry in the Mississippi and South Sea Bubbles* (London, 2012).

——, *The Rise of Financial Capitalism: International Capital Markets in the Age of Reason* (Cambridge, 1990).

Newman, Steve, 'Second Sighted Scot: Allan Ramsay and the South Sea Bubble', *Scottish Literary Review*, 4 (2012), 15–33.

Nicholson, Colin, *Writing and the Rise of Finance: Capital Satires of the Early Eighteenth Century* (Cambridge, 1994).

North, Douglas and Barry Weingast, 'Constitutions and Commitment: The Evolution of Institutions Governing Public Choice in Seventeenth-Century England', *Journal of Economic History*, 49 (1989), 802–32.

O'Kane, Finola, *Landscape Design in Eighteenth-Century Ireland: Mixing Foreign Trees with the Natives* (Cork, 2004).

O'Regan, Philip, *Archbishop William King of Dublin (1650–1729) and the Constitution of Church and State* (Dublin, 2000).

Paul, H. J., *The South Sea Bubble: An Economic History of its Origins and Consequences* (London, 2010).

Pincus, Steve, *1688: The First Modern Revolution* (London, 2009).

Pittock, Murray, *Scottish and Irish Romanticism* (Oxford 2008).

Place, G. W., 'Parkgate and the Royal Yachts: Passenger Traffic between the North-West and Dublin in the Eighteenth Century', *Transactions of the Historic Society of Lancashire and Cheshire*, 138 (1988), 67–83.

Powell, Martyn J., *The Politics of Consumption in Eighteenth-Century Ireland* (Basingstoke, 2005).

Quinn, Stephen P., 'The Glorious Revolution's Effect on English Private Finance: A Microhistory, 1680–1705', *Journal of Economic History*, 61 (2001), 593–615.

Reamonn, Sean, *History of The Revenue Commissioners* (Dublin, 1981).

Robbins, Caroline, *The Eighteenth-Century Commonwealthman: Studies in the Transmission, Development, and Circumstance of English Liberal Thought from the Restoration of Charles II until the War with the Thirteen Colonies* (Cambridge, MA, 1959).

Robertson, John, *The Case for Enlightenment: Scotland and Naples, 1680–1760* (Cambridge, 2005).

Rodgers, Nini, *Ireland, Slavery and Anti-Slavery: 1612–1865* (Basingstoke, 2009).

Rogers, Pat, 'Literary Art in Defoe's Tour: The Rhetoric of Growth and Decay', *Eighteenth-Century Studies*, 6 (1972–73), 153–85.

——, 'Plunging in the Southern Waves: Swift's Poem on the Bubble', *The Yearbook of English Studies*, 18 (1988), 41–50.

——, '"This Calamitous Year": A *Journal of the Plague Year* and the South Sea Bubble', in *Eighteenth Century Encounters* (Brighton 1986), pp. 151–69.

Roseveare, Henry, *The Financial Revolution, 1660–1760* (London, 1991).

Ryder, Michael, 'The Bank of Ireland 1721: Land, Credit and Dependency', *Historical Journal*, 25 (1982), 557–82.

Satsuma, Shinsuke, 'The South Sea Company and Its Plan for a Naval Expedition in 1712', *Historical Research*, 85 (2012), 410–29.

Saville, Richard, *Bank of Scotland, A History, 1695–1995* (Edinburgh, 1996).

Scott, W. R., *The Constitution and Finance of English, Scottish, and Irish Joint Stock Companies to 1720*, 3 vols (Cambridge, 1912).

Selgin, George, 'Those Dishonest Goldsmiths', *Financial History Review*, 19 (2012), 269–88.

Shea, Gary S., 'Sir George Caswall vs. the Duke of Portland: Financial Contracts and Litigation in the Wake of the South Sea Bubble', in *The Origins and Development of Financial Markets and Institutions from the Seventeenth Century to the Present*, ed. Jeremy Attack and Larry Neal (Cambridge, 2009), pp 121–60.

Simms, J. G., *Jacobite Ireland, 1685–91* (London, 1969).

——, *The Williamite Confiscation in Ireland 1690–1703* (London, 1956).

Sneddon, Andrew, *Witchcraft and Whigs: The Life of Bishop Francis Hutchinson* (Manchester, 2008).

Stasavage, David, *Public Credit and the Birth of the Democratic State: France and Great Britain, 1688–1789* (Cambridge, 2003).

Storrs, Christopher (ed.), *The Fiscal-Military State in Eighteenth-Century Europe: Essays in Honour of P. G. M. Dickson* (Farnham, 2009).

Stratmann, Silke, *Myths of Speculation: The South Sea Bubble and 18th Century English Literature* (Munich, 2000).

Talbott, Siobhan, 'British Commercial Interests on the French Atlantic Coast, c.1560–1713', *Historical Research*, 85 (2012), 394–409.

Temin, Peter and H. J. Voth, 'Riding the South Sea Bubble', *American Economic Review*, 94 (2004), 1654–68.

Tenison, C. M., 'The Old Dublin Bankers', *Journal of the Cork Historical and Archaeological Society*, 1 (1893), 17–18, 36–8, 54–6, 102–6, 120–3, 143–6, 168–71, 193–7, 221–2, 241–3 and 256–60.

Truxes, Thomas, *Irish-American Trade, 1660–1783* (Cambridge, 1988).

——, 'London's Irish Merchant Community and North Atlantic Commerce in the Mid-Eighteenth Century', in *Irish and Scottish Mercantile Networks in Europe and Overseas in the Seventeenth and Eighteenth Centuries*, ed. David Dickson, Jan Parmentier and Jane Ohlmeyer (Gent, 2007), pp. 271–300.

Vickers, Daniel, 'The Northern Colonies: Economy and Society, 1600–1775', in *The Cambridge Economic History of the United States I*, ed. Stanley L. Engerman and Robert E. Gallman (Cambridge, 1996), pp. 209–48.

Victory, Isolde, 'The Making of the 1720 Declaratory Act', in *Parliament, Politics and People: Essays in Eighteenth-Century Irish History*, ed. Gerard O'Brien (Dublin, 1989), pp. 9–29.

Wall, Maureen, 'Catholics in Economic Life', in *The Formation of the Irish Economy*, ed. L. M. Cullen (Cork, 1968), pp. 37–51.

Walsh, Patrick, 'The Bubble on the Periphery: Scotland and the South Sea Bubble', *Scottish Historical Review*, 91 (2012), 106–24.

——, 'Club Life in Late Seventeenth and Early Eighteenth-Century Ireland: In Search of an Associational World c.1680–c.1730', in *Clubs and Societies in Eighteenth-Century Ireland*, ed. James Kelly and Martyn J. Powell (Dublin, 2010), pp. 36–52.

——, 'Free Movement of People? Responses to Emigration from Ireland, 1718–30', *Journal of Irish and Scottish Studies*, 3 (2010), 221–36.

——, 'The Irish Fiscal State, 1690–1769', *Historical Journal*, 56 (2013), 629–56.

——, 'Irish Money on the London Market: Ireland, the Anglo-Irish and the South Sea Bubble of 1720', *Eighteenth-Century Life*, 38 (forthcoming 2014).

——, *The Making of the Irish Protestant Ascendancy: The Life of William Conolly, 1662–1729* (Woodbridge, 2010).

Watt, Douglas, *The Price of Scotland: Darien, Union and the Wealth of Nations* (Edinburgh, 2007).

Wennerlind, Carl, *Casualties of Credit: The English Financial Revolution 1620–1720* (Cambridge, MA, 2011).

Whatley, Christopher A., *Bought and Sold for English Gold? Explaining the Union of 1707*, 2nd edn (Edinburgh, 2001).

Whelan, Kevin, 'An Underground Gentry: Catholic Middlemen in Eighteenth-Century Ireland', *Eighteenth-Century Ireland*, 10 (1995), 7–68.

Yn-Casalilla, Bartolomé and Patrick K. O'Brien with Francisco Comín Comín (eds), *The Rise of Fiscal States: A Global History, 1500–1914* (Cambridge, 2012).

Unpublished Theses

Forbes, Suzanne, 'Print, Politics and Public Opinion in Ireland, 1690–1715' (Ph.D., University College Dublin, 2012).

McGrath, C. I., 'The Irish Revenue System: Government and Administration 1689–1702' (Ph.D., University of London, 1997).

Smyth, Alan J., 'The Social and Economic Impact of the Williamite War on Ireland, 1688–91' (Ph.D., Trinity College Dublin, 2013).

Works of Reference

Johnston-Liik, E. M., *History of the Irish Parliament, 1692–1800: Commons, Constituencies and Statutes*, 6 vols (Belfast, 2002).

Matthew, H. G. C. and Brian Harrison (eds), *Oxford Dictionary of National Biography* (Oxford, 2004).

McCusker, John, *Money and Exchange in Europe and America, 1660–1775: A Handbook* (London, 1978).

McGuire, James and James Quinn (eds), *Dictionary of Irish Biography*, 9 vols (Cambridge, 2009).

Index

Printed and bound by CPI Group (UK) Ltd, Croydon, CR0 4YY

23/04/2025

14661042-0001